Story and Situation

Theory and History of Literature
Edited by Wlad Godzich and Jochen Schulte-Sasse

Story and Situation
Narrative Seduction
and the Power of Fiction

Ross Chambers
Foreword by Wlad Godzich

Theory and History of Literature, Volume 12

University of Minnesota Press, Minneapolis

Published by the University of Minnesota Press,
2037 University Avenue Southeast, Minneapolis, MN 55414
Printed in the United States of America.
Second Printing, 1985
Library of Congress Cataloging in Publication Data

Chambers, Ross.
    Story and situation.
    (Theory and history of literature; v. 12)
    Bibliography: p.
    Includes index.
    1. Fiction—Technique. 2. Narration (Rhetoric)
3. Fiction—History and criticism. I. Title.
II. Series.
PN3383.N35C48 1984   808.3   83-14787
ISBN 0-8166-1295-1
ISBN 0-8166-1298-6 (pbk.)

For David, who makes love simple

Tout langage dit *je suis
acte de quelqu'un* avant de signaler
autre chose.

Paul Valéry

Contents

Acknowledgments

My thanks go to the students at the University of Chicago and the University of Michigan with whom I thought (taught) my way through some of the ideas in this book and to the many friends and colleagues in different places who have helped me with its argument. Without the work of Lucien Dällenbach, my own would scarcely have been possible, and Mary Maclean has been a constantly supportive adviser and critic. Peter Brooks and the anonymous readers of the University of Minnesota Press made a number of helpful suggestions. In the latter stages, the help and advice of the series editors, Wlad Godzich and Jochen Schulte-Sasse, proved invaluable.

Versions of chapters 4, 5, and 6 appeared in the journals *French Forum* (5, 3 [1980], 220-238), *Poétique* (41 [1980], 22-38), and *MLN* (96, 4 [1981], 771-791). For permission to reprint in revised (and in two cases translated) form, I am grateful to the editors. Parts of the argument in chapters 1, 2, and 9 were used in "Narrative Point" (*Southern Review* [March 1983]) and "Schwob's *Les Sans-Gueule* and the Anxiety of Reading" (in *L'Hénaurme Siècle*, ed. Will McLendon and Wolfgang Drost [Heidelberg: Carl Winter Universitätsverlag, to appear]) and reappear here with permission.

Finally, for devoted work at the typewriter and word processor, respectively, my warm thanks go to Daphne Swabey and, especially, Bill Mitchell.

R.C.

After the Storyteller...
Wlad Godzich

Ross Chambers is a critic of modest pretensions: Eschewing the current tone of theoretical pronouncements, he prefers to analyze the way in which stories make their point. He does so with unparalleled rigor and clarity and in full cognizance of the methodological and theoretical debates that animate the branch of literary studies we have recently taken to calling narratology. In the process, he not only provides an evaluation of the achievements and the shortcomings of this field, but forces us into a fundamental reflection on narrative and its fate.

I.

Narratology arose from the seemingly common-sensical observation that stories are told in a variety of media: in verbal narratives, myths, cartoons, dance, mime, film, in the kind of music we call programmatic, and even in stained-glass windows. If such is the case, it has been argued,[1] then stories, or more properly their narrative component, should be studied in their own right, without reference to the medium in which they are cast. This approach, dealing with the universe presented in the stories rather than with the mode of that presentation, was quickly labeled "grammatical" by its practitioners since it did not consider the more semantic dimension of the stories' signification. Historically, it is associated with the international movement we call French Structuralism (Todorov, Barthes, Lévi-Strauss, Gerald Prince, A.-J. Greimas, Thomas Pavel). It is character-ized by a search for the invariant components of all narratives and their mode of articulation; specific kinds of articulatory configura-tions permit then the establishment of a taxonomy of narratives. We owe to this approach the elaboration of an important body of analytical terms and procedures that have given the study of narra-tive a certain technical veneer and considerable descriptive power. As a result, this field of research seems to have taken on more of a scientific standing in accordance with the hypothetico-deductive protocols of the linguistics upon which it has modelled itself. In this respect, the narratological structuralists have drawn upon the funda-mental work of the folklorist Vladimir Propp[2] as well as that of the morphologist André Jolles.[3]

But as soon as the very real accomplishments of this approach are brought to bear upon literary studies, in the study of verbal narra-tives, a new set of problems arises, and it is in the manner of addres-sing these problems that narratology as a branch of literary studies has come into being, gathering under its label works, such as Henry James's Prefaces and Wayne Booth's *Rhetoric of Fiction,* as well, that, in the aftermath of its emergence, appear to be its forerunners. For, uninformed as such works may be of the properly structural properties of narrative, they are nonetheless concerned with a story's mode of being in language. The structuralists, if they did not know it already, rapidly discovered that their initial methodological decision to bracket away the medium and the mode of presentation of narrative could at best serve as a delaying tactic. Eventually the scientific precision and elegance of their descriptions not only failed to clear up or dispel some of the traditional problems of narrative analysis, it actually recast them into more puzzling ones. While such a problematization may have represented a tangible gain in the appreciation of the complexity of the problems at hand, it was still somewhat of an embarrassment, if not outright discomfiture, to its formulators who saw themselves suddenly facing such old standbys of narrative analysis as point of view. To their credit, the narratol-ogists did not give up their project but rather expanded its scope to include these new problems, thus giving narratology its present compass and place in literary studies.

The articulation of the first set of problems—those of narrative structure—with the second—those that arise in conjunction with a study of the mode of presentation—has been effected by means of a distinction, originally drawn by the Russian Formalists, between *fabula* and *sjuzhet*: the story as a series of events and the story as it is told in narrative.[4] In English this distinction is generally rendered as *story* and *discourse,* which have been conveniently defined by Jonathan Culler as, respectively, "a sequence of actions or events, conceived as independent of their manifestation," and "the discursive presentation or narration of events."[5] But, as Culler goes on to show in his important article, this articulation is far from constituting a happy resolution. Rather, insofar as it can be called an articulation at all, it is one of necessary non-conjunction, and, frequently, of outright incompatibility. On the one hand, the analysis of the story, in Culler's sense of the term, proceeds on the common-sensical assumption of a logical and temporal priority of events over their rendition in the discourse, while, on the other, it is the empirically verifiable lot of narratological analysis to constantly come upon events in narratives, that, far from being prior givens that the discourse of the narrative is merely relating, are the products of discursive forces or constructs fulfilling discursive requirements. Such an inversion in the relation of story and discourse does not merely violate what both common sense and theory require as their logical ordering but condemns narratology to a permanently cleaved state: the analyses of story and of discourse cannot be free-standing; yet, as soon as their mutual dependency is acknowledged and, in the concrete carrying out of analytic work, the absent one is brought forth—regardless of whether one started with story or discourse—it proves to be a perturbatory element rather than a resolving one, and the totalization one hoped for is irremediably gone. As Culler puts it:

Neither perspective, then, is likely to offer a satisfactory narratology, nor can the two fit together in harmonious synthesis; they stand in irreconcilable opposition, a conflict between two logics which puts in question the possibility of a coherent, non-contradictory science of narrative.[6]

This manner of bringing to bear upon each other two components or aspects of what until then was presumed to be a single entity, in order to show that they are incompatible and yet are bound to each other, is generally associated with the procedures of post-structuralism. The latter has been quite hard not only on narratology, reducing it, as Culler does in his discussions, to a tragic critical practice— tragic because at once inescapable and doomed to alternate, without the possibility of totalization, between its dependent constituents— but on narrative as well, especially that part that is called story.

The best example of this is the one that would be said to be foundational of deconstructive practice. It is the well-known fragment of

The Will to Power in which Nietzsche shows that causation is not a state of affairs in the world but the rhetorical figure called meton-ymy.[7] Again Culler's summary and discussion are to the point:

Causation involves a narrative structure in which we posit first the presence of a cause and then the production of an effect. Indeed, the very notion of plot, as E. M. Forster taught us, is based on causation: "the king died, then the queen died" is not a narrative, although "the king died, then the queen died of grief" is. . . . [F]irst, there is cause; then, there is effect; first a mosquito bites one's arm, then one feels pain. But, says Nietzsche, this sequence is not given; it is constructed by a rhetorical operation. What happens may be, for example, that we feel a pain and then look around for some factor we can treat as the cause. The "real" causal sequence may be: first pain, then mosquito. It is the effect that causes us to produce a cause; a tropological operation then reorders the sequence pain-mosquito as mosquito-pain. This latter sequence is the product of discursive forces, but we treat it as a given, as the true order."[8]

Clearly, what is at stake here is no longer the relatively parochial issue whether a science of narrative can be erected, but the very question of the cognitive value of narratives. If tropological opera-tions and discursive forces order the sequence of events in stories, and do not do so in any predictable manner but only *may* do so, then we can never know from a narrative what the actual sequence of events in a given instance may have been, or what caused what. Such a narrative may give us pleasure or hold our interest, but it is useless from the point of view of cognition: it offers no reliable knowledge about that which it purports to relate.

As long as the narrative is a self-proclaimed fiction, such as a short story or a novel, there is not much harm. But we rely upon narratives in many other than the fictional area, and foremost in history, which we take to be the very opposite of fiction. Yet, if it is true that narratives give us no reliable knowledge of what they purport to relate, then they are all fictions, including those of history. At that point, I can no longer evaluate two differing historical accounts on the basis of their veracity, that is of their accuracy with respect to the events they relate, but on some other criteria, perhaps even aesthetic ones such as style or internal coherence. Moreover, since what is being asserted of narratives' fictionality here must clearly be taken to apply to all narratives, past and present, then it follows that reliance on some historical accounts or on explanations of a historical, that is narrative, character, could have been determined by considerations other than those of truthfulness, perhaps even by aesthetic ones such as pleasure. What I have taken to be the regularities, continuities, and discontinuities of history, are perhaps, since the latter has been known to me through narratives, no more than the products of tropological operations or discursive forces, and their reassuring recurrence from historical narrative to historical narrative may just be a testimony to their power, their status as master narratives, or, even more simply, the result of ideological manipulation. But the large explanatory systems, the ideologies of liberalism, Marxism, nationalism, etc., the self-foundational narratives of religions—what Jean-François Lyotard calls the "grands récits" in his account of their present recession[9]—are constructed in the form of narrative themselves. From a post-structuralist perspective, explanatory regresses built upon narratives can no longer lay any claim to knowledge; although they certainly need not vanish as a result, they can no longer command the authority that once was theirs.

There is a stinging irony here: once upon a time it was claimed, under Marxian auspices, that "men made history," that human beings were the subjects of history. Now, with the equation of history and narrative,[10] that claim becomes the derisory one that "men make stories," that human beings are the subjects of stories. Yet, while this scaled-down claim has little of the sweep of its prototype, it does have the advantage of any truism: it gains assent. We do tell stories. It also shifts the focus away from *what* stories are about, from what they recount, to *who* is telling the story to *whom*, or as Ross Chambers puts it in the following pages: stories *relate* speakers and listeners in an act of communication they constitute. The question of *what* is recounted will not, however, be so easily dismissed. Even when the focus is shifted onto the communicative act, it persists, but in a new guise: by virtue of what does the speaker, the storyteller, spin the tale?

II.

This, of course, is the very question that Walter Benjamin addresses in his essay "The Storyteller."[11] His inquiry proceeds on the assumption that the storyteller and his function are in a state of decline. Though the immediate historical reference is to the aftermath of the Great War, the process must have started earlier since the references to the period in which the storytellers flourished clearly establish that they preceded our modernity: peasants told the stories of the land that they toiled and thus endowed it with a dimension of temporal continuity; seamen related tales of the lands to which they had sailed and thus extended (made continuous) the space of human experience; and the artisans, who in the years of their apprenticeship had to roam the land as journeymen but then settled to practice their craft, achieved a conjunction of both the temporal and spatial dimensions, earning their class the title of the storytelling university (p. 85).

In all three instances of storytelling, the enabling condition of the storyteller is experience, and it is clear that, for Benjamin, the ability to exchange experiences, to pass them from mouth to mouth, is the fundamental function of stories and their telling. He considers it an "inalienable" right, the "securest among our possessions" (p. 83). Yet, as I noted earlier, his essay begins with the observation that we are losing this possession presently, and that we are losing it because experience is falling in value.

Benjamin does not go into the causes of this devaluation here, although he does give some hints. As I have argued elsewhere,[12] the rapid expansion of markets in the 15th and 16th centuries necessitated an equally rapid acquisition of the types of knowledge we call information and know-how. The traditional mode of lengthy individual apprenticeship with several master practitioners in different locations proved inefficient under such circumstances and had to be replaced by a form of learning no longer based on experience but on mediation. Instead of acquiring experience directly or through the stories the master would have told them, the students (no longer apprentices) increasingly learned their trade from the systematic expositions of the most efficient practices in the profession presented in the forms of models and not as records of actual activity. This was even truer for those forms of economic and socio-political activity that require knowledge of vastly different sectors of the market and the society. Book learning thus came to replace direct acquisition of experience, and, as Benjamin observes, it gave rise to a desire for a form of knowledge that would no longer be guaranteed by the life experience of its propounder—the master—but that would instead be "understandable in itself" and subject to "prompt verifiability" (p. 89), namely information. At the same time, information is not so much stored in order to be reflected upon and to serve as a guide for one's future practice as it is consumed. Instead of contributing to the growing awareness of the individual's continuity with others in space and time, that is to what has been traditionally called wisdom, it fragments time and space even further, isolates the individual even more from others, and indeed by its news-like obsolescence, its incompleteness and inherent recalcitrance to totalization, it unmoors the individual from such values as he or she may have acquired, especially since the latter are no longer determined by the inherited wisdom of the collectivity or the precepts of religion but by the momentary needs of the market. Although it was meant to supplement experience, and not supplant it, mediated knowledge destabilized it and, in the process, produced the condition characteristic of our modernity, in which we find ourselves caught in the gap between the lessons of acquired experience and the values fostered upon us in the various apparatuses of mediation.

This is where literature, and art in general, came in. Already previously, the storyteller not only recounted personal experience, but, in the narrative in which he or she couched it, endowed that experience with meaningfulness. While the lived experience of the storyteller was, as Benjamin saw, the condition of his or her authority, the efficacy of the telling lay in the fact that it articulated learnable modes of endowing experience with meaningfulness. Literature will increasingly rely upon this capacity of narrative. We may observe, for example, that the large-scale explosion of narrative literature in the 18th and 19th centuries was preceded by several decades of memoir writing in which the writer, like the storyteller earlier, appealed to the authority of lived experience in the recounting of his or her life. Similarly, the epistolary novel provides the means for reflecting upon experience and thus serves as a guide to it. Its future was to be the novel of manners. The aesthetic function of art, in other words, was, paradoxically, to become a mediator itself, but a mediator that would deliberately play the role of a supplement to a fragmentalized and unmoored experience, and thus hold open the possibility of totalization. Narrative form was particularly well suited to such a task because of its special mode of articulating temporality: what was fragment today could be completed tomorrow.

We may wish to pause and reflect upon the movement of our reflection so far: on the one hand, we have seen that the attempt to develop a science of narrative as a branch of literary studies was thwarted, but in a curiously undebilitating fashion, by the inescapable necessity of maintaining at once two incompatible approaches, the analyses of story and discourse, and that moreover the only apparent achievement of narratology—outside of the development of its technical apparatus and the production of some illuminating textual exegeses—is to have provided the means for a devastating attack upon narrative, an attack that has resulted in the invalidation of the claims made on behalf of all explanatory regresses narrative in form while, on the other hand, we have seen that the increasing mediation of daily life has resulted in the fragmentation of experience and the dethroning of the storyteller but, at the same time, in the granting of greater power to the aesthetic function of art, and to narrative art-forms in particular. Our own movement does not escape the process it describes: the analysis of the fragmentation of the study and status of narrative propelled us into narrative form ourselves. Such a happenstance is too curious not to deserve some attention. And this is where a reading of Ross Chambers's *Story and Situation* proves necessary.

III.

To reiterate: Ross Chambers is a scholar of modest pretensions. He knows better than to write either a systematic treatise on narrative or a history of its development. Rather, he focuses on that element of lived experience that we have in relation to all stories when we ask: what's the point? He starts then with what seemed like the derisory conclusion that human beings are the subjects of stories, but instead of reading in it the truism that we do tell stories, he subjects it to the same kind of analysis that recognized in the Marxian quotation that "men make history" not a statement of fact but an admonition, a call to revolutionary action, the expression of a desire. That human beings are the subjects of stories means then that the communicative act in which a story is told is constitutive of its participants, that it is an experience itself, and not merely a way of talking about experience, though it is that as well. But whereas the experience told in the story is, as Benjamin saw, dependent on the authority of the teller, the experience of the telling, lived equally by teller and audience, writer and reader, narrator and narratee, is a function of the authority of the story.

Chambers readily accepts Benjamin's observation of the decline of the authority of the storyteller, but he sees it as leading to the necessity for the story to take on more authority itself. Forced to function more autonomously and without the claim to respect and attention that the storyteller could put forward, the story, functioning like a commodity in the market, must take on the aura of art in order to maintain itself. Divorced from the lived experience of the teller who previously stood as its guarantor, it must become part of ours. Since in the mediated universe that is ours we are no longer engaged in processes of intersubjective communication, that is we no longer conceive of knowledge as consisting in the acquisition of personal experience and the sharing of that experience with others, but rather we model our concept of knowledge upon the acquisition of information about an object so that our subjecthood is defined in the cognition of objects, be they things, ideas, or other human beings, the story, commodified as it has become, will take on the guise of an object rather than being a process between human beings. In this way, we will indeed become its subjects, just as students of narrative become narratologists as their object dissolves in their cognitive undertaking.

But, as Chambers is quick to observe, when stories assume the status of objects, they do not do so with the passivity of reified entities, things. They begin to exert powers of their own, and foremost among them, those of seduction. As the reader will quickly discover, Chambers has written a very detailed account of the ways in which seduction becomes the only recourse of entities reduced to objecthood under our present model of cognition.[13] Since the latter is a model known to us, if at all, from the perspective of the subject, Chambers's account provides a wholly new outlook on something we thought we knew. It permits him to retrace ground covered by others, but by doing so from his special vantage point, he makes us aware of how different the configuration of that ground is from the impression we had formed. It becomes clear as one proceeds that in the communicative act in which a story is told in the age of its commodification, the subject, whether as teller or narratee, is in the weak position; yet that is the position from which we had judged the entire encounter. Chambers's modesty then was the recognition of a necessity, a coming to terms with the existing state of affairs. It also represents an attempt to practice criticism from a position other than that of a pre-formed subjecthood coming to invest an object given to it readymade, inert and powerless. For Chambers, the object to be known knows that it is such an object, and that it is an object of desire. What is the critic then to do?

IV.

In a fine example of *mise-en-abyme* in his own text, Chambers gives us a model of his practice in his seventh chapter where he subjects Henry James's *The Figure in the Carpet* to close scrutiny. This tale, that so fascinates critics because it depicts our lot, stages the desire of the critic to achieve subjecthood, not only cognitively but socially, by penetrating the secret of the author. Chambers shows that the narrator-critic conceives of the penetration of this secret as the appropriation of what Vereker, the author, calls "the particular thing I've written my books for."[14] In other words, the critic conceives of his task in accordance with the model of subject-object cognition. But the text, represented in *The Figure in the Carpet* by the figure of the author who, in a crucial scene, stands *on* the rug of the narrator-critic's bedroom,[15] refuses to submit in such a fashion and begins to play what Chambers calls a cat-and-mouse game, in which its powers of seduction and its mastery of the communicative situation give it the upper hand. As Chambers puts it, the text's "true superiority over the critic does not lie in [its] possession of a secret so much as it results from [its] successful deployment of discursive strategies for which the younger man is not a match."

We recognize here our point of departure: the attempt to elicit from the text its narrative structure, its secret, runs into the text's discursive forces or tropological operations that render the task impossible. The critic is stymied, but not undone. What is undone is the critic's reliance upon the model of subject-object cognition that presupposes that the path to knowledge for a subject requires the appropriation and "thesaurization" of the object. But this model is deconstructed in the text as it is by post-structuralism in relation to the claims made for narrative. But James's text shows that this need not be the end of the story, in either instance. Chambers observes that the figure of Vereker recedes from this point onward in the tale, and the focus shifts to the relation of the narrator to other critics. In the painstaking analysis that follows, Chambers leads us to the scene of the revelation of the narrator-critic's practice, which occurs when the narrator tells Drayton Deane his story, that is the very story the reader is reading: "I told him in a word just what I've written out here." In other words, once the critic abandons the framework of a subject-object cognition, with its scientific pretensions, and focuses on his or her relations to others, s/he will produce a story that will indeed relate him or her to others, and in this manner the critic will indeed lay the secret bare.

Chambers, as I have written, has no scientific pretensions. His rigorous analyses of nineteenth-century art-tales[16] bring to light the variety of modes in which they play the cat-and-mouse game of communication. In the process, as by now we should expect, Chambers tells us a story, or rather at least two stories: one is that of the art-tale from Poe to Joyce, passing through Balzac, Flaubert, Nerval, and James; the other we are less quick to notice until we observe that the texts that Chambers has chosen to reread could be said to constitute the canon of narratology: "The Purloined Letter," "Sarrasine," "Un Cœur simple," etc. This is also then the story of narratology from Barthes, Lacan, Derrida, to J. Hillis Miller, Shoshana Felman, and Wolfgang Iser. But these are stories the reader will have to read by him- or herself; otherwise, what's the point?

...comes the storyteller.

NOTES

1. For this argument, cf. Tzvetan Todorov, *La Grammaire du Decaméron* (The Hague: Mouton, 1969).

2. *Morphology of the Folktale* (Bloomington: Indiana Research Center in Anthropology, 1958); Russian original published in 1928. For a discussion of the problematic relation of the French structuralists, especially Lévi-Strauss, to Propp's work, see: Anatoly Liberman, "Introduction," to Vladimir Propp, *Theory and History of Folklore* (Minneapolis: University of Minnesota Press, 1983).

3. *Einfache Formen* (Tubingen, 1968); original published in 1929.

4. Victor Shklovsky, "Parodijnyj roman. *Tristram Shandy* Sterne," in Jurij Striedter, ed. *Texte der russischen Formalisten,* Vol. I (Munich: Wilhelm Fink Verlag, 1969), 245-300.

5. "Story and Discourse in the Analysis of Narrative" in Jonathan Culler, *The Pursuit of Signs. Semiotics, Literature, Deconstruction* (Ithaca: Cornell University Press, 1981), p. 169-170.

6. Ibid. p. 187. Culler provides several examples of such analytic dilemmas. One that deserves consultation in its own right is Cynthia Chase's "The Decomposition of Elephants: Double-Reading *Daniel Deronda,*" *PMLA,* 93:2 (March 1978), 215-227.

7. Friedrich Nietzsche, *Werke,* ed. K. Schlechta, vol. 3 (Munich: Hanser, 1966), p. 804.

8. Jonathan Culler, *The Pursuit of Signs,* p. 183.

9. *La Condition post-moderne* (Paris: Minuit, 1979); in English, *The Post-modern Condition,* translated by Geoffrey Bennington and Brian Massumi (Minneapolis: University of Minnesota Press, 1984).

10. An equation that is not meant to state that history as the temporal dimension of human existence is a narrative. Rather, since history has been knowable only through the kind of narratives that we call history, it is properly unknowable unless its dependence upon narrative form can be broken. Obviously, this is far too complex a subject to be treated in a note. One would need to differentiate at least between the positions of Foucault and Derrida, who debated the issue among themselves. Derrida's arguments can be found in: "Cogito et histoire de la folie," *Revue de Métaphysique et de Morale,* 68 (1963), 460-494; in English translation in *Writing and Difference,* translated by Alan Bass (Chicago: University of Chicago Press, 1978), 31-63, and in "A propos de 'Cogito et histoire de la folie,'" *Revue de Métaphysique et de Morale,* 69 (1964), 116-119. Derrida's essays were occasioned by the publication of Michel Foucault, *Folie et déraison: Histoire de la folie à l'age classique* (Paris: Plon, 1961); partially translated as *Madness and Civilization: A History of Insanity in the Age of Reason* (New York: Pantheon, 1965). Foucault's reply to Derrida is contained in the expanded version of the book published under the title *Histoire de la folie* (Paris: Gallimard, 1972).

11. "Der Erzähler. Betrachtungen zum Werk Nikolai Lesskows," *Gesammelte Schriften,* II. 2, Werkausgabe vol. 5 (Frankfurt: Suhrkamp, 1980), 438-465; in English: "The Storyteller. Reflections on the Works of Nikolai Leskov," *Illuminations,* translated by Harry

Zohn (New York: Schocken Books, 1969), 83-109. For convenience's sake, references will be to the English version.

12. "Die politische Ent stellung des Post-Strukturalismus," *Hefte für kritische Literaturwissenschaft* 5, edited by Jochen Schulte-Sasse (Frankfurt: Suhrkamp, 1984).

13. Chambers is aware of the work of Jean Baudrillard on seduction (*De la Séduction* [Paris: Galilée, 1979]), though not of the more recent but closer in tone essay on strategies (*Les Stratégies fatales* [Paris: Grasset, 1983]). In any case, Chambers differentiates between strategy which he defines as the "Practice of those who are masters of the terrain" and tactics, defined as the practice of those who are not in control of the situation (see the last chapter). Chambers takes seduction to be a tactic even though it leads to a mastery of the situation. It is also obvious that the critic cannot resort to strategy—hence Chambers's cautiousness vis-à-vis theory—but must rely on tactics.

14. Henry James, *The Novels and Tales of Henry James. The New York Edition.* Vol. 15 (New York: A. M. Kelley, 1970), p. 230.

15. I owe this observation to Samuel Weber whose reading of the tale converges with, and nicely supplements, that of Chambers. See the third chapter of his forthcoming *Institution and Interpretation* (Minneapolis: University of Minnesota Press).

16. The choice of the art-tale for this study strikes me as being, in Chambers's own terms, strategic. The presumption of completion and finition that is so important a part of the argument for the commodification of the art-tale, makes it a privileged object of study. By contrast the novel calls for the kind of inquiry we associate with Mikhail Bakhtin. This may also account for the fact that all narratologists, dependent on the subject-object model, choose to write about short stories, their protestation that it is for pedagogical reasons notwithstanding. Chambers's forthrightness is refreshing. It remains to be seen whether the critical option of a return to narrative is possible in the case of longer prose, or whether the latter forces us into the meantime between the two storytellers.

Story and Situation

Chapter One
Story and Situation

With the waning of structuralism, it has become clear that, in general terms, meaning is not inherent in discourse and its structures, but contextual, a function of the pragmatic situation in which the discourse occurs. Indeed, there is some debate—fired principally by the extreme monism of Stanley Fish[1] —as to whether it makes *any* sense to attempt to distinguish text from context, although to many it does seem that meaning is precisely the *perception of a relationship* between discourse and its context (however difficult it may be, in purely formal terms, to distinguish one from the other). As far as narrative goes, common language has always recognized the contextual nature of meaning through the concept of "point": the "same" story can have a quite different point when it is told in different situations. Consider, for example, a "faggot" joke told by gay people among themselves, by straight people among themselves, by a straight person to a gay person and even, just conceivably, by a gay person to a straight person. In each of these cases, the significance of the story is determined less by its actual content than by the point of its being told, that is, the relationships mediated by the act of narration. That is why, when one looks hard at stories, it becomes extremely difficult to distinguish them from their *telling*, so true is it that people "do things with narrative,"[2] just as they do with words. A story is always, as Barbara Herrnstein Smith reminds

3

us,[3] someone telling someone else that something happened (be it fictionally or otherwise), and this narrative act is always available as a vehicle whereby people may "do things"—that is (and the double meaning is itself significant), *relate*.

In light of such everyday observations, it seems strange that literary criticism and theory have paid so little attention to the performative function of storytelling, preferring to limit themselves arbitrarily to the study of narrative structure and the discourse of narration conceived in each case as a set of relationships internal to a context-free text. As a consequence, we possess a fine "grammar" of stories, deriving from the work of Propp, Greimas, Bremond, Todorov, Prince, and others.[4] We possess, too, a useful "rhetoric" of narration, elaborated by Booth and especially by Genette,[5] as a grammar of possible relationships between text as narration ("discourse") and text as narrated ("story"). All this work has been summated, added to, and worked into a synthesis by Seymour Chatman in a handbook entitled, precisely, *Story and Discourse.*[6] But what is lacking is recognition of the significance of situational phenomena—of the social fact that narrative mediates human relationships and derives its "meaning" from them; that, consequently, it depends on social agreements, implicit pacts or contracts, in order to produce exchanges that themselves are a function of desires, purposes, and constraints. We owe it to the *Rezeptionsästhetik* movement in Germany that there is now some perception of the act of reading as based on a relational "contract" with a text (cf. the work of W. Iser[7]) and as a historical, that is, historically determined *and* determining, process (cf. the work of H. Jauss[8]), and Philippe Lejeune has elaborated a contractual definition for the genre of autobiography.[9] But the implications of the contextual nature of meaning for the analysis of *narrative texts themselves* remain to be explored; and the main title of this book, echoing Chatman's, is meant to focus attention onto the need, not simply to read texts in situation (which is inevitable) but also to read, in the texts, the situation that they *produce* as giving them their "point." O. Ducrot[10] has long insisted that all discourse is *sui*-referential and describes itself as an act; my contention will be that, for reasons to be elaborated a little later, literary narrative, as represented by the short story as an "art tale," includes as part of its self-reference system specific indications of the narrative situation appropriate to it.[11]

There is plenty of evidence in the literary tradition that the creators, unlike contemporary theorists, have been aware of storytelling as an event that presupposes a situation and mobilizes social relationships so as to give it performative force. A *locus classicus* is Othello's storytelling in the house of Brabantio, which from being an act of social civility (he tells the story of his adventurous and heroic life to introduce himself and entertain his hosts, as a good guest should) imperceptibly merges, through Desdemona's reaction, into an act of courtship (*Othello*, I, iii):

> My story being done,
> She gave me for my pains a world of sighs:
> . . . she thank'd me
> And bade me, if I had a friend that lov'd her,
> I should but teach him how to tell my story,
> And that would woo her. Upon this hint I spake: . . . .

But when, in the council chamber, Othello tells the Duke and the Senators the story of this tale-telling courtship, his narrative now has the force of a judicial defense (against Brabantio's accusation that he has won Desdemona by magic)—and its success as a defense is indicated by the Duke's under-the-breath comment: "I think this tale would win my daughter too."

Of course, Othello's claim of innocence is disingenuous and Shakespeare is working an irony, for it is clear that the very success of Othello's "spellbinding" narration is a confirmation of Brabantio's accusation. The Moor has introduced his story thus:

> I will a round unvarnish'd tale deliver
> Of my whole course of love; what drugs, what charms,
> What conjuration, and what mighty magic,—
> For such proceedings I am charg'd withal—
> I won his daughter.

So much hurt innocence itself arouses suspicion, and the scene invites interpretation as an illustration of the power of words: their power to seduce (in the original tale telling) and their power to disculpate (in the retelling), in short, their power to *charm*, in both the strong and the weak senses of the word, their "mighty magic." But it is the special property of the theatre that "words" can never be proffered there independently of a represented context, so the audience of *Othello* sees the Moor working his verbal charms through the *situational* power of his noble presence, and they also undergo the seduction of his magnetic personality, much as the Duke does. In addition, in the case of the scene in the council chamber, the playwright has significantly weighted the balance in favor of Othello's charm by sketching a political situation: the Republic is in danger, the Senate *needs* Othello. Political exigencies, personal presence—without these contextual circumstances, Othello's stories would be less *telling*, their magical power less strong.

If in the theatre the role of situation is to some extent a matter of acting and *mise en scène*, phenomena independent of the verbal text, the genre of the fable is a simple illustration of the fact that a text may supply, through textual means, a contextual situation that gives force, and point, to its storytelling. La Fontaine cannot have been unconscious of the fact that the "morals" to his fables—in addition to sketching an interpretative possibility—gave didactic force and moral significance to what might otherwise have been taken as mere fun. But one particular fable (VIII, 4) takes as its actual subject matter "Le pouvoir des fables" and indicates in a striking way that this power derives from situational circumstances. An Athenian orator, unable to stir his fellow citizens to a sense of political urgency, unable even to hold their attention, switches to another mode of discourse and begins a story. All ears, the crowd responds to the device of suspense: "Et Cérès, que fit-elle?" This is the traditional question ("What happened next?") that reveals, in situational terms, the thrall exercised by a narrator over a narratee; and La Fontaine's orator now profits from the power he has acquired to upbraid his audience for its indifference to the affairs of state, leaving his story unfinished:

> A ce reproche l'assemblée,
> Par l'Apologue réveillée,
> Se donne entière à l'Orateur . . . .

La Fontaine is making a relatively trivial point (about the power of stories to attract and hold attention) and a rather more significant one concerning the relationship between storytelling and the art of government, for the tale is set in the framework of a mock-modest apologia of fables addressed, at a time of delicate political significance in the affairs of France, to Louis XIV's ambassador to England, M. de Barillon. Louis Marin has studied the intricacies of this fable's own illocutionary manipulations at length;[12] the point most relevant to my present concerns is the absolute insignificance of the Athenian orator's tale *in itself.* It is a story with no intrinsic meaning: it has the form of a story but (in its fragmentary form) does not make sense *except* as a device for getting attention from the crowd. It is literally uninterpretable *except* within the framework of the total situation. In this, it is not unlike the so-called "anecdotes" the characters in Ionesco's *La cantatrice chauve* tell one another; these are antistories, formal parodies of story structure that are literally pointless in themselves and derive their point solely from the social relationships they mediate. (Here again, a dramatist profits from the automatic context provided by theatrical *mise en scène*.)

But a contemporary novelist who has given thematic significance to the contrast between storytelling that is worthless in its content and the situation that endows it with vital human significance is Manuel Puig, the author of *El beso de la mujer araña*.[13] Two men are in an Argentinian prison cell together: an apolitical homosexual window dresser, Molina, and Valentin, a *macho* political activist. To while away the time, the middle-aged Molina tells Valentin, in loving detail, the plots and settings of Hollywood movies and Nazi propaganda films he remembers from the forties—art forms the young activist can only regard as trash, and socially oppressive trash at that. But, as the novel develops, these narrations come to express something essentially independent of their unworthy content: Molina's concern for and protective care of the younger man. And gradually they come to mediate the developing relationship between the two, in the course of which each changes, Valentin discovering tenderness under Molina's influence and the value of feelings while Molina learns from Valentin the solidarity of *all* the oppressed and the importance of political resistance. In short, it is a love affair conducted per medium of storytelling, and in the course of which tawdry plot outlines acquire, through their loving telling, a totally unexpected situational "point."

— I'm curious . . . would you feel much revulsion about giving me a kiss?
— Mmm . . . . It must be a fear that you'll turn into a panther, like with the first movie you told me.
— I'm not the panther woman.
— It's true, you're not the panther woman.
— It's very sad being a panther woman; no one can kiss you. Or anything.
— You, you're the spider woman, that traps men in her web.
— How lovely! Oh, I like that. (pp. 260-261)[14]

What is common to these three rather random examples is the evidence that stories are not innocent and that storytelling not only derives significance from situation but also has the power to change human situations. The change can be a reinforcement (as when Othello's power, momentarily shaken, perhaps, by Brabantio's accusation, is strengthened by his tale to the Senate), or it can produce a reversal (as when the Athenian narrator produces political awareness in his apolitical hearers or when Puig's queen becomes an activist while his *macho* learns to feel, and to feel homosexually. There is, in each case, a transformation *that itself has narrative structure,* but it is a transformation that affects relationships and produces history, impinging on the affairs of Venice, the course of events in Athens (or Louis XIV's Europe), or the social situation in a contemporary dictatorship. Of course, what I have just called "history" is itself a fiction, not only because it has conventional narrative structure but also because it is the object of a fictional narrative (*Othello,* "Le pouvoir des fables," *El beso de la mujer araña*), and Hayden White might see further evidence here of the difficulty of distinguishing between what is called "fiction" and what is called "history."[15] But my point is that the texts do clearly distinguish between narrative discourse itself and the circumstances *in* which, and *on* which, it may have an impact. And in this thematization of the impingement of storytelling on history lies the lesson that needs to be drawn by narrative theory: meaningfulness is not exhausted (and indeed it may be completely missed) by analysis of narratives in terms of their supposed internal relationships alone.

In a companion volume, I plan one day to examine more specifically the relationship between narrative and history, taking as my focus the problematics of storytelling in circumstances of social violence. But, for the present, what I am suggesting is, then, that narrative is most appropriately described as a transactional phenomenon. Transactional in that it mediates *exchanges* that produce historical change, it is transactional, too, in that this functioning is itself dependent on an initial *contract,* an understanding between the participants in the exchange as to the purposes served by the narrative function, its "point." Although narrative content is not irrelevant, of course, it is this contractual agreement as to point that assigns meaningfulness to the discourse. In this respect, literary texts yield plentiful evidence of their own awareness of the transactional basis of narrative interactions. For example, among the texts studied later in this book, Poe's "The Purloined Letter" includes, at the centerpoint of the text, a moment in which Dupin exchanges the letter for a fat check from the Prefect of Police—a manifest enactment of the exchange value of fiction ("letters") in the economic marketplace and a reminder that economic forces form part of the situation that makes Poe's fiction meaningful. "Une belle histoire contre une nuit d'amour"—this is Roland Barthes's reminder that the inner story in Balzac's "Sarrasine" is also a *récit-marchandise.*[16] The point of the story lies in its intended function of bringing Mme de Rochefide to bed. That she breaks the pact derives from complex reasons having to do with her experience of the story, and of the storytelling, itself: in short, like Puig's novel, it illustrates the power of narrative to change relationships. In Nerval's "Sylvie," the contractual arrangements on which the narration's success depends are spelled out in the metanarrative discourse of the text: it is not a romance, we learn, but perhaps a personal document of some kind, and the appropriate reader is one who will read with the heart ("bien des coeurs me comprendront"). Thus, a specific type of reading— nondistanced and empathetic—is called for, and another type of reading (rational and distanced) is excluded from being able to *understand* the text, that is, from being able to give it its true point.

Henry James's tale "The Figure in the Carpet" revolves around a challenge—the challenge of an author to a critic, who is enjoined to develop an accurate reading of the secret figure in the author's work; and James Joyce's "The Dead," as an examination of the artist as "pennyboy," a parasite giving meretricious words in exchange for hospitality, foreshadows a contrastingly different relationship of art to the world. Other texts (such as Flaubert's "Un coeur simple") are less specific in indicating their own contractual basis, but it is only on the strength of such agreements that narratives can exert their impact and produce change.[17]

So, it is my further suggestion that the study of narrative as transaction must open eventually onto ideological and cultural analysis of these enabling agreements, that is, onto what Clifford Geertz might call "thick description."[18] "Sarrasine" is as embedded in the male-female relationships of Paris in the 1830s as "The Purloined Letter" is in a certain American mercantilism, while "Sylvie" presupposes, with its bid for "understanding," the desperate estrangement, in the bourgeois culture of the 1850's in France, of such marginal figures as the poet, the dreamer, the lover, *le fou*. Similarly, "The Figure in the Carpet" and "The Dead" propose in their different ways striking images of alienation, in the little world of literary criticism remote from the "vulgar" and in the figure of Gabriel Conroy, ill at ease in the (vulgar) Dublin society to which he panders, without being able to become the messenger of a reality radically opposed to that society. It is beyond my powers to do more, in the pages to come, than hint at what such "thick description" of the texts' implied and explicit contractual bases might be. Yet it would be disingenuous of me to pretend that, in conducting relatively formal and entirely text-based studies of the apparatus—the discursive *dispositifs*—by which a small group of nineteenth-century texts designate themselves as contractual phenomena and produce the transactional situation that gives point to their narratives, I am doing more than lay some preliminary foundations for a study of the social implications of literary narrative.[19]

Seduction and Alienation

My critique of the narratological tradition conveniently encapsulated by Seymour Chatman is not, then, that this tradition fails to explore the pragmatics of literary narrative in the sense of the empirical circumstances in which literary texts come to be written and read.[20] It is rather that, in concerning itself with literary texts, it has neglected those features in them—those textual indices of contractual and transactional understandings—that themselves realize the narratives as communicational acts and open them, as verbal structures, onto a world of events and change. Not the actual historicity of texts, but the markers, within them, of historical situation—these are what a renewed narratology, concerned with the phenomenon of point, might take as its object.

By way of exemplification, it is necessary to anticipate the results of the analyses that occupy the body of this book. One of its major conclusions will be that the nineteenth-century texts examined here identify with extraordinary constancy their narrative situation by recourse to a metaphor of seduction. The transaction that gives them narrative point is perceived as mobilizing the forces of desire (here a desire to narrate and a desire for narration) and as doing so, situationally, in ways that lie outside the cultural norm of, let us say, "legitimate" exchange (here, the type of exchange of information called communication). Leaving for the conclusion a slightly more detailed examination of the modes of narrative seduction and some suggestions regarding the possibility of generalizing this model (both within the corpus of literary texts and within the general phenomenon of verbal narrative), I will content myself now with drawing attention to the result itself—narrative communication in some important nineteenth-century French and English short stories conceives itself as a matter of seduction—and with proposing a possible interpretation, or "reading," of this phenomenon (for it is not really a "thick description") in terms of the historical circumstances of literary production in the modern period.

As Denis de Rougemont in his time[21] and René Girard[22] more recently have pointed out, adultery and seduction have for centuries been the mainstay of novelistic subject matter in the West. In this respect, narrative literature has been a major medium, as Tony

Tanner points out in a brilliantly suggestive study of *Madame Bovary*,[23] for affirming the disruptive truth of desire in a social universe governed by the order of codes and laws. But that narrative as a communicational act should itself begin to lay claim to seduction as its own *modus operandi* is likely, upon examination, to prove to be a relatively modern phenomenon, and one related, most probably, to the development to which Walter Benjamin refers when he distinguishes between the traditional storyteller as the conveyor of experience and the modern novelistic narrative as posing a question: what is the meaning of existence?[24] I mean that, when narrative ceases to be (perceived as) a mode of direct communication of some preexisting knowledge and comes instead to figure as an oblique way of raising awkward, not to say unanswerable, questions, it becomes necessary for it to trade in the manipulation of desire (that is, the desire to narrate must seek to arouse some corresponding desire for narration) to the precise extent that it can no longer depend, in its hearers or readers, on some sort of "natural" thirst for information. The distinction I will be making in chapter 3 between "narrative" authority and "narratorial" authority depends on some such shift from the function of transmitting information, on the one hand, to an operation, on the other, best described, albeit vaguely, as the arousing of "interest."

Such a shift is certainly the sign of a more radical and profound change, one that has affected the perception of communication in general and literary communication in particular. It is important to realize that the phenomenon of alienation, identified by Marx as a consequence of the shift in modes of production characteristic of modern industrial-capitalist-urban civilization and further refined by Georg Lukács in the concept of "reification,"[25] does not affect solely the *producers* of literary texts in the nineteenth century, as social beings involved in class relationships (most frequently as members of the dominated intellectual fringe of the dominating commercial and industrial bourgeoisie) and as participants in a system of marketplace forces that makes writing a form of labor and the literary work a commodity. What has been said a page or two back will suffice, perhaps, to show the awareness in the texts themselves of their dependency on such social conditions as these, among others. But the modern age is one also in which the literary text itself, as a form of communication, undergoes the process of reification, becoming *specialized* as "artistic" communication and more particularly *autonomized* as "text," that is, as a form of communication cut off from the circumstances of "direct" communication and freed both from the intentionality of an authorial subject and from the determination resulting from a specific recipient (henceforth abstracted into the concept of "the reader"). Deferral and mediation, the conditions of "interpretability," now become the necessary conditions of meaningfulness for literature. This is not the place to attempt a historical reconstitution of the long process by which literature has come finally to be defined less as a positive act of direct communication (a concept still dominant, surely, in the eighteenth century and persisting, of course, right through the nineteenth and into the twentieth) and more as an alienated discursive practice, a mediation in which both what is mediated and the agents of mediation have become infinitely problematic. The evidence for the gradual change is, in any case, inscribed in the texts themselves, in their production of the seductive model as a figure of the precondition of their communicational success.

For it is not paradoxical but entirely consistent with the overall circumstances of middle-class society that the condition of "outsider" imposed on the literary text (that is, its alienation from the more normal, or dominant, systems of communication and exchange) is the source of its value. Because of its isolation from an immediate communicational situation, literature becomes interpretable and as such *productive* of meanings, *rich* in significance. The assumption that the right thing to do with a literary text is to interpret it and that the interpretive process involves first isolating a text (as structure) before "recontextualizing" it (and recontextualizing it again and again) so as to realize its potential of ongoing meaningfulness has become in our present-day practice so automatic and unexamined that we scarcely recognize its significance as an indicator of our general social circumstances and of our alienated approach to language in particular. Yet it means that, if literature no longer has a use value (by which I understand the sort of value an act of direct communication might have), it has entered into the system of exchange value, in which its significance, or worth, is a function of its interpretability as a complex sign for which other discursive signs can be substituted. However, in order to realize this potential value, the alienated text must first be read, and its seductiveness appears, then, as the necessary means whereby such a text succeeds in acquiring a readership and inserting itself into the new interpretive contexts that will actualize its meaningfulness. In short, such seductiveness is the sign that, like other commodities that must find a place for themselves on the market of exchange, literature is aware of its alienated status and seeks to realize the potential for value that that alienation confers on it.

One could put this another way by saying that seduction goes hand in hand with the "readerliness" or "readability" of literature — understanding these terms in the slightly technical sense given by Roland Barthes to the concept of *lisibilité*,[26] which I will explore further in the next chapter. If readability (or interpretability) is the power literary texts have of producing meanings, a power achieved by virtue of the reification of literary discourse into "text," then seduction is the inevitable means by which the alienated text achieves value by realizing its potential of readability. However, if this readerly quality of text is a function of textual alienation, then we need not be surprised to discover, in the analyses that follow, that textual seductiveness relies in growing measure on techniques and conceptions of art that today we associate rather with the notion of the "writerly" (*le scriptible*). Dupin's "smokescreen" of words, the thematics of lack in "Sarrasine," the stylistics of complexity and disorder in "Sylvie" — and, more obviously still, the claim to textual "simplicity" in "Un coeur simple," the implications of the figuring of text as figuration in "The Figure in the Carpet," and the valorization of "noise" in "The Dead" — all these are aspects of textual self-definition in writerly terms; they show an increasing sense of text, in Barthes's seminal formulation, as *ourselves writing, "nous en train d'écrire,* avant que le jeu infini du monde (le monde comme jeu) ne soit traversé, coupé, arrêté, plastifié par quelque système singulier (Idéologie, Genre, Critique) qui en rabatte sur la pluralité des entrées, l'ouverture des réseaux, l'infini des langages."[27] In the story to be told in this book about nineteenth-century narrative, an insistent strand will concern the pressure within the readerly texts of the period of a sense of the writerly. And an implication of this story — I believe it to be Barthes's implication also — therefore will be that the readerly and the writerly are not so much clearly defined and crisply opposed categories as they are stages in a continuous historical evolution of the literary text in the age of its alienation.

What is the writerly text, indeed, unless it be one that has realized to the fullest possible extent the implications of textual autonomy — the self-same implications explored by the readerly text in a less radical way? Standing genuinely on its own as a purely verbal construct, the writerly text realizes the maximum specialization of text, its highest degree of reified objectivity. It tends, therefore — and this will be a strand of the narrative developed in this book — to realize itself as a seductive *object,* one very largely dependent, that is, on the willingness of its readership to be seduced, as opposed to the seductiveness of the readerly text, which is much more strongly centered in a sense of its own power to take the initiative and to develop an *active* seductive maneuver. What is at stake in the writerly text, as Barthes phrases it, is to "faire du lecteur, non plus un consommateur, mais un producteur du texte."[28] Consequently, as one moves from the readerly to the writerly, one can perceive a shift in emphasis in the texts' own analysis of their transactional status, from a sense of (seductive) *authority* exerted by the text to a sense of the (still seductive) *dependency* of the text on the act of reading that is to realize it, in its complexity and plurality, as writing. And in my own analysis of the modes of narrative seduction in the conclusion, I will move similarly from the question of establishing and maintaining authority to a question of what I will call duplicity, understanding by this the textual understanding of the necessarily *dual* input (of text and reader) into the communicative event and the consequent acknowledgment, in texts, of the irreducible *otherness* of the reader whose involvement in the textual processes is, nevertheless, a precondition of their success.

With this recognition of the otherness of the "seducee" of literary seduction, we will have come full circle; for the alienated text recognizes in this way to the fullest extent the degree of its alienation, in the unclosable gap between text and reader on which its status as literature depends. But at the same time, the problems of literary pragmatics reappear in a new guise and with a different emphasis. If it is the alienation of literary discourse as a social phenomenon that produces modern literature, self-defined as a seductive communicational act, how are we to account for the *success* of literary narrative—in view of the "gap" that cannot be closed, the irreducible (and constitutive) otherness of its readership— in nevertheless producing a seduction, exerting an influence, entering history, changing the social world? The question now is not what are the social forces that make literature a necessarily seductive phenomenon, but how, in social terms, does the seduction actually work? What, to recall Othello's metaphor, is the "mighty magic" that enables alienated narrative to exert seductive force? This is the problem—that of the relationship between the outsider and power— that I will be grappling with in the companion and successor volume to this one. I will suggest here only that contemporary thinking, notably in the work of Michel Serres and René Girard, about the necessary inclusion of the outsider role (the "scapegoat," the *tiers exclu*) in any account of the genesis, maintenance, and evolution of social "order" must provide the essential framework for any account of the historical effectiveness of alienated literary narrative. And the very powerful theory of mimetic desire that we owe to René Girard has certainly much to offer as an approach to understanding how a real reader can come to identify with, or at least relate to, the purely fictional "seducee" produced within a literary text as the object of its seduction. When we are seduced, are we not always seduced into conforming ourselves with an image: the simulacrum of one whom we believe can be loved?

NOTES

1. See *Is There a Text in this Class?* (Cambridge, Mass.: Harvard University Press, 1980) and, for another monistic view of the reading-text relationship, F. Rutten, "Sur les notions de texte et de lecture dans une théorie de la réception," *Revue des Sciences Humaines,* 177 (1980-1981), 67-83.

2. Cf. J. L. Austin, *How to Do Things with Words* (New York: Oxford University Press, 1965).

3. See B. H. Smith, "Narrative Versions, Narrative Theories," *Critical Inquiry,* 7, 1 (autumn 1980), 213-236, p. 232; and R. Scholes, "Language, Narrative and Anti-narrative," *Critical Inquiry,* 7, 1 (autumn 1980), 204-212, p. 209: "Narrative is a sequencing of something for somebody."

4. Notably V. Propp, *The Morphology of the Folktale* (2nd ed.) (Austin: University of Texas Press, 1968); A.-J. Greimas, *Sémantique structurale* (Paris: Larousse, 1966), and *Du Sens* (Paris: Éd. du Seuil, 1970); Cl. Bremond, *Logique du récit* (Paris: Éd. du Seuil, 1973); T. Todorov, *Grammaire du Décaméron* (La Haye: Mouton, 1969); G. Prince, *A Grammar of Stories* (The Hague: Mouton, 1973).

5. See W. C. Booth, *The Rhetoric of Fiction* (Chicago: University of Chicago Press, 1961); G. Genette, *Figures,* III (Paris: Éd. du Seuil, 1972) ("Discours du récit," 65-273). The latter is translated as *Narrative Discourse* (Ithaca, N.Y.: Cornell University Press, 1980).

6. *Story and Discourse: Narrative Structure in Fiction and Film* (Ithaca, N.Y.: Cornell University Press, 1978).

7. See especially *The Act of Reading: A Theory of Aesthetic Response* (Baltimore: Johns Hopkins University Press, 1978), translated from *Der Akt des Lesens* (München: Fink, 1976). For a survey of reading theory, see also W. Daniel Wilson, "Readers in Texts," *PMLA,* 96, 5 (October 1981), 848-863.

8. Two convenient compendia are *Pour une esthétique de la réception* (Paris: Gallimard, 1978), and *Toward an Aesthetic of Reception* (Minneapolis: University of Minnesota Press, 1982).

9. See in particular *Le pacte autobiographique* (Paris: Éd. du Seuil, 1975).

10. See *Dire et ne pas dire* (Paris: Hermann, 1972) and O. Ducrot et al., *Les mots du discours* (Paris: Éd. de Minuit, 1980).

11. Some aspects of this understanding of literary communication are treated by contributors to S. Suleiman and I. Crosman, eds., *The Reader in the Text: Essays on Audience*

and Interpretation (Princeton, N.J.: Princeton University Press, 1980); see in particular the essays of M. Beaujour (325-349), G. Prince (225-240), Peter J. Rabinowitz (241-263), and N. Schor (165-182).

For self-reflexivity and the notion of point in nonliterary narrative, see William Labov, *Language in the Inner City: Studies in the Black Vernacular* (Philadelphia: University of Pennsylvania Press, 1972), p. 366: "But there is one important aspect of narrative which has not been discussed . . . . That is what we term the *evaluation* of the narrative: the means used by the narrator to indicate the point of the narrative, its raison d'être . . . ."

For a cultural conception of narrative point, see Livia Polanyi, The American Story: Cultural Constraints on the Meaning and Structure of Stories in Conversation (doctoral dissertation, University of Michigan, 1978); see also "So What's the Point?" *Semiotica*, 25, 3/4 (1979), 207-241, and "What Stories Can Tell Us about Their Teller's World," *Poetics Today*, 2, 2 (winter 1981), 97-112. Polanyi perceives point as being what the narrative is (agreed to be) about, a matter she sees as subject to negotiation within culturally imposed constraints (relating to what is worthy of being made the subject of a story). My contention is, however, that point derives from the narrative situation itself, from what the narration is (perceived to be) doing, the relationships it mediates, and changes; and it is the perception of the narrative situation that I see as being subject to cultural analysis (Geertz's "thick description"). Polanyi never tells us, of the stories she collected at her dinner table, why they were told but only what, culturally speaking, makes them tellable.

12. In *Le récit est un piège* (Paris: Éd. de Minuit, 1978), 15-34 ("Le pouvoir du récit").

13. Translated as *The Kiss of the Spiderwoman* (New York: Knopf, 1979).

14. For an analysis that anticipates the argument of this book by demonstrating that film is the narrative model of the novel as a whole, see Frances Wyers (Weber), "Manuel Puig at the Movies," *Hispanic Review*, 49, 2 (spring 1981), 163-181.

15. See *Metahistory* (Baltimore: Johns Hopkins University Press, 1973) and *Tropics of Discourse* (Baltimore: Johns Hopkins University Press, 1978).

16. See *S/Z* (Paris: Éd. du Seuil, 1970), p. 95. Translated as *S/Z* (New York: Hill and Wang, 1974), p. 89.

17. For more extended commentary on the texts mentioned in this paragraph, see the following chapters.

18. See *The Interpretation of Cultures* (New York: Basic Books, 1973). Livia Polanyi's work (see note 11) might be regarded as "thick description" of stories, but not of the narrative situation as such.

19. These words were written before the appearance of Fredric Jameson, *The Political Unconscious: Narrative as a Socially Symbolic Act* (Ithaca, N.Y.: Cornell University Press, 1981), which sets out (pp. 74-102) the program of what such a study might attempt to accomplish.

20. On the empirical study of literature, see the special issue of *Poetics* on this topic (10, 4/5 [1981]) and particularly "Empirical Studies in Literature: Introductory Remarks" by Siegfried J. Schmidt (317-336).

21. *L'Amour en Occident* (Paris: Plon, 1939). Translated as *Love in the Western World* (New York: Harcourt Brace, 1940).

22. *Mensonge romantique et vérité romanesque* (Paris: Grasset, 1961). Translated as *Deceit, Desire and the Novel* (Baltimore: Johns Hopkins University Press, 1966).

23. *Adultery in the Novel* (Baltimore: Johns Hopkins University Press, 1979).

24. "The Storyteller," in H. Arendt, ed., *Illuminations* (New York: Schocken Books, 1969), 83-109.

25. See "Reification and the Consciousness of the Proletariat" in *History and Class Consciousness* (Cambridge, Mass.: MIT Press, 1971), 83-222.

26. See *S/Z*, pp. 9-12 (translation, pp. 3-6).

27. Ibid., p. 11.

28. Ibid., p. 10.

Chapter Two
Self-Situation and Readability

Much of the specific conceptual apparatus deployed in this book is unoriginal. It derives from modern research into the interpretability of literary texts, their self-interpreting specularity and their readerly availability to hermeneutic operations. It derives, too—why make a mystery of it?—from the already long tradition of narrative analysis, with its "grammatical" branch reaching back to the formalism of Vladimir Propp and largely developed by French structuralism, and especially its "rhetorical" branch, influenced seminally by the perspectivism of Henry James and which has flourished particularly in English-speaking countries. If I wish to extend the narratological tradition and go beyond it, it is by bringing together these two strands of literary theory—the theory of narrative and the theory of textual interpretability—into a proposal concerning the interpretability of narrative.

What, strikingly, has led twentieth-century narratology to ignore the phenomenon I have designated as "point," the meaningfulness that arises from a relationship between discourse and situation, text and context, has been a certain fidelity to the limiting presuppositions of its founders. The structural tradition has rarely displayed any suspicion of the objective status of its analyses: it believes in a stable and immediately knowable text, directly available to classificatory operations that are themselves neutral and innocent of interpretive bias. The narrative grammars at our disposal—the grammar of functions and indices in Barthes,[1] that of actantial roles in Greimas,[2] the sets of relationships (chronological, causal, logical) codified by Todorov, Bremond, or Prince[3]—all presuppose a narrative *énoncé* that does not "shift" in different reading circumstances; and it is only recently that, for example, Barbara Herrnstein Smith[4] has warned that "variants" cannot with impunity be reduced to a single model and Gerald Prince has shown awareness of the interpretability of stories.[5] Similarly, the Jamesian mimesis of the individual consciousness as a "reflector" or filter of narrative information has profoundly influenced the study of the "rhetoric" of narration, with its narrator-narratee (Prince)[6] and implied author-implied reader pairs (the latter deriving from Booth),[7] its distinctions between "who sees?" and "who speaks?" (Genette),[8] and its concern with "focalization" (Genette, Bal).[9] The model here is, again, that of a stable text whose characteristics are determined by an overriding vision and/or voice that takes responsibility for the act of narration and determines "our" understanding, as readers, of character and event. The discipline, in other words, is deeply rooted in the psychology and metaphysics—the ideology—of the individual "subject" or self, and of discourse as being controlled by that self.

I am far from rejecting the pertinence of such a model, especially to the nineteenth-century texts that have in large measure generated it. But it is necessary to see also that the literary text, deploying as it does its narrators and narratees, its implied authors and implied readers, does not thereby become a determinate (and determined) act of communication. Its characteristics as a literary text derive precisely from its autonomy (what in the previous chapter I called its alienation), the autonomy we give it as readers, an autonomy that cuts it off from "original" or determining circumstances of narration, such as a controlling individual consciousness, a "subject" solely responsible for meaning. These are, of course, the characteristics of interpretability, the availability to the activity of reading that enables the text to produce ever new meanings. Such a text can be treated as a stable or inert thing, predetermined by an intentionality (whether that of a fictional consciousness or that of an author), only at the risk of severely impoverishing it and depriving it of what gives it its value as literary discourse. But the interpretability of literary narratives implies that "point" in their case requires a special definition. Their point, as literature, is to admit (and invite) a range of interpretations, that is, to display the possibility of having, as individual narratives, any number of points. I want to suggest, in other words, that the mechanisms of interpretability, in literary narratives—the mechanisms that introduce some indeterminacy into their self-determination of point—are those that give them their point as literature. But since this is done by self-situation, it is necessary to begin by going back to the pragmatics of storytelling in general, for distinctions like that between discourse and situation, or text and context, operative as they may be in the analysis of everyday communicational acts, are in an important sense irrelevant to the literary text, which we define as autonomous discourse and in that way as situationless and context free. A critique of the text-context distinction, an exploration of the textual character of so-called context and, inversely, of the contextualizing force inherent in text, is therefore necessary, to pave the way toward some understanding of the phenomenon of self-situation, which is itself the key to textual interpretability.

Relevance

A theorist very much alive to the contextual character of meaning—that is, the type of "meaningfulness" I am calling point—was Gregory Bateson, whose definition of story introduces a key word: "A story is a little knot or complex of the species of connectedness we call relevance."[10] On the same page, he gives a definition of relevance that sounds as if it refers only to a presumed internal coherence of the story text ("any A is relevant to any B if both A and B are parts or components of the same 'story' "), but the very circularity of these definitions—a story is composed of relevant items; relevant items are those that belong in the same story—shows clearly that relevance (as internal coherence) derives from something external to the story and is the perception of coherence as a function of narrative situation. Those parts of a story are relevant to each other that, taken together, constitute the story's relevance to its situation; and relevance is thus, ultimately, the perception of a relationship between story discourse and story situation. As such, it involves minimally a story teller and a hearer, and some measure of agreement between them as to the significance or point of their joint participation in the discourse situation.

Defined in this way, what Bateson calls meaning results from an act of selection, the production (if one will) of form from out of the discourse as substance; or, to change the metaphor, it is a negentropic ordering of textual chaos. Such a principle of selection can only be a function of situation. The utterance "It's cold out!" can be a meteorological observation in certain circumstances, or it can have merely phatic function (equivalent to a greeting when the speaker has just come in from outside), or again it can be a warning ("Watch your health!") or an order ("Dress warmly!") or an invitation ("Stay in with me!") in others. More accurately, the same utterance may have *any* of such forces in given pragmatic circumstances; *which* of them it has will be a matter of choice (and agreement) on the part of those involved in the act of communication, who determine the observation's relevance. Or, to take an example of story, a class in folklore hears "Little Red Riding Hood" as something comparable to a grammatical example for analysis; its relevance derives from a pedagogical interaction between professor and class. A child being put to sleep by an affectionate adult hears it as a confirmation of love and a source of security, that is, as part of an affectional interaction. If these transactional agreements break down —as, for example, when the folklore student is put to sleep in class by "Little Red Riding Hood" or the sleepy three-year-old wakes up and comments on the structure and motifs of the tale—it means that there has been a misunderstanding as to relevance. (We will see that it is largely as a way of counteracting such possible "misunderstandings"—the quotation marks indicate my own skepticism as regards the reality of literary "misunderstanding"—that literary stories of the kind I will be examining are so careful to include in their self-referential apparatus indications as to the situation that bestows relevance on them.)

But Bateson's definition is important also because it is deliberately formulated in such a way as to include nonverbal stories (e.g., the growth of an organism or the evolution of a species) as well as verbal ones. For that reason it is useful to us, although our concerns are exclusively with verbal stories, in presenting a warning. A long humanistic tradition, which has been challenged only relatively recently, predisposes us to think of "man" as the producer of his discourse and of discourse as a kind of malleable tool available to us for whatever purpose we may wish to bend it. In this light, stories are produced by a storyteller for the benefit of a hearer, and it is agreements between those two that determine the relevance of a given story. But, just as it is possible to define a chicken as an egg's way of producing another egg, so it is important to realize that the human can similarly be thought of as an *effet de sens*, that is, a product of the symbolic order as much as the symbolic order is a product of the human. The two orders form an inextricable "little knot or complex," so true is it that relevance is a two-way street;

the relevance "we" perceive in a story is at one and the same time the story's way of defining "us," and roles such as "storyteller" and "hearer" are slots without which a story cannot exist (it would literally be pointless) but which equally the story gives substance to by coming into existence as an event. In this respect, the fact—yet to be demonstrated—that literary stories produce by textual means their own narrative situation (that is, minimally, a storyteller and hearer together with the agreements constitutive of relevance) is a somewhat troubling one, since it suggests that illocutionary situations in general (including "real world" ones) may equally be analyzed not as existing prior to, but as products of, a discourse that is constitutive of them. (I will be suggesting, of course, that the real-world reader need not, and indeed should not, be bound by the narrative situations produced in the texts as vital to their relevance and that these in turn need to be relativized in the reading process as part of the *text*, not the context; but this freedom to read textually produced narrative contexts in the light of new contexts of reading does not in itself demonstrate that contexts can be defined independently of discourse. However "free" my critical discourse may make itself of the narrative situations produced in my target texts, the new contexts I am determining in which to read the texts are inextricably bound up with the discourse—minimally, *my* discourse—that produces them.)

In using the vocabulary of semiotic and rhetorical analysis and the conceptualizations of speech-act theory—terms such as "speaker-message-hearer" or "narrator-story-narratee," distinctions such as that between "discourse" and "situation"—I am implicitly accepting in what follows a common-sense world in which speakers produce discourse for hearers, as opposed to speakers and hearers being produced by their shared discourse, and in which situation somehow preexists discourse. Yet, the major thrust of the research represented by the essays in this book is that certain types of literary storytelling consistently produce *by textual means* a narrative situation that gives point to the narration, a narrative situation describable in terms such as "speaker," "hearer," "narrator," "narratee," and so forth, but *indistinguishable from discourse itself.*[11] My analytic model is, in this sense, in philosophical disagreement with the model produced by the analysis, and the disagreement is all the more flagrant because the situation of literary communication is itself one in which the situational slots corresponding to notions like "speaker" and "hearer"—that is, such notions as "author" and "reader"—are so notoriously difficult to give substance to. One's whole experience of being a reader gives support to the view that the communicational roles are textual products, rather than the reverse.

But I do not believe my philosophical stance is contradictory so long as it is recognized that terms such as "narrator" and "narratee," for example, have a theoretical status exactly equivalent to the fictional status ascribed in the texts, and by the texts, to the participants in narrative situations; the theoretical terms, in fact, mirror the fictional situations and like them produce fictive entities that it would be naive to mistake for realities. The subtitle of this book is intended to suggest, among other things, that one of the important powers of fiction is its power to theorize the act of storytelling *in and through the act of storytelling.* If this is so, then literary theory ought to have little difficulty in acknowledging the derivative, and hence fictive, status of its own conceptual apparatus. (But, this being said, it should be an important priority of narrative theory to produce a conceptual apparatus less misleading because less simplistic in its presuppositions, and in this the literary branch of the theory is well placed to take the lead.)

So, it is because I am dealing with classical and (in Barthes's terms[12]) "readerly" texts (*textes lisibles*) that my own theoretical apparatus is "classical" in its terminology and assumptions and implies the existence of communicational situations in which relatively stable and coherent instances (like the "narrator" and the "narratee") combine in relatively stable agreements regarding "meaning" and "point." Unlike "writerly" texts (*textes scriptibles*), such texts, as Barthes says, are "adonnés à la loi du Signifié" and characterized by a "pluriel limité"; in them, and hence in my analysis, the selective process whereby structures are perceived and meaning created through the act of reading is assumed to be *determinable* within quite narrow limits and *controllable* — determinable and controllable, in my view, by the textual production of narrative situations — within a cultural context in which intelligibility, coherence, and order are prime values. "Readerly" texts, then, in my understanding of the matter, are those that determine themselves by textual means as complying with the conditions of *readability.* The type of relevance they assume and that enables us to recognize them as classical texts is such as to imply careful and somewhat restrictive acts of self-definition that limit the range of their interpretability and restrict their literary "point" to a quite strictly channeled form of meaningfulness. If the first power of fiction is the power to theorize itself as narrative act, the second power it wields is, then, the power to control its own impact through the act of situational self-definition.

But if the texts theorize in this way the conditions of their own intelligibility, it is necessary to theorize on their behalf the *need* they thus manifest to control and determine their meaning. My thesis will be that the textual self-reflexivity such a need implies is perhaps not exclusive to literary narratives of this classical kind but that it is certainly a necessary part of their apparatus and that this is so for quite specific reasons. So, before asking what exactly is meant by a text producing self-reflexively its own narrative situation, I will first look briefly into why such a phenomenon should be characteristic of certain types of literary narrative.

Situational Self-Reflexivity

My assumption is that the "literary," as a quality of certain texts, is not a characteristic of the texts *as such* but that it is a contextual phenomenon in the sense that it is produced either by the situation in which the texts are read or by the situation that the texts themselves produce as being their appropriate reading situation or—of course—by both. In the cultural history of the West, the notion of "literature" with the aesthetic and autotelic function it is generally understood to have today is a relatively recent invention: it seems to be a product of the early nineteenth century, or at most of the eighteenth century.[13] As a specific pact between text and reader, involving a decision concerning the right use to be made of a body of discourse, an understanding as to the appropriate way of making meaning with a text, the "literary" is best defined as a mode of reading and hence as essentially situational in character.

Indeed, attempts to distinguish in a purely formal (situation-free) way between "literary" discourse and "nonliterary" discourse are always open to invalidation by the very simple process that consists of taking a piece of discourse formerly classified as "nonliterary"— say, a piece of journalistic prose, the unselfconscious narrative of William Labov's storytellers, the expository prose in which Roman Jakobson describes the "poetic function" of language—and demonstrating either that the "nonliterary" discourse has formal features associated with "literary" discourse or that, by the use of appropriate framing (contextualizing) devices, that is, by a shift in the reading perspective, it can *become* literary. This shift involves certain mental operations that *structure* and *fictionalize* the discourse; and these, in turn, are techniques for actualizing the discourse as *deferred communication*.[14] Such a message is significant to the extent that it is perceived as available for interpretation because free of any *original* situation that would close and limit its meaning, and hence open to the ongoing interpretations that may be suggested by its insertion into a theoretically infinite number of new contexts. Except in a trivial sense, such texts are originless, their meaning is unfixed and unfixable because it is subject to a kind of "drift" as the discourse figures in constantly renewed and unrepeatable situations. Their status as art in our culture consequently implies an interpretive history, from which they derive the "polysemic" quality Barthes has so frequently stressed.[15]

But in society there are many forms of discourse that are meaningful because they are available for ongoing insertion into new contexts; such things as jokes and advertisements, for example—although their iterativity functions differently (the joke fails if it is repeated to the same hearer, the advertisement succeeds if the same recipient perceives it frequently)—are, like literature, fictions of this kind. Consequently, we have institutions, academic, journalistic, and commercial, whose function it is to classify such discourse by determining what is to be regarded as "literature": schools and scholars establish the literary "canon," journals decide to review or not to review (or they review differently according to literary "importance"), bookstores (and libraries) put "fiction" and "poetry" here, "nonfiction" there, and so forth. But it becomes advisable, also, for texts that are specifically produced as "literary" and whose meaningfulness consequently depends on their being read as such to *designate themselves* accordingly. This implies designating the literary reading situation as the one that gives them "point," since only that situation —and nothing intrinsic to themselves—can make them meaningful.[16]

In short, the self-reflexivity of literary texts is part of an apparatus whereby they can ensure that they are read as literary and thus make their claim to an interpretative history. My point is not the banal observation that literary texts are or may be self-referential, nor am I talking about the self-referentiality of the autotelic text, focused on a Jakobsonian "poetic function" to the detriment of other, communicational functions. I am saying that certain texts are, in a specific way, *situationally* self-referential and that these texts have recourse to a form of self-referentiality that analyzes them in their communicational function and actualizes them as communicational acts, specifying the conditions—the necessary understandings between reader and text—for them to be successful as acts of literary communication.

Clearly, all the texts we classify as literary do not necessarily correspond to this description: texts may become literary without making a specific self-claim to "literarity." But such textual self-consciousness does appear to be characteristic *at least* of the "literary" age, that is, of the period of our modernity dominated by the current alienated sense of the literary as structured, fictional discourse bidding for an interpretative history. More specifically—and this is my limited claim in this book—situational self-reflexivity is perhaps the *notable* characteristic of the type of text that, after Barthes, I call "readerly"—those whose polysemy is channeled within fairly strict limits of meaning, as opposed to the more radical semantic indeterminacy that characterizes "writerly" texts, those that have derived from the "révolution du langage poétique" of the late nineteenth and early twentieth centuries.[17] There is a reason for this. "Readerly" texts claim the power to produce new meanings in ever new circumstances (they lay claim to status as artistic discourse), but at the same time they are concerned, if not to claim a single univocal sense as central to their meaning, then at least to define the range of possible meanings that they can admit, to the exclusion of other possible meanings and relevances. This is what is meant by their "readability." It is as if for them the deferring of meaning from which they benefit as art requires careful control so as not to get out of hand—and it would be possible to show in many texts of the nineteenth century, for instance, that their sense of writing as a phenomenon of entropy, of slippage, or of drift is carefully balanced by a negentropic appeal to the act of reading as an ordering, fixing, or channeling phenomenon.

My claim is that situational self-referentiality is the key device by which this paradoxical claim in "readerly" texts—the claim to ongoing meaningfulness *and* a restricted range of significance—is made. This is because, in situating itself as art (i.e., in bidding for an interpretive history) such a text cannot avoid projecting a conception of the artistic function that is limiting because specific (being by definition culturally determined and indeed inescapably ideological in its provenance). Notions such as those I have been using—"fiction" or "art," for instance—are subject to as many definitions and redefinitions as there have been artists producing literary texts and readers reading them. In the final analysis, each text that designates itself as "art" or as "fiction" subscribes to a conception of the artistic or the fictional that is valid for that text alone; in other words, it projects a reading situation that is uniquely the right one for that particular piece of discourse. Furthermore, such situational self-reference is most often generic in its thrust; taking for granted the proposition "I am art" or "I am fiction" and the ideology of art (or fiction) such a proposition may presuppose, it specifies: "Read me as this type of art (fiction), not that"—romance, not realism; philosophical, not psychological; social comedy, not metaphysical drama, et cetera. Consequently, the self-referential text inescapably forecloses itself in the very act of opening itself to ongoing meaningfulness.

To my mind, it follows that the reader, who is in a position to perceive the ideological and cultural constraints that have limited the text's self-conception, has a responsibility to free the text from its own limitations. In other words, one should not allow one's own mode of reading to be determined exclusively by the text's situational self-reflexivity—that is, by the ideology of art to which the text happens to subscribe. On the contrary, by reading this self-situating as *part of the text*, one should free oneself to recontextualize it (that is, interpret it) along with the rest of the text. Thus, it may become necessary for a text whose self-claim is to social observation to be recontextualized in terms of metaphysics or for a supposedly realist novel to be read as romance; more generally, the text needs to be thought of in terms other than those available to it in the historical and ideological circumstances of its own production. This is not so much out of an exigency of freedom on the reader's part (although we *must* be free to make use of the texts of the past in our own reading circumstances) as out of respect for the text's own founding claim to the status of art: it is only in this way that the textual power to make ongoing meaning can be preserved and rescued from the text's own tendency to limit its meaningfulness. But a necessary first step in this liberation of the text consists of identifying both the limitations it puts on itself and the means whereby it does this, so that they can be relativized in the act of reading; and that is the role that can be performed by a reading of the situational self-reflexivity—the devices of readability—of so-called "readerly" texts.

For a handful of short French and English narrative texts of the nineteenth century, such is the task the present book attempts to perform. In contenting myself with analyzing their self-situating devices and describing the terms in which they produce themselves as literary communications, I am aware of stopping short at the stage of ideological distancing that would enable a true recontextualizing reading to take place. In limiting myself to so small and limited a corpus, I am aware also that it is pitifully unrepresentative, not only of such vast categories as "literature," "narrative," or "fiction," but even of relatively smaller classes such as "nineteenth-century fiction" or "the short story." Perhaps, however, my texts *can* be seen as representative in some sense of the class of "readerly" texts, and the mode of analysis I have adopted can be seen as transferable, *mutatis mutandis,* to the "readerly" narrative in general and to other "readerly" genres.

Moreover, the fact that all the texts are short stories is not due exclusively to the relative ease with which such brief texts can be analyzed in sufficient detail to produce broadly convincing results; it follows from a hunch that in the nineteenth century the short story was the artistic form of narrative par excellence—comparable in its relationship with the more monumental narrative genres to the situation of the *Lied,* or art song, in relation to the symphony or the opera—and that, as a result, the ideologies of art involved in their textual self-contextualizing might be more readily visible there, because more self-conscious, than in other texts. Baudelaire was fascinated by Wagner but followed Poe in praising, and practicing, the shorter lyric forms for their poetic intensity. In pursuing some of the secrets of the "readerly" narrative in a few shorter examples of the form, I assume that the intensity of their artistry holds at least a few keys to the presuppositions and practices of nineteenth-century narrative art in general.

Textual Mirrorings

By what means does a text produce its own narrative situation? Or, to put it another way, what is the textual object of a situational reading of text? The resources of language include markers of what E. Benveniste calls *énonciation* ("utterance"), as opposed to *énoncé* ("statement"): the pronoun system, the tense system, modes of deixis.[18] O. Ducrot and his group have shown in turn that innocent little words like *mais* or *d'ailleurs* cannot be correctly analyzed in their linguistic function except situationally.[19] Consequently, the functioning of the literary text as speech act is inscribed in its linguistic substance and is readable there. But the more text-specific mode of making meaning, including situational meaning, is by repetition, reflection, and mirroring of all kinds. The specular text is one that assumes that it is readable—or is assumed to be readable— by virtue of its coherence, that is, by virtue of the fact that it has parts that can be perceived as similar to one another, and that as a consequence each part can also be related by its similarity to the text as a whole. This insistence on similarity does not, of course, exclude difference—the difference without which parts would be indistinguishable from each other and from the whole and without which there can be no production of meaning. But it implies that significant differences can be perceived only against a background of sameness, rather than the contrary, and consequently that reading such texts is based essentially on a process of comparison.

Such a reading technique presupposes, more particularly, that a given segment of text, in specular relationship with another such segment or with the text as a whole, can be conceived as a "model" of the text, or text segment, to which it is compared; and such a model can be, among other things, a model of narrative situation. However, these so-called "models" are by definition incomplete and partial with respect to the total text (since a part cannot coincide with a whole), and inadequate (by virtue of their differences) one to another. This means that the reading maneuver must consist of a (theoretically) indeterminate number of identifications of parts and acts of comparison between parts and parts, and parts and whole, until a multiple model of the text is built up. Moreover, the necessary difference (in similarity) between various segments of text means also that all so-called "models" must also be, to a greater or lesser extent, *antimodels,* that is, similar in the way that opposites are similar—and indeed, empirically, not only will it be seen that texts very frequently incorporate in their structure a true antimodel, or even a number of such antimodels (defining themselves in terms of what they are not), but also that *all* models can be as fruitfully considered in terms of their difference (as antimodel) as they can in terms of their similarity (as model). So a very significant part of the reading process consists of acts of discrimination determining whether a given "model" is to be taken as significant by virtue of its similarity (its direct applicability as model) or by virtue of its dissimilarity (its revelatory powers as an antimodel).

However, such reader discrimination is inversely important to the degree of *explicitness* of textual mirrorings. Texts frequently include quite explicit metanarrative discourse, or "commentary," such as the summing up in Nerval's "Sylvie": "Telles sont les chimères qui charment et égarent au matin de la vie. J'ai essayé de les fixer sans beaucoup d'ordre; mais bien des coeurs me comprendront . . . ." In such a case—unless one is dealing with an "unreliable narrator" or some other device of indeterminacy—the direct applicability of the model may be assumed. "Sylvie" is here describing its narrative content as "chimères" and thus determining a text-reader relationship based on an assumed agreement as to what constitutes illusion (illusion is part "charme," part "égarement"; it intervenes during youth). Given this understanding, which implies a certain maturity on the part of narrator and narratee, the speaking voice of the narrative ("je") now defines the relationship of writing and reading that pertains to the text. In it, the unmasterly and disorderly (entropic) process of writing is to be counteracted by a (negentropic) process of comprehension—reading as an ordering act, the "bringing together" (comprendre) in which the disordered subject ("je") of the writing becomes the ordered object ("me") of the reading activity. And this act is entrusted not to the intellect but to the feelings—the Rousseauesque coeur of the reader, while at the same time readers not capable of such an effort of intuitive comprehension, the "heartless" members of the reading public, are excluded. In this way, the text defines in quite specific and explicit terms its narrative situation and describes the conditions in which, by its own reckoning, it makes sense.

At the other end of the spectrum, the narrative situation of the text may be much more implicit, and it may need, for example, to be "read into" such relatively indeterminate features as effects of style. In this case, the process of comparison will bear, for example, on "dialogic" effects in the text, such as the contrast in Flaubert between the measured style of the narration ("Pendant un demi-siècle, les bourgeoises de Pont-l'Evêque envièrent à Mme Aubain sa servante Félicité") and the verbal slovenliness, the vulgarisms and errors, of the characters ("Un vestibule étroit séparait la cuisine de la salle où Mme Aubain se tenait . . . "; "Pour 'se dissiper', elle demanda la permission de recevoir son neveu Victor"). But here one would be overly hasty in assuming that narratorial style embodies a simple model, and characters' style a simple antimodel, of the narrative situation (one of "refinement," for example, versus "unrefinement"), since there is a sense in which each style comments on the other. The narrative situates Félicité, for example, through the incorrectness of her sociolect, but to the extent that her speech is an index of her "simplicity"—the goodness of her heart—the presence of Félicité's voice speaking in the text reflects inversely, and perhaps adversely, on the cultivated sobriety of the narratorial voice. There are short stories by Marcel Schwob in which the refined prose of the narration contrasts with underworld slang in the mouth of a protagonist without its being possible to determine which "level" of style is model and which is antimodel for the narration as a whole.

Does *fin de siècle* refinement or socially marginal discourse connote the language of art? If each does, can one be said to connote it in a positive sense and the other in a negative sense? One might conclude that here the artistic situation—the situation out of which the text speaks—is the one that these two models—each the antimodel of the other but not of "art" itself—connote jointly. But such a conclusion must be inferred from essentially implicit indices.

Among the important textual features that guide the reader's identification and comparison of significant repetitions and equivalences is intertextual reference, which must also be viewed in terms of a range of explicitness and implicitness, as well as of precision and imprecision—specificity and unspecificity—of focus. To designate specifically another text or work of art within a text is to invite the reader to correlate that text with the work mentioned (it may be a positive or negative correlation, or, of course, both) and hence to *situate* the text in terms of a literary or discursive context that serves as the interpretant, or criterion of relevance, and determines the selective process of reading. Thus, in "Sylvie," there is insistent intertextual reference to Rousseau, on the one hand, as novelist and, on the other, as philosopher, a reference that serves to relate certain segments of the text to the category of the "romanesque" and others to that of the philosophical—categories that, in this text, signify radically opposed narrative situations (i.e., they offer an antimodel and a model, respectively, of the text's own narrative stance).

However, such intertextual reference need not be so specific: Genette reserves the term "architextualité" for intertextual reference of broader range (e.g., generic in its scope).[20] Thus, in "Sarrasine," the narrator refers to Mme de Rochefide's taste for hearing "l'histoire de ces passions énergiques enfantées dans nos coeurs par les ravissantes femmes du Midi"—thus referring his own tale to the thematics of a broad range of romantic writing (Mme de Staël's *Corinne* and E. T. A. Hoffmann's *Des Teufels Elixiere*, for example). Again, the intertext may be quite specific but referred to only implicitly: I see an implicit intertextual reference to Dante, for example, in the reading scene at the end of "Sylvie," where the episode of Paolo and Francesca is, so to speak, turned upside down.[21] Finally, in the absence or apparent absence of intertextual reference, it is, of course, the reader who, as part of the communicational process of situating the text, furnishes an interpretant from the resources of his or her personal "library" of literary experience.

The range in degrees of implicitness and explicitness with which texts produce models of their own narrative situation correlates to some extent with the classical polarization of narrative in terms of *showing* versus *telling* (the "mimetic" narrative versus the "diegetic" narrative, in Gérard Genette's terms[22]). There are narratives that focus on their own status as narration—and these are the narratives that favor the more explicit modes of self-reflexivity—and narratives that historically have tended to background their status as narrative acts so as to focus attention on their content: in them, the story, so to speak, tells itself. Since the latter are no less art narratives than the former, although they rely rather more on the *ars celandi artem* and attempt to imitate what might be called a "natural" narrative situation—the manuscript-found-in-an-attic ploy, on the one hand, the story that "tells itself," on the other—such narratives might be referred to as *duplicitous.* The duplicity of the narrative situation they presuppose is such that a felicitous reading must comprehend its doubleness and respond both to the mimesis of "natural" narrative and to the artistic assumptions of the narrative as a whole; in short, it is a duplicity that does not function correctly unless it is seen through.[23] It follows that the indicators of narrative situation such texts propose cannot afford to be too explicit (they would give the game away); yet, they must be readable (or there would be no game); consequently, the more implicit modes of situational self-reference are the ones they favor. These presuppose a reader who is either alert enough to the techniques of *ars celandi artem* through literary experience or specifically alerted by the text—most often by some "ungrammaticality" or *invraisemblance* in the supposed "natural" narrative—to seek out and interpret these more indirect devices. Thus, in "Un coeur simple," a prime example of "duplicitous" narrative, the most important key to textual self-contextualization proves to be, rather unexpectedly, the "simplicity" of its protagonist, the maid Félicité—such, at least, is what I will suggest in chapter 6.

But if the distinction between the duplicitous narration and the self-designating narration is a worthwhile one (I will be proposing in my conclusion that there is a broader sense in which all narrative can be understood to be duplicitous), it is not surprising that one should be able to distinguish in similar terms between the two most significant devices used in nineteenth-century texts to produce their narrative situation through textual means. I am referring to two forms—one relatively explicit, the other relatively implicit—of embedding, or *mise en abyme,* the technique studied with masterly completeness by Lucien Dällenbach in *Le récit spéculaire.*[24] Dällenbach makes a number of important and useful distinctions, pointing out that embedding may function as a statement model (*mise en abyme de l'énoncé*), an utterance model (*mise en abyme de l'énonciation*), or a code model (*mise en abyme du code*). (And incidentally, this classification can be extended to other forms of textual mirroring; thus, a "commentary" can refer, for example, to the narrative content—"Telles sont les chimères . . ."—to the narrative act—"J'ai essayé de les fixer . . ."—or to the understandings on which it is based: ". . . bien des coeurs me comprendront"). For the purpose of situational narrative analysis, all three of these functions are relevant (since a reference to the text as *énoncé* cannot help betraying an attitude to that *énoncé* and hence affecting the narrational relationship involved, as in the case of the word "chimères" in "Sylvie"), but utterance models and code models are particularly apposite in that they refer directly to the narrative situation, one by "mirroring" the act of narration (and hence the actors involved and the relationships among them), the other by mirroring the code of understandings that makes the narration as act a meaningful one. As a matter of fact, the distinction between *énonciation* and *code* is probably at best a heuristic one, so true is it that the "code" implies an enunciatory situation in which to function while inversely "enunciation" or "utterance" presupposes a code, without which it would be pointless. Be that as it may, these are the functions of embedding that, in the essays that follow, will be called upon time after time as evidence of the texts' situational self-reflexivity.

However, the distinction that correlates with that between self-designating and duplicitous narrative concerns not the function but the mode of embedding. There is, in situational terms, a relatively explicit mode (I call it "narrational" embedding) and a relatively implicit one (which I call "figural" embedding). "Narrational" embedding is not "l'histoire dans l'histoire" (in the terms of J. Ricardou's pioneering title[25]) but narrative act within narrative act, narrative situation within narrative situation: it implies the representation, internally to the fictional framework, of a situation involving the major components of a communicational act (emitter-discourse-recipient)—and very frequently the mirroring within a story of the storytelling relationship itself: narrator-narration-narratee. "Figural" embedding, on the other hand, consists of the incorporation into the narrative of a "figure" (in the sense of a personage but also in the sense of an image) that is representative in some sense of "art," or of the production and reception of narrative, that is, of narrative "code" or "enunciation." Thus, in "Sarrasine," the narrator's intimate storytelling relationship with Mme de Rochefide is embedded in the storytelling relationship of the tale as a whole. This is "narrational" embedding; whereas in "The Purloined Letter," Dupin's production of a screen of pipe smoke, representing a function of discourse, or in "Sylvie," the references to watchmaking or lacemaking that appear as images of narrative art, or again, in "Un coeur simple," the stuffed parrot and the *reposoir* that serve as antimodels of "art" — all these can be classified as examples of "figural" embedding.

I know of no rule requiring "narrational" embedding to appear in self-designating narratives and "figural" embedding in duplicitous narratives; on the contrary, it is clear that both may appear (or not) in either kind of narrative, although "narrational" embedding appears relatively discreetly in duplicitous narrative. But it does seem that, by virtue of their relative degrees of explicitness and implicitness in mirroring the text as narrative act, the two types of embedding are of inverse significance *to the reader* of each type of narrative. In self-designating narratives, the presence of "narrational" embedding provides an immediate clue to the situational model the text is producing; in duplicitous narratives, in which "narrational" embedding is either absent or very reduced in function, the reader's reliance on "figural" embedding is proportionately greater.

This is because "narrational" embedding admits of specific analysis in terms of the components of the communicational situation. A "narrator" and a "narratee" can be identified and the status of each analyzed in terms of qualities (in Greimas's terms, their *être*) and performance (their *faire* — modalized as it may be in terms of *vouloir faire, savoir faire, pouvoir faire*).[26] The *faire* in this case being accomplished by means of a *dire* (the communicational act itself), the latter is open to actantial analysis, and by this means the relationship between narrator and narratee can be described in terms of their respective positions in regard to power, knowledge, and desire. Thus, in the embedded narrational situation of "Sarrasine," a narrator with specific qualities (e.g., maleness) is using his storytelling as a means of influencing (specifically, seducing) a narratee, also endowed with specific qualities (e.g., femaleness) — an act whose performance and outcome are determined by the precise relationship of power, knowledge, and desire distributed between the two. But "figural" embedding, on the other hand, does not have initial status in terms of a represented communicational situation; its status is that of a component in the primary narrative (an actor, an element of the setting, or even a figure of style) and its communicational significance is a latent one only, awaiting actualization through a specific act of interpretation by a reader. Thus, in "Sylvie," lacemaking or clock-making form part of the *savoir-faire* of two characters, Sylvie and Père Dodu, who are themselves engaged actantially in a narrative sequence concerned with actions (the voyage of *"je"* to the Valois), not communication. For these skills of the characters to become figures of narration depends on a reader's being capable of the appropriate act of metaphorization.

However, and to conclude, whatever the value of these distinctions (self-designating versus duplicitous texts; narrational versus figural embedding), the frequency with which the device of embedding itself appears in the texts under consideration is a phenomenon that invites some reflection. It is perhaps not accidental that embedding is so important a feature of "readerly" texts, those that exploit the power of fiction both to produce and to limit meaningfulness. Less explicit than metanarrative commentary, for example, embedding (even "narrational" embedding) allows for relatively intense interpretive involvement on the part of the reader (who must decide, for example, whether a specific embedded feature is a model or an antimodel of the text in question, or something in between) and thus produces a degree of textual polysemy. But, on the other hand, to the extent that it does model the narrative situation, embedding (even "figural" embedding) limits the reader's options in approaching the text, and it does so in a way that is more precise and explicit, more directive of a specific reading, than, say, dialogic interplay between segments of the text, or features of style. Opening up interpretive options while simultaneously programming them, determining a narrative situation without imposing a single interpretation of the narrative content, embedding defines and limits but defines and limits a *range* of reading options.[27] As such it constitutes the central device by which the "readability" of the "readerly" text is produced, a proposition that will be illustrated and explored in the examples that follow.

Models and Antimodels: "The Open Window"

A story that concerns the power of fiction—analyzed as a function of narrative situation—is Saki's "The Open Window." (See appendix A). The questions are: How does the text theorize its own impact? What power, in what situation, does the tale lay claim to? How does this claim relate to the fictional power directly represented in the text? Or, putting it another way, is the textual representation of fictional power a model or an antimodel of the text's own power? Certainly, the initial readability of the text derives from two narrational embeddings—Vera's story to Framton Nuttel about her aunt's "tragedy" and her story to the aunt about Framton's Indian adventure—which form a double utterance model and demonstrate a set of situational conditions for the success of fiction. These lie essentially in a relationship of inequality between narrator and narratee, one of whom is "very self-possessed" and adequately informed about the pragmatic situation, while the other is either suggestible and insecure (like Mr. Nuttel) or gullible (like Mrs. Sappleton) and in any case receives the story in a kind of referential void. Mr. Nuttel and Mrs. Sappleton know nothing about each other or their respective histories, that is what frees Vera to romance about them; and although it may not be consonant with the text's grapholect to read Mr. Nuttel as "nutty" and Mrs. Sappleton as a "sap," he is certainly in need of a nerve cure and she is capable of cohabiting with Vera without perceiving her niece's inveterate mythomania. Vera's name, on the other hand, signifies her "epistemological" superiority over her interlocutors: the access she has to the "truth" and her consequent ability to distinguish "truth" from "fiction," with a view to producing a duplicitous confusion of the two. As for her self-possession, it takes the form of narrational skill, mastery of her means, as is abundantly illustrated by her acting ability, her voice faltering and her eyes staring at all the appropriate moments. Vera is a personification of narrative "authority."

But Vera, it is true, is an ironic name for a professional fictionalist. "Romance at short notice was her specialty": this metanarrative comment about Vera serves to make her activity as fictionalist a figure of the text itself (in other words, the character appears as a figural embedding by which the text characterizes itself as "romance at short notice" and the product of a "specialty"). The link between the internal narrations and the text itself as narrative act—in short, the readability of the text—is produced by this equivalence, for one need not know much about Saki to perceive the relevance to the text's own situation of words such as "romance" (with its latter-day connotations of literature as entertainment), "at short notice" (cf. the conditions of journalistic production), and "specialty" (the practice of literature as a more or less technical pursuit, or "skill," rather than, say, as an everyday activity engaged in by all). The textual claim, then—as it emerges from this equivalence—is distinctly self-effacing; the text is saying something like "Do not give me more importance than I deserve: I am not great literature, just a trivial although workmanlike divertissement. And, like Vera's romancing, I am false."

However, if one carries the comparison of the text with its narrational embeddings a little further, it becomes clear that Vera's storytelling is less of a model and more of an antimodel of the text's own narrative situation. The narrator of "The Open Window" is clearly not seeking to produce in the narratee anything like Framton Nuttel's "loss of nerve" and precipitate flight; nor does he keep the narratee in the dark (about Vera's myth making) as poor Mrs. Sappleton remains in the dark. Although he exercizes considerable narrative mastery and "self-possession" by withholding some essential information until the end, thus practicing the form of power called suspense, the final sentence makes the relationship between himself and the narratee different from that in the embedded narratives in a number of important ways. Unlike Mr. Nuttel, the reader is reassured, not scared out of his or her wits (there are no ghosts, only fiction); unlike Mrs. Sappleton, the reader is informed, not deluded by false explanations (there were no pariah dogs, only fiction); so that, unlike both, the reader is not given illusory information about pragmatic circumstances (like the apparent "fit" between Vera's discourse and the hunters' return or Framton's flight). But he or she *is* given a strong hint about the true illocutionary circumstances (by means of the genuine "fit" between Vera's specialty and the fictional status of the narrative itself). In short, the difference between "The Open Window" as narrative act and Vera's acts of storytelling lies in the status of Saki's narrative as a *self-designating* fiction: it is genuinely informative about the illocutionary circumstances appropriate to it, whereas Vera produces illusory information about the pragmatic situation.

This difference comes about, of course, because in the narrative situation of the text there are *no* pragmatic circumstances to be judged true or false. Unlike Vera, the narrator of "The Open Window" operates from the beginning in exactly the same referential void as the narratee: there is simply no "real-life" experience common to both—I mean, something equivalent to the hunter's return or Framton's flight—that the fictional discourse could be made (prospectively or retrospectively) to match, in conjunction with which it could exercize its power and against which its truth or falsity could be measured, so that, unlike Vera's romancing, the text's claim to power can lie only in its being *recognized* by the reader, and treated as, fiction. What this means is that the text is claiming to be, like Vera's discourse, a discursive framework, but one that (unlike hers) encloses a *complete* referential void and has only the *latent* power of relating in a meaningful way to the pragmatic experience of its readership—perhaps future experience (as Vera's hunting story foreshadows the return of the hunters) or perhaps past experience (as Vera's Indian story accounts retrospectively for Nuttel's flight).

I am able to say this because of the final example of figural embedding in the text, the one which—as opposed to the narrational embeddings that function in important ways as antimodels as well as models—provides the most direct model of the text as a whole. I am referring, of course, to those suspiciously "open" windows on an October day—the circumstance on which Vera seizes to make her own fictions work, but which stands more generally as a model for the idea of a framework opening onto a void but doing so pregnantly (in such a way that experience *may* fill it and make it meaningful).

We can say, then, that whereas Vera's stories constitute *mise en abyme de l'énonciation,* or models of utterance, the windows are *mise en abyme du code*—they specify what must be understood for the story, as fiction, to succeed. However, by virtue of their intertextual reference, and their classification as "romance," Vera's stories are also relevant to the code. The fifteen-year-old is clearly a reader of the pulp of the period: stories of widows deranged by their grief or of adventure in imperial outposts. And she uses these lurid fictions precisely as their status as romance requires: as empty frameworks available to make pragmatic experience (in this case, a decorous formal visit between parties, none of whom has any interest in the others) into a more meaningful circumstance. "I hope Vera has been amusing you," says the aunt. "She has been very interesting," says Nuttel.

Again, the text dissociates itself, of course, from Vera and her concept of romance: *its* subject matter is not outlandish things like pariah dogs and hunting disasters but—precisely!—a boring visit, the *same* boring visit Vera so effectively enlivens with fiction. So the antimodel is again a model, since, as romance, the text is claiming for itself the same function as Vera performs: to make "interesting" the banal circumstances of the everyday (and specifically, the everyday of the Edwardian upper middle class, a milieu in which the most disturbing event of the day is apt to be someone's tracking mud into the living room). It does it, following Vera's model, by an admixture of "romance" or fiction, in short by the character of Vera herself, through whose agency the return of the hunting party becomes a spectral visitation, and the *gaucherie* of a disturbed young man is suddenly part of the White Man's Burden.

But these transformations are false, gratuitous, and ephemeral, in short, just "romance," as the deflationary final sentence makes clear. The text itself, as "romance" also, makes no greater claim. "Thick description" of the narrative contract implied here would be very relevant, for, by implication, the text is defining its readership as the Mr. Nuttels and the Mrs. Sappletons of this world, the class of leisured English gentlefolk who ask of literature, not that it touch life and.transform it, but only that it entertain. The "open window" of the text cannot frame any experience except that of a "restful spot," of rural society centered on the rectory, where things happen "just in time for tea" and where colonial violence (on which the comfort of the society objectively reposes) is so remote as to be, at best, subject matter for adventure stories, "romance." In this world, "tragedies [seem] out of place": it is a world where only romance is meaningful—and meaningful because, precisely, it does not seek to be "meaningful" but only to entertain. Vera's variety of romancing is *disturbing* because it brings visionary phenomena and extraneous violence into *contact* with this isolated "restful spot," thus producing madness and disorder. In this final sense, she is again an anti-model, for Saki's romance holds such things at bay, by labeling them "romance" precisely—while it still exploits their power, as romance, to make the dreary round of middle-class life, factitiously, into something "interesting" and "very amusing."

The Limits of the "Readerly": "Les Sans-Gueule"

By contrast with "The Open Window," Marcel Schwob's "Les Sans-Gueule" (see appendix B) exemplifies those texts that, rather than functioning as self-designating narrative acts, present themselves—duplicitously—as concerned only with their content: in this case, an account of the treatment of a rather extraordinary medical "case." That the text might be producing *itself* as a "case for treatment" is a hypothesis that depends entirely on a figural reading of this narrative content, in which the "case" *in* the text is taken to be indicative of the "case" *of* the text, so that the problem of treatment becomes a figure for the problematics of reading. "Problematics" because—again by contrast with the Saki story—"Les Sans-Gueule" is in this respect something of a *cas-limite*. Although it determines its readability and delimits its interpretability by means of the classical technique of figural embedding, it does so in such a way as to define the situation that makes sense of it as one of "unreadability," since reading is projected as a situation of unresolvable anxiety as regards sense. Consequently, an aporia is produced in the text as narration (we are invited to read but to read its unreadability), and this is mirrored in the figure itself (the story of the Sans-Gueules—the "embedded" figure is in fact coterminous with the text itself) by a similar but reverse coupling of the impossibility of reading with a requirement to read, in which the impossibility of reading is posed as the condition in which one reads.

Structurally, the story pivots (between the hospital segment and the domestic episode) on a description of the anxiety to which the "petite femme" is subject by reason of the need to choose between two featureless—not faces—but "surfaces":

Elle allait éternellement de l'un à l'autre, épiant une indication, attendant un signe. Elle guettait ces surfaces rouges qui ne bougeraient jamais plus. Elle regardait avec anxiété ces énormes cicatrices dont elle distinguait graduellement les coutures comme on connaît les traits des visages aimés. Elle les examinait tour à tour, ainsi que l'on considère les épreuves d'une photographie, sans se décider à choisir.

This passage makes it clear that her careful scrutiny does succeed in distinguishing something equivalent to a "face"—the scars have markings that can be discerned "comme on connaît les traits des visages aimés." But her anxiety stems from the impossibility of discerning a sign that would give *one* of the Sans-Gueules, *but not the other*, a face (the face of her husband): she cannot choose between them. So the problem is not to produce meaning by humanizing the faceless surfaces she is scanning; the problem is to opt for one rather than the other as being the "true" or "right" choice, the one that corresponds to her lost husband. The anxiety she displays in attempting to "read," that is, to "treat" or to "cure," the undifferentiated text (the "coutures" figure the *cousu*, the sewn-together quality of text) does not derive from a difficulty of *figuration* but from the difficulty of choosing one such figure, or face (French *figure*) to the exclusion of another. In short, the problematics of reading she is thus enacting derives from the classical conception of meaning as being unique and determinable and subject in consequence to acts of discernment as to the rightness or wrongness of specific "readings": it is reading of the "readable," not the *scriptible.*

That "treatment" in the story is bound up with a problematics of choice is something that emerges from the thematics of both the hospital segment and the domestic segment, which mirror each other in significant ways. Choice intervenes at both the beginning and the end of the story. Initially, it is the arbitrary selection (as one might choose to "read" text A as opposed to texts B, C, . . . , N) by which the two Sans-Gueules are singled out from all the other victims of war as candidates for treatment. A medical orderly "les prit par curiosité surtout"; the surgeon "fut surpris du cas, et y prit intérêt." At the end of the story, the equally arbitrary choice of the woman, singling out one of the men and allowing the other to die (as one "reads" according to one meaning, thereby excluding other possible meanings), mirrors the initial act of selection.

In the hospital, once the surgeon decides to treat his patients, his intervention has an immediate humanizing effect: they learn to smoke, an activity that the text equates with inarticulate discourse and inchoate communication:

Cependant ils guérirent tous deux. . . . Accroupis dans leurs couvertures, ils respiraient le tabac . . . . Et chaque échappement du brouillard gris qui jaillissaient entre les craquelures de ces masses rouges était salué d'un rire extrahumain, gloussement de la luette qui tressaillait, tandis que leur reste de langue clapotait faiblement.

But it is at this point that it becomes necessary to distinguish them one from the other—the woman arrives, anxious to identify her husband. Her inability to do so provokes a stage of hesitation, "elle était dans une affreuse perplexité," which is broken only by her decision to take both men home with her, that is, to defer her choice.

At home, their treatment continues. Once more, it has a humanizing effect, consisting as it does in the establishment of a true communicational relationship between them and the woman. Already at the hospital this process had begun:

Elle se pencha vers eux: elle parla à l'oreille de l'un, puis de l'autre. Les têtes n'eurent aucune réaction,—mais les quatre mains éprouvèrent une sorte de vibration,—sans doute parce que ces deux pauvres corps sans âme sentaient vaguement qu'il y avait près d'eux une petite femme très gentille . . . .

Now, at home, it continues. She names them—an act constituting a kind of inverse response to the surgeon's treatment, by which they acquired the power to produce smoke discourse, and thus instituting a kind of dialogue.

Ils étaient "ses deux singes", ses bonshommes rouges, ses deux petits marins, ses hommes brûlés, ses corps sans âme, ses polichinelles de viande, ses têtes trouées, ses caboches sans cervelle, ses figures de sang . . . .

This act (equated by the sentence structure with her nursing) is notable because, like her attention to their scars, it is an act of figuration. By employing the figure of metaphor, she is giving the faceless surfaces a human "face" (*une figure*), or, in other words, she is making them meaningful. But although she now produces a kind of animal response from them (they are sometimes "comme deux chiens folâtres," sometimes "semblables à des animaux repentants"), they remain indistinguishable from each other, and undistinguished in her affections.

It is an intervention from the hospital (reproducing the effect of her previous arrival there) that forces her choice—a choice that, by now, however, has been further complicated by the erotic involvement between the Sans-Gueules and the woman.

Elle leur baisait parfois leurs affreuses coutures, et s'essuyait la bouche tout de suite après, en fronçant les lèvres, en cachette. Et elle riait aussitôt, à perte de vue.

As a result of this divisive choice, the "couple" formed by the woman and the faceless pair will become a triangle: thus, it produces jealousy, decline, and death—but without resolving the woman's dilemma: "lorsque le malade fut mort, toute sa peine se réveilla." Although she has perhaps killed her husband (the rightful choice), she cannot hate his happy rival: "elle courut, haineuse, vers l'autre Sans-Gueule, et s'arrêta, prise de sa pitié enfantine . . . ." The story thus ends in kind of stasis of continued hesitation.

At a number of points, the text is explicit that the two Sans-Gueules pose the problem of meaning. At the outset, they are a "double cicatrice arrondie, gigantesque et sans signification," and later, "les deux coupes rouges couturées reposaient toujours sur les oreillers, avec cette même absence de signification qui en faisaient une double énigme." If there is a suggestion here that they are, metaphorically speaking, a speechless mouth ("double cicatrice arrondie," "deux coupes rouges couturées"), then the erotic atmosphere at the end finds its justification in the idea that the cure for their speechlessness—the answer to the problem of meaning—lies in love, that is, not just in the establishment of a mutual (or mouth-to-mouth) relationship that produces communication but also (and here's the rub) the selection of one individual by another. Since it is the two Sans-Gueule together who form the mouth (even though each is equipped individually with a "palais béant" and a "tremblant moignon de langue"), the selectivity of love can only be self-defeating, and the production of meaning can only destroy the totality that offered the possibility of meaning. In this way, then (as ever), the erotics of text and the aesthetics of text are identical, and the problematics of meaning is identified with what René Girard would call mimetic desire.[28]

The operation of *figuration*—that is, the form of "treatment" that bestows powers of expression and a human "face" on the couple's undifferentiated surface, an operation equivalent to the act of reading—is governed by the same self-defeating conditions. The couple develop a "double cri rauque," they produce "sons aigus et modulés, mais sans puissance syllabique," or "cris inarticulés"; they learn to respond with body language, like pet animals, to the woman's care; but this *virtuality* of meaning is not realized by the woman's attempt at differentiation between them. The individual who remains alive, joyful as he is, does not acquire individual features, articulated language, or the power to make meaning: he is still just "le misérable mannequin rouge qui fumait joyeusement, en modulant ses cris"; her anxiety has not been relieved but rather has been intensified by her act of choice. So, the phrase that records the woman's final hesitation, as one Sans-Gueule lies dying and the other survives, is particularly apposite: "Alors, dans une incertitude haletante, elle dévisagea de nouveau ces deux têtes sans visages." The operation of choice can only lead to a new *dévisagement,* that is (to make the pun explicit), on the one hand, a return to the undifferentiated surface of facelessness and, on the other, to continued anxious scrutiny, in the hope of discovering the sign that will differentiate *meaningfully* between the undifferentiables.

Of course, the equivalence between the text (as narration) and the case recounted in the text (as figure) is not impaired by the obvious fact that Schwob's text is far from being literally "sans figures." On the contrary, it employs many specific rhetorical figures. It introduces figures also by parallelism and other types of textual equivalence and repetition (thus, for example, the sentences that make smoking equivalent to speech or the woman's care for the Sans-Gueules equivalent to naming them by metaphor; or again, the equivalence between the text as a whole, qua text, and the "case" recounted in the text). Far from being without figures, there is a sense in which the text is all figures (and of course, it is frequently asserted, after Nietzsche, that all language is inescapably figuration). But a text that is all figuration poses the problem of indifferentiation no less surely than do the couple who are "de même taille, et *sans figure,*" and the anxiety of reading such a text may produce, through the necessity of giving it a face, of making sense of it (privileging certain figures and patterns of figures but not others—as I am doing, precisely, in the present reading), is structurally the same as the anxiety of the "petite femme" scrutinizing "ces énormes cicatrices dont elle distinguait graduellement les coutures comme on connaît les traits des visages aimés."

Yet, the paradox remains: "Les Sans-Gueule" is a "readerly" text that uses the device of "readability"—its power as fiction to determine the reading situation that makes sense of it—in order to criticize the notion of readability and the presuppositions concerning the nature of meaning it implies. Although in this sense the story genuinely foreshadows the undecidability inherent in more modern, "writerly" texts, I do not believe this is a case of textual self-deconstruction, in which equal weight, so to speak, should be given to the two sides of an unresolvable aporia between "readability" and "unreadability." There are three reasons for this—or rather, I see the text subscribing preferentially to the notion of determinacy of meaning in three ways.

First, by presenting as unusual, exceptional, and indeed horrible its "case" of indifferentiation, it problematizes, certainly, the classical conception of how one might "treat" a text for meaning, but without any alternative conception being produced in or by the text. The anxiety of reading is thus seen, on the one hand, as inevitable (given the phenomenon of textual indifferentiation) but, on the other, as exceptional (given the unusualness of the case). However, if the phenomenon of indifferentiation was thought of in a generalized way, the anxiety would itself disappear, since it derives from a conception of meaning that would then be untenable (as we now know from our familiarity with "writerly" texts).

Second, the narrational tone of the storytelling is as self-assured and classical as the case related is unprecedented and baffling, and on two occasions, at least, the narrator sets himself off from his characters as the possessor of insights regarding the meaning of the Sans-Gueules' behavior, the beneficiary of a certain readability in them that is otherwise denied. Thus, ". . . les quatre mains éprouvèrent une sorte de vibration, sans doute parce que ces deux pauvres corps sans âme sentaient vaguement que . . . ," and ". . . une jalousie animale, née de sensations avec des souvenirs confus peut-être d'une vie d'autrefois." The adverbs *sans doute* and *peut-être* are sops to the Cerberus of narrational verisimilitude, an attempt to mask the narrator's privilege: the observations are nevertheless clearly addressed by a knowing (if not all knowing) narrator to a narratee who is assumed to be equally capable of reading meaningfulness into the Sans-Gueules and their story.

And—finally—behind this narrator lies an implied author who

displays similar faith in meaning by producing the figure of the Sans-Gueules as a guide to the meaning of the text, in conformity with classical narrative techniques. That the meaning this technique conveys is one that subverts the possibility of meaning does not impair the primacy of the technique itself and its presuppositions as to the nature of meaning: although it sets up a tension between the classical narrative as an act of *narration* and the more problematic thematic content of the story, the narrative as *narré*, the story remains firmly "readable." "Content" is never separable from the meaning it acquires in the communicational situation; just so, in "Les Sans-Gueule," the situation of "unreadability" implied by the narrative content is outweighed by the narrational act of producing that situation and, therefore, by the situation of "readability" implied by the narrative techniques. The situation produced *in* the text proves subordinate to the situation produced *by* the text, by virtue of the principle formulated by Valéry: "Tout langage dit je suis acte de quelqu'un *avant de signaler autre chose*" (I have changed the emphasis). Thus, although we have a text in which the embedded figure (the story of the Sans-Gueules) and the narration proper are, in formal terms, indistinguishable one from the other, one has to conclude that the former is the antimodel—not the model—of the actual textual situation.

What does this mean? Just as it was necessary in the case of "The Open Window" to read the text's own situational self-contextualizing (as "romance") in the light of the text's own cultural circumstances (its pact with the genteel readership of Edwardian England), so too the tension in "Les Sans-Gueule" between the situation of "unreadability" in the embedded figure and the "readability" of the narration can be interpreted as a sign of the text's cultural situation and more specifically its transitional status in historical terms. There is an unresolved conflict in the implied contract with the reader that reflects a cultural context involving ideological disagreement. Among the understandings assumed to prevail between text and reader is a set of assumptions concerning the "readability" of texts and another set of assumptions that posit the "unreadability" of texts (when they are approached, at least, in the light of the first set of assumptions). Here, the first set of assumptions, which looks to the past, is still dominant; the second, forward-looking set has not imposed all of its implications.

One might relate this situation to the social conditions prevailing in France in the aftermath of the Franco-Prussian war and the Commune. As is frequently the case after a national defeat, there was a perceptible weakening in authority structures (reflected in the—gradual—transition from the authoritarianism of the Second Empire to the relatively democratic structures of the Third Republic), but delayed in this case by the strong reassertion of the power of the ruling bourgeoisie, throughout the seventies, in the vigorous repression of the Commune. The "decadence" in France, to which Schwob's writing can be assigned, is understandable as an emergence of repressed and marginalized forces consequent on the weakening of authority, and its beginnings coincided more or less with the amnesty and the return to Paris of the surviving *communard* exiles, that is, with a period of relaxed, but still vigilant, control.

In Schwob's text, the maintenance of authority is figured most notably by the hospital as a social institution, with its role of treating and if possible curing an "ill" caused by the war—an ill dramatized here by the shell that so sharply divides before and after, face and facelessness. It is to the hospital that the woman comes in search of prewar order (her husband); and at the point when her own will to distinguish between the Sans-Gueules flags, it is a reminder from the hospital that compels her to choose. However, this authoritarian pressure to restore a situation of "readability" operates in a situation of weakened authority. It cannot be insignificant that it is the male figures—the visibly phallic but castrated Sans-Gueules, with their uselessly flapping remnant of tongue—who have lost control of language; while the task of restoring readability, the authority to make meaning, is now entrusted to a woman—and to a woman described in insistently diminishing terms, as "la petite femme," "vraiment gentille," "avec des moues enfantines." The etymology of the word *infant* (*in-fans*, unable to speak) is relevant: it is now the turn of those deprived of the power to speak to make meaning.

This reversal of roles is significant when one bears in mind the fact that in previous literary treatments of "unreadability"—texts such as Balzac's "Sarrasine" or Nerval's "Pandora"[29] —it is a "feminine" figure who signifies the disquieting absence, the central void (Zambinella's status as castrato, the Nervalian "femme sans coeur") that problematizes meaning. The emptiness has here extended to the male, and instead of being concealed at the "heart" and productive of illusion, it now spreads across the visible "sur-face" and displays a problem, an ill that cannot be ignored. Concomitantly, the situation ceases to be one of seduction and fascination exercized by the text woman on an unsuspecting male and instead becomes one in which an anxious effort of recuperation must be performed by a feminized (weakened) subject on the fatally damaged male text—an effort at "treatment" that, although it has now become a genuine act of love, is insufficiently strong to cure an ill that has become irreversible.

If "Les Sans-Gueule" reproduces a transitional situation, perhaps nothing much has really changed to this day: when one hears in a classroom "deconstructive" philosophy being expounded in the language of "logocentrism," the communicational situation is no more or less incoherent than that of "Les Sans-Gueule." But to the extent that definitions of "writing" *have* changed in our culture, and of reading as a consequence, a text like "Les Sans-Gueule" is valuable in marking—not so much the moment of transition, which is, of course, difficult, if not impossible, to pinpoint—as the fact of a transition and thus in establishing the historicity of the "readerly" (readable) text, the pressure within it of an emerging "writerly" mode. So, although the juxtaposition of "The Open Window" with "Les Sans-Gueule" does not reproduce the roughly chronological ordering of the studies that are to follow, it may serve, then, already —while acting as a reminder of the continued dominance of the "readerly" text into our own century—as an introduction to the polarization between "readerly" and "writerly" that marks the modern alienated narrative and, in broad terms, organizes the sequence of studies that compose this book, as they map the emergence of the "writerly" within essentially "readerly" texts.

Alienation—Saki's "Romance at short notice was her specialty" neatly encapsulates the reification, through specialization, of the narrative function as the production of fiction—produces the mechanisms and devices of authority characteristic of the "readerly" text, with its emphasis on control; and the self-possession of Vera has much in common, at a fundamental level, with Poe's Dupin. But, as the alienated text becomes more blandly and imperviously autonomous, like Schwob's faceless creatures, the responsibility will shift rather to the reader, whose anxiety in the presence of a closed-off surface of writing becomes an object of textual awareness and whose act of love appears as the necessary requirement, not even for the text's "cure," but for its survival. Narrative interpretability has its roots in a situation that both these texts identify, in the final analysis, as pathological, in a world of hospitals and nerve cures. The formal and methodological considerations of this chapter are thus placed in an important perspective by the texts themselves, and one should not lose sight of this perspective in reading the, again, somewhat technical studies of textual self-situation that follow.

NOTES

1. "L'Analyse structurale des récits," *Communications*, 8 (1966), 1-33.
2. *Sémantique structurale* (Paris: Larousse, 1966), *Du Sens* (Paris: Éd. du Seuil, 1970).
3. T. Todorov, *Grammaire du Décaméron* (La Haye: Mouton, 1969); Cl. Bremond, *Logique du récit* (Paris: Éd. du Seuil, 1973); G. Prince, *A Grammar of Stories* (The Hague: Mouton, 1973).
4. "Narrative Versions, Narrative Theories," *Critical Inquiry*, 7, 1 (autumn 1980), 213-236.
5. "Because such aspects as theme, symbol or point have to be explained at least partly in terms of a receiver, they are the domain of a theory of interpretation (a theory of semiotics, if you will) and the ultimate task for narratologists will be to link their grammars with that theory." "Aspects of a Grammar of Narrative," *Poetics Today*, 1, 3 (spring 1980), 49-63, p. 63.
6. G. Prince, "Introduction à l'étude du narrataire," *Poétique*, 14 (1973), 178-196.
7. *The Rhetoric of Fiction* (Chicago: University of Chicago Press, 1961).
8. "Discours du récit," in *Figures*, III (Paris: Éd. du Seuil, 1972), 65-273.
9. Ibid.; Mieke Bal, *Narratologie* (Paris: Klincksieck, 1977).
10. *Mind and Nature* (New York: Dutton, 1979), p. 13.
11. The situation is exactly similar to that relating to the distinction in traditional narratology between story and discourse, whose interdependency and mutual implication are demonstrated by Jonathan Culler in his essay "Story and Discourse in the Analysis of Narrative," chapter 9 of *The Pursuit of Signs: Semiotics, Literature, Deconstruction* (Ithaca, N.Y.: Cornell University Press, 1981), 169-187.
12. See *S/Z* (Paris: Éd. du Seuil, 1970), pp. 9 et seq.; also Susan Suleiman, "Redundancy and the 'Readable' Text," *Poetics Today*, 1, 3 (spring 1980), 119-142, and "Repetition, Redundancy and Readability in Modern Fiction" (to appear).
13. For debate on the issue, however, see R. Wellek, "What Is Literature?" in P. Hernadi, ed., *What Is Literature?* (Bloomington: Indiana University Press, 1978), 16-23.
14. This sentence perhaps requires some expansion. I am implying that, just as "structure" may be regarded as the actualization of certain features of articulate language so as to produce "text," fiction is the actualization, in certain contexts (e.g., literary) and for certain purposes (e.g., interpretation), of the fictive quality inherent in discourse in general, and in storytelling in particular (on this point, see my conclusion). These operations function in such a way as to produce "reading" as the communicational act that treats text as an object of understanding rather than as the medium of transmission of a given meaning—hence, actualizing the deferral that may itself be taken to characterize all human communication.
15. Notably in *Critique et vérité* (Paris: Éd. du Seuil, 1966).
16. I am mindful of Stanley Fish's point that texts do not exist independently of our reading (i.e., interpretation) of them and of my own point that "relevance is a two-way street." But before they are read, texts get written, and the writing also occurs *in situation:* consequently, the features our reading discovers (or produces) in them are, among other things, discoverable/producible in terms of a historical act that generated the text. It is the circumstances of the historical act that are my focus here, although clearly this is a hypothetical (interpretive) object.
17. For an interesting attempt to specify what readership means in and for such texts, see Vincent Kaufman, "De l'interlocution à l'adresse," *Poétique*, 46 (avril 1981), 171-182.

18. See *Problèmes de linguistique générale,* I and II (Paris: Gallimard, 1966 and 1974).

19. See *Les mots du discours* (Paris: Éd. de Minuit, 1980).

20. See *Introduction à l'architexte* (Paris: Éd. du Seuil, 1979), 87-89. On intertextuality in general, see also Julia Kristéva, *Séméiotiké: Recherches pour une sémanalyse* (Paris: Éd. du Seuil, 1969), esp. p. 255; *Poétique,* 27 (1976) (special issue on "Intertextualités"); Laurent Jenny, "Sémiotique du collage intertextuel," *Revue d'esthétique,* 3/4 (1978), 165-182; Michael Riffaterre, *Semiotics of Poetry* (Bloomington: Indiana University Press, 1978), esp. 115-160, and *La production du texte* (Paris: Éd. du Seuil, 1979), passim. There is a useful general bibliography in *New York Literary Forum,* 2, 1978 ("Intertextuality: New Perspectives in Criticism"), 293-298. In my final chapter, I return to intertextuality in the context of the problem of narrative authority.

21. For further analysis of these texts, see chapters 4 and 5, respectively.

22. See "Discours du récit," in *Figures,* III.

23. For a more complex discussion of duplicity, see chapter 3, where I introduce a distinction between "mimetic" duplicity—the kind discussed here—and "textual" duplicity; and chapter 6, where these terms reappear and recombine. As foreshadowed in chapter 1, and as will be noted in the concluding chapter, all the forms of duplicity relate to a single phenomenon, the characteristic duality of the narrative situation in circumstances of alienated communication.

24. (Paris: Éd. du Seuil, 1977). Other studies by Lucien Dällenbach closely relevant to the studies in this book are "Du fragment au cosmos (*La comédie humaine* et l'opération de lecture, I), *Poétique,* 40 (novembre 1979), 420-430; "Le tout en morceaux (*La comédie humaine* et l'opération de lecture, II)," *Poétique,* 42 (avril 1980), 156-169; and—for a careful theoretical study of the function of embedding with respect to the act of reading—"Réflexivité et lecture," *Revue des Sciences Humaines,* 177 (1980-1981), 23-37.

25. See *Problèmes du nouveau roman* (Paris: Éd. du Seuil, 1967), 171-190.

26. See *Sémantique structurale* and *Du Sens.*

27. Lucien Dällenbach extends this function interestingly to "writerly" texts, seeing the ambiguity of embedding as a factor of textual indeterminacy: "La leçon de la fable est que seul se prête à la lecture un texte ajouré et que la mise en abyme . . . est cet outil ambigu qui permet aussi bien de combler les 'blancs' quand ils abondent, de les creuser quand ils se raréfient, ou de les creuser en les comblant, comme dans *Le Voyeur* où elle tisse à la fois le plein et le vide de l'étoffe, la lisibilité et l'illisibilité du texte-dentelle,—mais toujours en vue de lui assurer, quant à sa lecture, une manière d'autoréglage" ("Réflexivité et lecture," p. 37).

28. See *Mensonge romantique et vérité romanesque* (Paris: Grasset, 1961) and *La violence et le sacré* (Paris: Grasset, 1972), which has been translated as *Violence and the Sacred* (Baltimore: Johns Hopkins University Press, 1977).

29. On "Sarrasine," see Barbara Johnson, "The Critical Difference," *Diacritics,* 8, 2 (July 1978), 2-9; reprinted in *The Critical Difference: Essays in the Contemporary Rhetoric of Reading* (Baltimore: Johns Hopkins University Press, 1980), 3-12. On "Pandora," see R. Chambers, *L'Ange et l'automate: Variations sur le mythe de l'actrice, de Nerval à Proust* (Paris: Minard, 1971), and Michel Jeanneret, *La lettre perdue: Écriture et folie dans l'oeuvre de Nerval* (Paris: Flammarion, 1978).

Chapter Three
Narratorial Authority
and "The Purloined Letter"

Narrative and Narratorial Authority

To tell a story is to exercise power (it is even called the power of narration), and "authorship" is cognate with "authority." But, in this instance as in all others, authority is not an absolute, something inherent in a specific individual or in that individual's discourse; it is relational, the result of an act of authorization on the part of those subject to the power, and hence something to be earned. Thus, in conversation, I may be willing to give up my prerogative of turn taking[1] in order to listen to a particularly interesting, or useful, or funny report; and in literature, if Mary Louise Pratt's analysis is accurate,[2] I am prepared to divert my attention away from the various possible objects that might engage it and toward a particular text, in the expectation of some intellectual or aesthetic gain from that text. Etymology tells us that the narrator is one who *knows*;[3] one might infer that the narratee's motivation in authorizing the act of narration lies in the prospect of acquiring "information." The storyteller, as Walter Benjamin insists—although he distinguishes in this respect between storyteller and novelist—is one who has "experience" to impart.[4]

However, imparting one's experience incorporates a problem; for to the extent that the act of narration is a process of disclosure, in which the information that forms the source of narrative authority is transmitted to the narratee, the narrator gives up the basis of his or her authority in the very act of exercising it. This is not unlike the well-known paradox of the teacher, who, to the extent that he or she is successful in educating the young, thereby renders them independent of the need for education and hence less likely to accord their educator the authorization to teach. There is no need to insist on the various well-known "tricks of the trade," used by teacher and by narrator, to "maintain interest," as it is called: divulgence is never complete, the telling of the ultimate secret is indefinitely deferred — and it most often transpires, in art as in education, that there *is* no ultimate secret. The fact does remain, however, that at the end of a "successful" narration, the interest that authorized the act of narration has been destroyed.

It is plausible to assume, then, that at bottom the narrator's motivation is like that of the narratee and rests on the assumption of exchanging a gain for a loss. Where the narratee offers attention in exchange for information, the narrator sacrifices the information for some form of attention. Consequently, there is a sense in which the maintenance of narrative authority implies an act of seduction, and a certain transfer of interest (on the narratee's part) from the information content to the narrating instance itself (be it the person of the narrator, as in "real-life" situations, or, as in the reading situation, the narrative discourse itself). This is never more the case than when the narrative content is acknowledged to be fictional, that is, noninformative (in the conventional sense of the term): the "point" of the narration can only lie then in its obtaining from the narratee a specific type of attention (to which the information divulged may certainly be germane but cannot be essential). It will be my assumption that in the type of narrative with which I am concerned (let us call it, on the analogy of the term "art song," the modern "art story") the production of art is what compensates for the divulgence of (fictional) information and that the texts' production of themselves as "art" has as its object the gaining of a new kind of authority (in the form of the reader's attention, respect, and indeed fascination) in exchange for the purely narrative authority being progressively lost. For the sake of clarity, I will refer to this new kind of authority as "narratorial" (versus "narrative") authority: it is the "art" of seduction.

Texts such as "Sarrasine" and "Sylvie," it will be seen,[5] specifically thematize narration as a seductive act. Balzac's narrator tells the story of Sarrasine in an effort to bring Mme de Rochefide to bed; Nerval's narrator tells his life story to the women he hopes will "save" him by responding to his love and solving the enigma of his dispersed attachments. But in each case the text specifically distances itself from narration as seduction and claims for itself—implicitly in Balzac's case, explicitly in Nerval's—other powers. The Balzacian narrator appears as a philosopher who expects of his narratee an equivalent degree of philosophical detachment (as opposed to the involvement of seduction); the Nervalian narrator, while also siding with the philosophical against the *romanesque,* asks not for detachment and distance, but for understanding—and the story he tells functions as a way of obtaining from the narratee such sympathetic adherence to an adventure that both narrator and narratee are assumed to perceive as folly. In short, the denial of narrative seduction *in* the texts diverts attention from the seductive program *of* the texts, with their manipulation of the narratee in the name of "understanding" (philosophical or sentimental).

"The Purloined Letter" is not concerned thematically with seduction, but its focus on the fascinating figure of Dupin perhaps works in a similar way to divert attention from the text's own seductive program. Here, too, there is a differentiating technique, Dupin's fascinating discourse being framed by the narration of the story as a whole and to some extent distanced by the play between Dupin's narratorial style and that of the general narration. Although it is thus dissociated from the text as a whole, Dupin's seductive and enigmatic discourse is simultaneously taken up and incorporated into the total narrative project; and this is not simply because the ascendancy Dupin exerts over the other characters, including the narrator (Dupin's nameless friend), is transmitted to the reader through the agency of this latter personage. It is rather that the narratorial advantages of Dupin's style of discourse (what I call "duplicity") are combined, in the narration proper, with the narratorial advantages of another style (that of "self-reflexivity" or self-designation). In short, the issue is complicated, in "The Purloined Letter," by a certain question of disclosure.

If a text relies, for its point, on its artistic ("narratorial") success, the transaction with the reader fails unless the narratee perceives that art is being produced; it becomes necessary, then, for the narrator to divulge the fact that the illocutionary relationship between narrator and narratee involves this new source of "interest."[6] But one of the more durable axioms of Western aesthetics has it that the greatest art lies in the concealment of art and that the production of art—and hence, the gain in narratorial authority—is the greater when the art narrative is apparently nonart, that is, a form of communication concerned principally with its own referent (i.e., "what it is about," the narrative information being divulged). Hence, there is a constant tug-of-war between conflicting strategies — between narrative *self-referentiality* whereby the story draws attention to its status as art and forms of narrative *duplicity* whereby the story pretends to be concerned only with its informational content and yet reveals in unobtrusive ways (usually by slight discrepancies) that this is not so.

Duplicity versus self-reference as artistic modes form the very substance of "The Purloined Letter" when one chooses to read it in terms of narratorial authority, and as a text concerned with its own illocutionary situation. The narratorial mode of Dupin and that of the narration itself represent a range of possibilities as between textual duplicity (with its reliance on the acumen and skilled guesswork of the narratee) and the techniques of self-reflexivity (which still, of course, require a narratee attuned to the literary codes that make self-reference possible). The order of the discussion that follows will suggest a hierarchical order in which the framing (self-referential) narration is seen as commenting, in a sense, on the (duplicitous) narratorial practices demonstrated by Dupin within the narrative, and there is certainly in the text some degree of ironic distancing of this kind. Yet, the total effect is cumulative: although the fascination and sense of enigma produced by Dupin's duplicity are dispelled in the self-revealing artistic reference of the general narration, the two combine in a mutually reinforcing way in supporting the effectiveness of art as the exercise of a "narratorial," not "narrative," authority and hence in promoting a relational, not informational, concept of discourse.

These central questions of situational import, concerning the relationship implied by the text between the text and the reader, can be approached particularly directly in "The Purloined Letter," because the narrative content itself displays an acute awareness of the relational (and therefore situational) character of understanding. Jacques Lacan, the author of the most powerful and influential reading of "The Purloined Letter" in the public domain, was drawn to the text, he says, by the story Dupin tells of the game of "even and odd," which Lacan saw as illustrating the necessary precedence of the *symbolic* (the "signifier") over the subject. The "lucky" schoolboy who wins so frequently at the game by "identifying" with his opponents' thought processes is not, Lacan says, a Kantian subject miraculously identifying with another subject, since "cette identification se fait non pas à l'adversaire, mais à son raisonnement qu'elle articule (différence au reste qui s'énonce dans le texte)."[7]

But the boy's success at identifying with his opponent illustrates not only Lacan's point about the role of the signifier but also the thematic significance in the text of duplicity and its oppositional correlative, second-guessing, as a mode of understanding (by contrast with the more simpleminded attempts at uncomplex and unmediated "identification," such as the Prefect's straightforward assumptions about the criminal mind he is dealing with) and hence as a model of communication that perceives it as a game—a "game of puzzles"—in which one may "win" or "lose."

Jacques Derrida,[8] in criticizing Lacan's reading for its supposed imposition on the text of a psychoanalytic "meaning" (the interpretation of the story in terms of castration—the letter as that which "manque à sa place," affirming a *given* in which "le manque a sa place") seems to miss something of the significance of Lacan's fascination with this communicational relationship, at once ludic and oppositional, as it is figured in the text. It is true that Lacan's reading is the "analyse fascinée d'un contenu" (p. 105) (why and how does the text so fascinate a reader like Lacan?) and that it misses the implications of the narrative framework. But this framework does not have solely the function Derrida attributes to it, of ensuring textual "dissemination" (the positioning, in terms of "difference," of "The Purloined Letter" with respect to literature and the world of discourse at large, and the Dupin trilogy in particular). The narration also relates in important ways to its content, the *narré*, and provides in the *narré* significant "clues" (in appropriately detective terminology) or models as to its own functioning as a performative discursive act: how it is (asking) to be received, what it assumes regarding the relationship between itself and its readership, what—in short—its point is as a narrative act. The game of "even and odd" is one such clue.

What is at stake in "The Purloined Letter," then—in "The Purloined Letter" as a narrative act that describes itself as a "game of puzzles"—is the gain or loss of narrative/narratorial authority. Consequently, I propose to look first at the thematization of questions of power and authority in the text, most particularly as they relate to the problem of disclosure. Derrida has pointed out to what extent the characters are "doubles" of one another: I propose to exploit this status by examining some of them as "models" (and "antimodels") of each other, and of the text as a whole, in terms of the exercise of authority through discourse. The Prefect of Police will thus be seen as a major foil to Dupin, but not so much in his detective work as in his prowess as a narrator (the two being, of course, closely related in any case): his failure in "narrative" authority sets off the success of Dupin's "narratorial" strategies. But the relationship of Dupin to the Minister will then lead me to examine the phenomenon of artistic duplicity as a mode of "narratorial" success, combining concealment with openness, disclosure with covertness, and to compare the different practices of duplicity each character exemplifies. Finally, it will be important to examine the character of the "general narrator" (as Lacan calls him) and his investment in the text as art, his function as the final foil to all the other power holders and narrative/narratorial authorities in the text: here the relationship of self-reflexivity to duplicity will be at the center of the analysis of narratorial authority in the text.[9]

The Prefect, the Minister, Dupin

Possession of "the letter" is possession of (political) power—that is why the Minister steals it from the "personage of most exalted station" (who, for simplicity's sake, will henceforward be referred to as the Queen). But this letter has some peculiar properties. For one thing, its contents are unknown to the reader; they are a secret that is never disclosed. (Is it a love letter? Does it contain evidence of a political plot?) For another, the power the letter confers on the Minister is, precisely, the power to divulge the secret:

". . . the disclosure of the document to a third person, who shall be nameless, would bring in question the honor of a personage of most exalted station; and this fact gives the holder of the document an ascendancy over the illustrious personage whose honor and peace are so jeopardized." (p. 209)[10]

Moreover, it is (more exactly still) not the divulgence of the letter but its possession, that is, the option of divulging it, that confers the power; and indeed actually to employ the letter in this way would destroy the Minister's "ascendancy." "With the employment the power departs" (p. 210). Hence, the necessary openness of the situation between the blackmailer and his victim: the Minister's ascendancy depends "upon the robber's knowledge of the loser's knowledge of the robber" (p. 209).

The Minister, then, ostentatiously does not disclose and retains power—there is some analogy here with the narrator's position as I have just presented it. That this situation embodies a "law" of the text is confirmed, *a contrario,* by the behavior of the Minister's initial opponents, who are reduced by the weakness of their position to partial (but in fact fairly full) disclosures concerning the letter.

The Queen confides to the Prefect "that a certain document of the last importance has been purloined from the royal apartments" (p. 209); the Prefect, in turn, comes to consult Dupin about the affair, saying, "I thought Dupin would like to hear the details of it, because it is so excessively *odd*" (p. 208). "Odd" means he has something of value to impart, but it shows, too, that he is an unmasterly narrator, one who does not understand the information he proposes to divulge, who does not truly "possess" it before he dispossesses himself of it. His authority—such authority as he has—derives solely from the political power of the Queen, whose agent he is, a power itself somewhat impaired in the present circumstances. Still, as a potential narrator, he does have information to give, in the form of "details"; and his incaution in thus risking his authority, in the face of the option he has of withholding what he knows, is specifically underlined by the text:

"I will tell you in a few words; but, before I begin, let me caution you that this is an affair demanding the greatest secrecy, and that I should most probably lose the position I now hold, were it known that I confided it to any one."

"Proceed," said I.

"Or not," said Dupin.

"Well, then. . . . (p. 209)

The weak narrative authority of the Prefect is conveyed to the reader in the subsequent section of text through the narrative situation the text enacts. Insensitive to the frame of mind of his hearers, who are of the condescending opinion that "there was nearly half as much of the entertaining as of the contemptible about the man" (p. 208), and oblivious to the irony in their comments and rejoinders, especially those of Dupin, he reveals himself to be as rhetorically deficient, in failing to "admeasure" himself to narratees who are in a clear sense already his "opponents" in a kind of "game," as he is intellectually deficient in perceiving only the details, and not the pattern, of the story he has to tell. His loss of authority to his narratees is consequently twofold: they possess a better understanding than he does of the information he has come to impart (since Dupin at least is able to tell him from the start that the problem lies in his not being able to see the wood for the trees: "perhaps it is the very simplicity of the thing that puts you at fault," p. 209), and they are able to "admeasure" themselves accurately to his limited intellect in a way that he cannot do to theirs.

In light of this, his childish attempt to salvage some narrative authority by withholding certain information from the pair is merely ludicrous. His would-be discretion is futile, either because he cannot maintain his evasiveness ("a certain document" soon becomes "a letter, to be frank," p. 210) or because this phraseology is in any case transparent (no one is in any doubt as to who is referred to by phrases such as "the illustrious personage" and "the other exalted personage," or what the issues are—Dupin later reveals that, as a "partisan of the lady concerned" and long-time opponent of the Minister, he is perfectly *au fait* with the political implications of the affair [p. 222]). What, in fact, the Prefect does (in response to a specific invitation: "Suppose you detail," said I, "the particulars of your search," p. 211) is to "blab": he pours forth a long string of "details" and "particulars"—a discourse that has its exact correlative in the philosophy of "nooks and crannies" and of leaving no stone unturned that presides over his search. Narrative divulgence, which he engages in to the point of indulgence (what is one to think of a police chief so anxious to advertise police methods?), is consequently the reverse of the same coin of which the failed search, and the baffled state of mind it produces, is the obverse: each is the sign of the Prefect's lack of authority, the latter with respect to the Minister's superior ingeniousness and the former (as we will see) by contrast with Dupin's combination of acuity and canny narratorial authority.

For these reasons, the Prefect's narrative cannot *advance* (it cannot move toward a culminating "point," since its only point is that he cannot see the point); it can only repeat itself, just as he is condemned to repeat, unproductively, his search. The narrative he proffers on his second visit is the (mercifully abbreviated) repetition of his initial tale: "I made the re-examination, however, as Dupin suggested—but it was all labor lost, as I knew it would be" (p. 213). And his final loss of authority, or admission of defeat, when Dupin produces the purloined letter and claims his reward, is therefore most appropriately signaled by his speechlessness. Without authority, one has nothing to say and no right to speak; and in a text such as this, which is so fundamentally concerned with illocutionary relationships and constructed of two opposed narrative situations (the Prefect's failed narrative about his failure, Dupin's successful narrative about his success), to be deprived of that form of power that is the power to disclose (or the right to narrate) is to disappear from the text. So, "This functionary . . . rushed at length unceremoniously from the room and from the house, without having uttered a syllable since Dupin had requested him to fill up the check" (p. 214).

"When he had gone, my friend entered into some explanations"—

the reduction of the Prefect to silence is the sign for Dupin immediately to take up the narrator's role, with a contrast that is, of course, total. The Prefect's preoccupation with monetary reward reveals his motivation as political (Dupin draws the connection [p. 116]). Dupin, in turn, accepts the Prefect's check, but it seems that his real reward is of a more histrionic kind: it lies in the functionary's discomfiture and in the astonishment induced by his theatrical production of the letter, not only in the Prefect but also in his friend ("I was astounded. The Prefect appeared absolutely thunder-stricken," p. 214). This parallel in the reactions of the policeman and the friend is important: it suggests a more hidden parallel between the handing over of the letter to the policeman and the "explanations" Dupin is now about to offer his friend, and it betrays the fact that Dupin's true gain is the production of fascination with, and admiration for, his genius, irrespective of whether this is achieved by narrative as an act of nondisclosure (as is the case with the Prefect) or narrative as an act of disclosure (as with his friend).

This parallel requires some explication, because, on the face of it, Dupin is exerting authority in two different ways, according to his audience. To the Prefect, no disclosure whatsoever is made; moreover, Dupin has already administered him a lesson in the art of maintaining (narrative) authority through nondisclosure by means of an anecdote:

". . . once upon a time, a certain rich miser conceived the design of spunging upon this Abernethy for a medical opinion. Getting up, for this purpose, an ordinary conversation in a private company, he insinuated his case to the physician, as that of an imaginary individual.

" 'We will suppose,' said the miser, 'that his symptoms are such and such; now doctor, what would *you* have directed him to take?'

" 'Take!' said Abernethy, 'why, take *advice,* to be sure.' " (p. 214)

However, the precondition of *narratorial* authority is that there be some narrative, and indeed, to his friend, Dupin enters at considerable length into a series of "explanations." The word, of course, is in significant contrast with the Prefect's "details" and "particulars": instead of obtuseness and confusion, the narrative this time displays mastery of its information. But it is a form of mastery that allows Dupin to be as prolix and expansive in his discourse as the Prefect himself while maintaining the firmest sense of authority.

He has first of all *chosen* his audience, disdaining the Prefect who is incapable of understanding his sallies, in favor of the friend who, being more receptive, forms a worthier "opponent" in what is to be for the latter something of a guessing game. In contradistinction to the Prefect, whose methods and thinking are adequate only for dealing with the *mass* of opponents (i.e., in his case, criminals), Dupin, like the Minister, is of the elite and disdainful of the mass—aristocratically, he quotes Chamfort to the effect that ". . . *toute convention reçue est une sottise, car elle a convenu au plus grand nombre*" (p. 217). The friend, then, is a worthy opponent, one capable of "admeasuring" himself to Dupin's mind (as the policeman cannot)—but not one capable of *winning* and hence of depriving him of his authority. The friend's role consists of asking clarifying questions and making corroborative comments or else of expressing surprise and raising easily demolished objections—in short, he is the foil to Dupin's brilliance, which he is there to appreciate and enjoy but not to *see through* (and it is in this latter sense that he is a companion figure to the Prefect).

For Dupin's alleged "explanations" are often closer to being enigmatic *pronouncements,* and they have as much the character of nondisclosure as of disclosure. From the beginning of the story, he has been portrayed not just as a pipe smoker (his friend and the Prefect both puff on meerschaums, also) but more specifically as one who uses clouds of pipe smoke as a measure of concealment: his more outrageous pieces of ironic flattery or of didactic lesson giving are directed at the Prefect "amid a perfect whirlwind of smoke" (p. 210) or "between the whiffs of his meerschaum" (p. 214). But when it comes to his dialogue with his friend, all notations of smoke production disappear from the text, because that function has now been taken over by his discourse itself.[11] His "explanations" are in two parts: theory and practice. The theoretical argument proceeds through clear enough stages: the story of the game of "even and odd" and the principle of identification with the opponent; the Prefect's error in supposing he is dealing with a common opponent and that all poets are fools; the discussion of the limited rationality of mathematics; and finally of the relative invisibility of the simple, the self-evident, the obtrusive. Two characteristics, however, make this argument quite difficult to *penetrate.* First, it takes the apparent form of a series of brilliant divagations on unrelated topics—Dupin disdains to indicate the logical structure, the *enchaînement,* of his argument, which has to be inferred by a hearer whose attention is constantly distracted by the second characteristic: the highly arguable character of propositions that range from the preposterous through the paradoxical to the enigmatic but that are presented with total assurance, as if not open to discussion (in short, as if self-evident).[12] The schoolboy's methods of "guessing" and of identification with the opponent *do not work;* on the other hand, the Prefect's plodding but exhaustive techniques of search *ought to have worked.* The challenge to the rationality of mathematics needs, in order to be coherent, to be complemented by some statement—which, however, is allowed to remain entirely implicit—of the value of the poetic mind. And the whole paragraph (p. 219) preceding the description of the puzzle game with maps and illustrating the invisibility of the evident is so enigmatic as to be itself a "game of puzzles."

Lacan goes so far as to speak of "le sentiment de poudre aux yeux" (p. 26) Dupin's argment produces—he is "pulling the wool over our eyes." I would prefer to speak of the duplicity of his argumentation, since Dupin is concealing by a smokescreen of words and brilliant paradoxes an unstated but self-evident proposition they nevertheless convey—a proposition concerning the need for, and value of, acumen. It is like the name in wide-spaced letters on the map, writ so large it cannot be discerned amid the mass of fine print. Needless to say, it is no accident that the concealed core of the argument is precisely a doctrine in which acumen and penetration are opposed to the Prefect's thoroughness. The Prefect's narration, it will be recalled, was an uncontrolled mass of details and particulars concerning a method of search that depends on the detailed and particular; Dupin's argument is a series of apparent divagations, covertly controlled by the notion of acumen and consequently requiring acumen in order to grasp their unstated ordering principle. As an exercise in authority maintained through such a combination of disclosure and nondisclosure, it contrasts with the Prefect's demonstration of authority lost while showing clear affinity with the Minister's technique of ostentatious concealment.

But Lacan is right to the extent that Dupin's argument (about acumen) requires two kinds of acumen on the part of the hearer: the acumen to grasp it (which the friend appears to have) and the acumen to see through it (which the friend does not have). The stance of self-evidence he adopts concerning the propositions he is putting forward protects the extreme vulnerability of his argument from the penetration of a critical eye—much as the Minister's employment of ostentation serves as a mode of concealment that is vulnerable only to the acumen of Dupin. One might say that Dupin's argument is all show without real substance, in the way that the Minister's use of the letter as an instrument of power depends on deployment, openness, and visibility, with the letter's actual contents being relegated, as unusable and irrelevant, to silence. The difference is that Dupin's duplicitous discourse, while it is vulnerable, survives the relatively uncritical scrutiny of the friend, and his authority remains intact—whereas the Minister's duplicity is laid bare by Dupin's acumen and his power demolished. Dupin does not use his acumen merely to *grasp* the Minister's maneuvers (as his friend understands his argument); he uses it also to *penetrate* the Minister's duplicity and to reveal the fraudulence of his techniques. So, between the theory and the practice in Dupin's narrative there is an apparent contrast: his theorizing exercises his friend's acumen (in the first sense), and his practice employs acumen (in the second sense) against the Minister's duplicity. The comparison between Dupin's duplicitous discourse and the Minister's technique of open concealment needs to be balanced, then, by some examination (which the contrast with the Prefect implies) of the correlation between Dupin's successful search procedures and the successful maintenance of authority in his narrative.

What is interesting is that, as a detective, Dupin adopts a practice that pits against the Minister's duplicity a form of duplicity that exactly matches and counters it. Under cover of green glasses, a spurious pretext, an animated conversation on a topic designed to distract the Minister's attention, he penetrates by virtue of his acumen through the smoke screen the Minister himself has set up— the pretense of languor concealing his real energy, the turning of the letter inside out and its disguised external appearance—to the principle of simplicity that controls the whole: concealment through hyperobtrusive display. This penetration, through acumen, of the ingenious Minister's duplicity corresponds exactly to the effort the friend was unable to provide in the case of Dupin's narratorial practice; yet the concealment of acumen beneath a deceptive screen (particularly the screen of words implied by the animated discussion) also matches the actual narratorial practice employed by Dupin in offering his "explanations." Dupin's practice as a detective, the practice of duplicity, is doubly successful: like his narratorial practice, it is not penetrated (by the friend, by the Minister), and it proves superior to the Minister's own practice of concealment, which *is* finally penetrated by one with greater acumen and more successful duplicity than he.

The question of the relationship between Dupin and the Minister, as exemplified by Dupin's coup in discovering and regaining the purloined letter, resolves then into that of the relative success and failure of two closely related, and well-matched, forms of duplicity. And since both Dupin and the Minister are poets, my suggestion will be that the story as a whole can best be understood as an examination of, or let us say a meerschaum meditation on, the advantages and disadvantages, the dangers and benefits of artistic duplicity as a mode of exercising narratorial authority. That artistic authority is superior to the authority of power is the primary tenet of the text: the political figures yield their authority to the poets, first the Queen to the Minister, then the Prefect to Dupin. But finally the Minister yields in turn to Dupin: what, then, of this rivalry between the two poets, their relationship of fraternal enmity (pointed up by the reference to *Atrée and Thyeste,* p. 222) and the victory of the one (who admits himself "guilty of certain doggerel," p. 211) over the other (who "as poet *and* mathematician . . . would reason well," p. 217)?

The essence of the similarity between them lies in the fact that each practices duplicity as the art of substituting an appearance for a reality. For the Queen's letter, the Minister substitutes on her table a "letter somewhat similar to the one in question" (p. 210), a hasty stratagem but effective enough to deceive the King, who does not perceive the substitution, if not the Queen. He then substitutes for the purloined letter the self-same letter but turned "as a glove, inside out, redirected and resealed" (p. 221)—the same letter, then, with the external appearance of another. What Dupin substitutes for the Minister's deceptive letter is yet another appearance, a careful *facsimilé* (the term is his [p. 221]) that reproduces the externals of the letter (but with a new text). Since the series of substitutions begins with, and is modeled on, the Queen's initial stratagem: ". . . she was forced to place it, open as it was, upon a table. The address, however, was uppermost, and, the contents thus unexposed, the letter escaped notice" (p. 210), we may say that the art of duplicity involves the production, and indeed the ostentatious display, of a deceptive externality intended to conceal an inner truth, the discovery of which would render the perpetrator vulnerable to loss of honor, dignity, or authority. Indeed, since the contents of the Queen's letter are never known, and even the police description of it consists of "a minute account of the internal, and especially of the external, *appearance* of the missing document" (p. 213) (my emphasis), it is almost as if there is no "inner truth" and certainly as if such truth is irrelevant to the game, in which only appearance counts. "Poudre aux yeux," certainly, wool over the eyes—but the *poudre* and the wool are of the essence.

This being so, what distinguishes Dupin from the Minister lies in the area of the "style" of duplicity each practices. The Minister's duplicity uses openness as its main ploy; Dupin's relies much more on concealment. The former's substitution of his own letter for the letter purloined from the Queen is performed in full view of the victim (since his power derives, as we know, from the loser's knowledge of the robber). And in "concealing" the purloined letter, he resorts to what Dupin calls "the comprehensive and sagacious expedient of not attempting to conceal it at all" (p. 220)—although, as we have seen, he does make a minimal effort at concealment by creating a new external form for the letter he proposes to display in its "hyperobtrusive situation" (p. 221). His, then, is the most audacious form of duplicity, the most breathtaking in its simplicity, but also the most rash, the one that is most at risk of being penetrated and hence of producing the most disastrous loss of authority. For his action to count as duplicity, it must involve a minimum of false appearances (simply to display the Queen's letter in unchanged form would not be duplicitous, it would merely be foolhardy); but such minimal disguise, under the sagacious scrutiny of such a one as Dupin, takes the form of *clues* (Why should a letter to D—— bear D———'s own seal? Why should its edges be "more chafed than seemed necessary" [p. 221]?) and leads to discovery and discomfiture. In terms of poetics, the Minister's device might be equated with realist texts so successful in imitating "natural" discourse that they *must* leave clues if they are to be deciphered as art ("seen through") at all, and thus benefit from artistic authority.[13] Such texts rely for narratorial effectiveness on a kind of internal inconsistency, the penetrability of their disguise.

By contrast, Dupin's practice of duplicity is more "honest," since it relies much more heavily on covertness. The substitution he performs in the Minister's apartment is done without the Minister's knowledge, and Dupin's power over him depends precisely on his remaining unaware of the deception being practiced on him. This corresponds not only to Dupin's reliance as a detective on green glasses and tactics of diversion but also to his narratorial practice of the verbal smoke screen. It is not that for Dupin concealment is all: again, the procedure would not be duplicitous but merely self-defeating if the Minister were not *eventually* to discover the trick and if the narratee were not, at least, to discover behind the smoke screen the doctrine of acumen. But in each case, penetration of the duplicity results not in a loss of authority (narratorial or political) on Dupin's part but in a confirmation and even a reinforcement of that authority. What the Minister discovers in penetrating the trick is a text, in Dupin's recognizable hand, that tells him in effect: "You are outwitted." What the narratee learns is also, in a sense, that he has been outwitted, for the text tells only of what one has already had to practice in reading it, the need for acumen. The "secret" is in the form of the words, writ large there, not somewhere behind that screen in the form of a discrete "message," and this is all the more the case if the spuriousness of the argument has also been detected: the narratee is then sent back to the puzzle of the discourse itself, wherein resides its true (duplicitous) essence—and so long as he puzzles, narratorial authority remains intact. One might think here, in contrast to realism, of the artistic practice of Mallarmé, whose textual obscurity "conceals" a message that is nevertheless "overt," since it is indistinguishable from the textuality itself. This, then, is a *textual* duplicity.

To summarize, it seems that the maintenance of artistic authority in "The Purloined Letter" is dependent on the practice of duplicity as a mode of divulgence and nondivulgence, of openness and covertness, at once. Certain tactical considerations dictate the superiority of a relative degree of covertness (which protects narratorial authority) over the corresponding degree of overtness, which may be brilliantly effective, yet necessarily carries with it a significant flaw by its need to incorporate a certain penetrability. Doubtless it is significant that, although the Minister is described as a poet, he is not given a narrative function in the story, he does not produce discourse as Dupin and the Prefect do. In historical terms, the poetics (or ideology of art) he presides over, that of realistic *mimesis,* owes little to Poe, whereas the lineage of Dupin—the practitioners of text as *écriture* such as Baudelaire, Mallarmé, and Valéry—has steadfastly acknowledged his mastery.

The General Narration

Yet, two further considerations need to be formulated regarding Dupin's practice of duplicity. The first is that he, too, risks a form of failure should he miscalculate his audience: the type of incomprehension displayed by the Prefect in the early part of the story, oblivious as he is to Dupin's smoke screen and to his irony, suggests that he would not perceive the art in Dupin's later narration, nor consequently would he recognize—that is, authorize—the narratorial authority being exercised. He would simply be confirmed in his view that poets are next to fools, and so Dupin is right not to divulge his secrets to him; but he does thereby miss a chance to exercise artistic authority. Such could be the case also of a narratee more acute than the friend, who might simply dismiss the "explanations" as spurious nonsense, without perceiving their narratorial artistry.

The second consideration is that Dupin's duplicity becomes so blatant in its excess of covertness (as the Minister's is blatant in its excess of overtness) that it begins to border on artistic self-reflexivity: there is something self-denunciatory about the histrionic display in which he delights, under the guise of offering "some explanations," and in the production of a verbose and somewhat self-conscious, if enigmatic and fascinating, text. The self-reference becomes explicit not only in his allusion to a chain of literary figures (La Rochefoucauld, La Bruyère,[14] Machiavelli, Campanella) who have allegedly preceded him in the art of mental identification with an adversary but also in Dupin's admeasurement of himself, the perpetrator of "certain doggerel," with the Minister, who is "poet *and* mathematician"; not to mention, finally, the specific status he achieves as producer of text through his pointed citation of Crébillon at the end (p. 222).

Self-reflexivity as a mode of exercising narratorial authority has over duplicity the signal advantage that it *cannot* be deceptive: the artistic "ascendancy" being laid claim to cannot be mistaken, even by a narratee as obtuse as the Prefect, for anything but what it is. So, it is significant that the narrative mode adopted by the general narrator of "The Purloined Letter" in the narration for which he takes responsibility, that is, that of the text as a whole, is the mode of self-reflexivity. It is as if, having drawn the lessons of the Minister's superior ascendancy over the Queen and the Prefect, and of Dupin's superior authority over him, it remains for the narrator to incorporate into his own art of narration the advantages of artistic indirection with the certainty of effect inherent in artistic self-designation.

I see a certain distancing on the part of the general narration with respect to Dupin in the slyness of the epigraph attributed to Seneca, which opens the text: *Nil sapientiae odiosus acumine nimio.* As translated in the most recent critical edition,[15] the phrase signifies "Nothing is more hateful to wisdom than too much cunning," and it is assumed to be a comment on the excessive cunning (and insufficient wisdom) of the Prefect, by comparison with Dupin. But the word *acumen* is precisely the word Dupin uses (p. 216) in favorable reference to his own abilities and in direct contrast with the mere "care, patience and determination" of the police. There is a sense, then, in which the Senecan phrase comments on Dupin's excessive subtlety and compares it unfavorably with true wisdom. Yet, at the same time, one needs to remember that the text is at pains to point out that Latin words are sometimes false friends: if, as Dupin says (p. 217), " 'analysis' conveys 'algebra' about as much as, in Latin, *'ambitus'* implies 'ambition,' *'religio'* 'religion' or *'homines honesti'* a set of *honorable* men," then it is possible that Seneca's *acumen* may not apply after all to Dupin's particular "set of notions regarding human ingenuity" (p. 216).[16] In its ambiguity, the epigraph functions then to set up an ironic distance between the narration itself and its principal actors, including Dupin, while in its refusal to divulge a clear meaning, it provides a notable example of the maintenance of narratorial authority through verbal art.

A similar refusal of the text to divulge is, of course, what is signified by the principal self-reflexive device in the tale—the letter, about whose actual and specific contents the reader remains totally uninformed while, as Lacan so clearly saw, its externality undergoes many substitutions. The letter thus signifies a conception of text in which the signifier is subject to constant "drift" while the signified remains elusive, if not altogether absent.[17] The opening paragraph of the text (before the motif of the letter has been introduced) provides corroborative self-reflexive imagery. In the "little back library or book-closet" (p. 208) that signifies the enclosed world of letters, the characters appear "intently and exclusively occupied with the curling eddies of smoke that oppressed the atmosphere of the chamber" (p. 208)—an image that is to take on the meaning of the screen of words as the text develops. However—not behind this screen so much as it is an accompaniment to it—the "luxury" of the meerschaum is doubled (as the signifier is doubled by its signified) by the mental luxury of "meditation"—an intellectual pursuit that does not provide an extralinguistic "meaning" but proves to be itself conducted per medium of language ("I was *mentally discussing* certain topics," p. 208) (my emphasis) and to refer intertextually— as Derrida points out—to other literary texts: "I mean the affair in the rue Morgue, and the mystery attending the murder of Marie Rogêt" (i.e., the two other items in the Dupin canon). Thus, at the point where the text enacts its own emergence from silence, the narrator's moment of choice between "proceed" "or not" ("for an hour at least we had maintained profound silence"), it does so amid an escort of reminders that significance derives from relations and referrals among signs, and not from the existence of some supposed preexisting content (which might be the narrator's "knowledge," the "information" he proposes to convey). Narrative authority (posited on information to be conveyed) has been replaced here by narratorial authority (based on the "undecidability" inherent in artistic signs), and textual self-reflexivity has less the (narrative) effect of producing information than the (narratorial) effect of confirming the text's elusiveness.

At the close of the tale, another emergence of text is enacted, this time by Dupin's substitution (in his *fac-similé* of the original purloined letter) of a text, in the form of a quotation from Crébillon père, for the blank that he feels it would be "insulting" (p. 222) to offer his reader, the Minister. Since the words:

> —Un dessein si funeste
> S'il n'est digne d'Atrée est digne de Thyeste

resume a tragedy of duplicity and second-guessing that turns on the existence of a compromising letter, the self-reflexive reference to "The Purloined Letter" itself is unmistakable; as is the inference that, in lieu of the blank contents of the Queen's letter (the always missing signified), what we have is the text of the tale itself, the signifier, the "whirling eddies" of words that signify through their inclusion, by intertextual referral, in the literary canon. Even the undecidability of such a text is again conveyed by the citation, for while there is some *équivoque* in Atrée's words within the context of the play, their exact bearing on the relationship of Dupin to the Minister is more than unclear in the context of the story. (Which of the two is Atrée? Which Thyeste? Whose *dessein* is being designated? In what sense is it unworthy of the one but worthy of the other?)[18]

At the midpoint of the tale, where the Prefect's narrative is interchanged for Dupin's, yet another substitution invites self-referential interpretation: in return for the Prefect's check, Dupin hands over the letter. A set of signs is exchanged for another set of signs, a "letter" for a "figure" (50,000 francs), in an episode that clearly embodies the text's conception of the relationship between the world of art and the world designated here as "political," that is, between two different value systems, aesthetic and economic, that both depend on the deployment of signs. If the handing over of the letter here signifies the exercise of Dupin's narratorial authority (both by his nondivulgence of "information" to the functionary and by the type of artistic divulgence represented by his explanations to his friend) and if by self-referential extension it also stands for the text itself as a whole, what is implied is that the *test* of narratorial authority is its exchange value against the script that has currency in the economic domain. That this is something of a fools' exchange is evident, since what the Prefect acquires is the equivalent of meerschaum smoke, the letter as signifier (although it is mentioned precisely here that he "cast a rapid glance at its contents" [p. 214]), while Dupin makes very clear his disdain for the money the Prefect so much respects (while pocketing his reward with some satisfaction).

In all these ways, then, the self-referentiality characteristic of the general narration proves to be a narratorial device, producing the text as a phenomenon of dissemination, like Dupin's own "whirling eddies" of words, but doing so in a nonduplicitous way. However, it would be misleading to abandon this discussion of the letter as the empty "place" that enables substitutions and exchanges of signs without pointing out that, for all its insistence on textual drift and the absent signified, "The Purloined Letter" does not deny meaning. Rather, it situates it, not in the domain of signs, but in the world of the relationships that signs serve to mediate.[19] Dupin has "a quarrel on hand . . . with some of the algebraists of Paris" (p. 217), and his disagreement with these specialists in signs (whose discipline depends precisely on the equivalence and substitutibility of signs) stems from the fact that "occasions may occur where $x^2 + px$. is not altogether equal to q" (p. 218) or, in other words, that situations alter the value of signs and meaning is contextual. "What is true of *relation*—of form and quantity—is often grossly false in regard to morals, for example" (p. 218)—that is, in regard to the world of human relationships. The letter about whose contents we learn so little is regularly described as to its address: when the Queen places the letter address uppermost on her table (p. 210), when the false address to D——— on the letter as disguised by the Minister alerts Dupin to the deception (p. 220), and when Dupin finally makes this false address the true one on the *fac-similé* that contains the text from Crébillon and justifies Lacan's statement of the story's moral (p. 53), that *"une lettre arrive toujours à destination."*[20] Hence, the process whereby a letter to the Queen becomes a letter to the Minister through the mediation of a false address forms the subject matter of the tale (its essential narrative reversal), just as much as the process whereby Dupin's text replaces the blank inner page. Not only this, but it is the *combination* of these two processes (the production of text *and* its insertion in a significant relationship) that gives point to Dupin's action in the culminating paragraph of the text. The self-referential point is evident: the meaningfulness of "The Purloined Letter" derives similarly from the substitution of text for absence (the story itself for the undivulged contents of the purloined letter) *and* from the production of a relationship between narrator and narratee that is mediated by the text in the way the relationship between Dupin and the Minister is mediated by Dupin's letter—a relationship, consequently, in which what is at issue is the matter of authority.

That communicational situations make meaning is signified, finally, not only by the insistence on "address" throughout "The Purloined Letter" but also by the motif of signature. The text of Crébillon, which is foreign to the relationship of Dupin and the Minister, is inserted into that relationship and thus acquires its cogency by the fact that, in signing it, Dupin takes responsibility for it and becomes its "author":

So, as I knew he would feel some curiosity in regard to the identity of the person who had outwitted him, I thought it a pity not to give him a clew. He is well acquainted with my MS., and I just copied into the middle of the blank sheet the words. . . . (p. 222)

The Prefect, too, must sign the check he hands over to Dupin in exchange for the lost letter—which signifies that here, too, it is the relationship that gives point to what would otherwise be the exchange of empty signs. If Dupin's signature on the letter to the Minister is a triumphant one, a measure of his success in the guessing game that has pitted him against a worthy opponent, the Prefect's signature is his admission of defeat, of confusion and bafflement in the presence of Dupin's superior genius:

For some minutes he remained speechless and motionless, looking incredulously at my friend with open mouth, and eyes that seemed starting from their sockets; then apparently recovering himself in some measure, he seized a pen, and after several pauses and vacant stares, finally filled up and signed a check for fifty thousand francs, and handed it across the table to Dupin. (p. 214)

In both cases, the act of signature acknowledges the role of authority in the relationships that give point to the deployment of textual signs.

What then, finally, of the signature appended to these pages? In the guessing game by which a critic pits himself against the superior genius, the narratorial authority of a text, does the signing of an essay signify "I have outwitted you" or "I concede defeat"? Am I playing Dupin to Poe's Minister, or the Prefect to Poe's Dupin? An interpretive essay has something in common with Dupin's exposure of the Minister's techniques of open concealment; but in the long run—as the form of words that recognizes the value of a literary text in the world of universities and scholarly journals—it is more like the

Prefect's check (in the world of economics) than it is like Dupin's missive to the Minister (in the world of "letters"); and in signing the present text I am happy to acknowledge both the relational character of the game of "even and odd" I have been playing with Poe's narrator and the defeat of my poor algebraic analysis as a way of admeasuring my intellect to that of my "opponent." However aware one may be of the ruses and stratagems by which narratorial authority produces and maintains itself, the act of reading can only ever, in the end, produce a kind of dumb homage to that strange ascendancy.

NOTES

1. See H. P. Grice, "Logic and Conversation," in P. Cole and J. L. Morgan, eds., *Speech Acts* (New York: Academic Press, 1975), 41-58.

2. *Towards a Speech-Act Theory of Literary Discourse* (Bloomington: Indiana University Press, 1977).

3. Latin "*narrāre* to relate, recount, supposed to be for *gnārāre*, relates to *gnārus*, knowing, skilled, and thus ultimately allied to KNOW" *(OED)*.

4. "The Storyteller," in H. Arendt, ed., *Illuminations* (New York: Schocken Books, 1969), 83-109.

5. See chapters 4 and 5, respectively.

6. This, of course, presupposes that the text is not prepared to place complete reliance on purely *extratextual* indicators (such as the mode of publication, etc.) — an assumption that nineteenth- and twentieth-century narratives appear to justify.

7. "Le séminaire sur *La lettre volée*," in *Écrits*, I (Paris: Éd. du Seuil [Coll. "Points"], 1970), 19-75. Future references to Lacan will be indicated by page numbers in the text. (For an English version, see *Yale French Studies*, 48 [1972].)

My focus on the text differs from Lacan's, and my debt to him lies principally in his having drawn attention to the features of the text that call for interpretation: the substitution of letter for letter and the substitutability of character for character; the fact that Dupin's substitution of letters only partially "repeats" the Minister's previous act of substitution (the latter being overt, the former covert); and finally the simple infractions of verisimilitude, the fact that the Prefect of Police's exhaustive search methods ought to have turned up the missing letter no less infallibly (perhaps more so) than Dupin's reliance on "acumen," and the fact that the "hyperobtrusive" place is not necessarily the best place to conceal an important document from persistent searchers. ("C'est là un leurre," Lacan says delightfully [p. 26], "dont pour nous, nous ne recommanderions l'essai à personne, crainte qu'il soit déçu à s'y fier.")

8. "Le facteur de la vérité," *Critique*, 21 (1975), 96-147. For a lucid critical account of the Lacan-Derrida confrontation that incorporates also many suggestive elements for a reading of "The Purloined Letter," see Barbara Johnson, "The Frame of Reference: Poe, Lacan, Derrida," *Yale French Studies*, 55/56 (1977), 457-505, reprinted in *The Critical Difference: Essays in the Contemporary Rhetoric of Reading* (Baltimore: Johns Hopkins University Press, 1980), 110-146. Following her, Norman N. Holland, in "Re-covering 'The Purloined Letter': Reading as a Personal Transaction" (in S. Suleiman and I. Crosman,

eds., *The Reader in the Text: Essays on Audience and Interpretation* [Princeton, N.J.: Princeton University Press, 1980], 350-370), insists on the relationship between the issue of authority in the text and that in the recent critical writing to which it has given rise.

9. The major trend of Poe criticism has been to give preeminent authority to Dupin, who is seen as a Romantic genius, a figure of "godlike omniscience," while the narrative "I" and the reader are allotted "the role of dull-witted dupes" (G. R. Thompson, *Poe's Fiction* [Madison: University of Wisconsin Press, 1973], p. 174; see also R. Daniel, "Poe's Detective God," in W. L. Howarth, ed., *Twentieth Century Interpretations of Poe's Tales* [Englewood Cliffs, N. J.: Prentice-Hall, 1971], 103-110). In distancing myself from this interpretation, I am not attempting to reverse this hierarchical ordering of the *characters* so much as to relate, one to the other, the *narrative instances* involved in the tale. The significance of Lacan's contribution in general has been to demystify the figure of the *"sujet supposé savoir"*; and it is in this perspective that I approach Dupin as narrator; but I am less interested in the personages as human "subjects" in either the conventional or the Lacanian sense than I am concerned with the functioning of discourse and discourse relationships.

I will be returning to the issue of authority and its relationship with seduction and duplicity in the conclusion, where it becomes the basis of a theory not only of "narrational" but also of "narrative" storytelling.

10. Page numbers following quotations from "The Purloined Letter" refer to Edgar Allan Poe, *Complete Tales and Poems* (New York: Vintage Books, 1975).

11. For a look at the smoke/words metaphor in Gautier, Baudelaire, Mallarmé, and Ponge, see my "Le poète fumeur," *Australian Journal of French Studies,* 16, 1/2 (1979), 138-150.

12. Can it be that Lacan's fascination with "The Purloined Letter" does not derive exclusively from the implications of the game of "even and odd"? Dupin's discursive practice offers a recognizable "model" of Lacan's own pedagogical style, with its combination of assurance, formal brilliance, and obscurity. (For acknowledgment of the issues of authority involved in the debate about "The Purloined Letter," see B. Johnson, "The Frame of Reference" in *The Critical Difference*; but see also Shoshana Felman's very subtle reading of Lacan's pedagogical style in "Psychoanalysis and Education: Teaching Terminable and Interminable," *Yale French Studies,* 63 [1982], 21-44, which appeared too late for me to be able to take it into account here.)

13. The "clue" as a claim to authorship, and hence to narratorial authority, is explicitly thematized at the end of "The Purloined Letter" through Dupin's need to let the Minister *know* that he has been duped, and by whom.

14. For this plausible correction of "La Bougive," see *Collected Works of Edgar Allan Poe,* ed. T. O. Mabbott (Cambridge, Mass.: Belknap Press, Harvard University Press, 1978), vol. III, p. 995.

15. Ibid., pp. 993-994.

16. *Lewis and Short* gives as figurative meanings of *acumen*: "A. *Acuteness, shrewdness, keenness, acumen* . . . ." The Seneca quotation has not been traced (probably it is a pseudoquotation), so its reference cannot be checked in the original context.

17. Lacan (pp. 39-40) proposes "La lettre détournée" as a more accurate translation of the title than Baudelaire's "La lettre volée." Equally apt would be "La lettre escamotée," since *escamotage* is the sleight of hand by which an object is made to disappear and (normally) a deceptive object is produced in its place—much as Dupin substitutes a deceptive letter for that addressed to the Queen, and much as, more generally, text substitutes in "The Purloined Letter" for the blank contents of the missing letter.

18. For a discussion of *Atrée and Thyeste*, see also B. Johnson, "The Frame of Reference" in *The Critical Difference,* p. 132.

19. For the insight that enables me to make this statement, I am particularly indebted to Charles Altieri, "Presence and Reference in a Literary Text: The Example of Williams' 'This Is Just to Say,' " *Critical Inquiry*, 5, 3 (spring 1979), 489-510. See also his *Act and Quality: A Theory of Literary Meaning and Humanistic Understanding* (Amherst: University of Massachusetts Press, 1981), chapter 4.

20. This is the formulation that drew Derrida's ire, as a denial of the phenomenon of dissemination. Barbara Johnson shows it to be more profound (and less univocal) in its implications than Derrida supposes; she interprets it to mean that "the letter's destination is *wherever it is read:* the place it assigns to its reader . . . . The letter's destination is not its literal addressee, nor even whoever possesses it, but whoever is possessed *by* it . . ." ("The Frame of Reference" in *The Critical Difference*, p. 144). She does not point out, however, that the story in fact enacts this philosophical point in its narrative structure, whereby the loss and return of the Queen's letter (on which Lacan and Derrida focus) appears as merely the occasion for a substitution of addressees (the letter to the Queen becoming Dupin's letter to the Minister in the course of the narrative and by means of the action of the story).

Chapter Four
Seduction Denied:
"Sarrasine" and the Impact of Art

The Power of Art

"Une nuit d'amour contre une belle histoire."[1] As has been mentioned, Roland Barthes rightly draws our attention to the exemplary character of "Sarrasine" as a figuring of the fact that no act of narration occurs without at least an implicit contract, that is, an understanding between narrator and narratee, an illocutionary situation that makes the act meaningful and gives it what we call a "point." In "Sarrasine," the contract is as close to being explicit as decorum allows: in accepting the very intimate circumstances of the rendezvous in which the narrator reveals the secret she wishes to learn and dispels the enigma surrounding the origins of the Lanty family by relating the story of Sarrasine, Mme de Rochefide accepts her own part of the bargain, which is to take the narrator as her lover, to give him, as he says, "le droit de vous obéir quand vous dites: Je veux" (p. 92).[2]

What Barthes does not point out is the equally exemplary character of the moment, at the end, when Mme de Rochefide breaks the bargain. The story told, she repudiates the initial contract and her response retrospectively gives the story quite a different point:

—Hé bien? lui dis-je.

—Ah! s'écria-t-elle en se levant et se promenant à grands pas dans la chambre. Elle vint me regarder, et me dit d'une voix altérée: Vous m'avez dégoûtée de la

73

vie et des passions pour longtemps. Au monstre près, tous les sentiments humains ne se dénouent-ils pas ainsi, par d'atroces déceptions?" (p. 110)

Story contracts are not always—indeed, not often—broken, of course; but what is exemplified by the dénouement of Sarrasine is that one does not narrate with impunity. To tell a story is an act, an event, one that has the power to produce change, and first and foremost to change the relationship between narrator and narratee. In simple terms, the possessor of knowledge has, by sharing his knowledge, lost the power over his hearer that that knowledge (and her curiosity) conferred on him; and Mme de Rochefide is now free to exercise in turn the power that the narrator's desire gave to her. But such a shift in the power relationships does not, of itself, suffice to explain why Mme de Rochefide is led to reject the narrator's suit. The question of *why* she so unexpectedly refuses what she had previously acceded to is one of those irritating difficulties of detail that have the function of provoking an interpretation, or reinterpretation, of a text by forcing us to read it as a whole in the light of the problem they pose.

Thus, for instance, at a superficial level, one might relate Mme de Rochefide's reversal to the general concept of woman that prevails in the text and is conveyed by words such as "coquetterie," "faiblesse," "mignardise": "C'était la femme avec ses peurs soudaines, ses caprices sans raison, ses troubles instinctifs, ses audaces sans cause, ses bravades et sa délicieuse finesse de sentiment" (p. 106). This opinion is that of Sarrasine and relates to Zambinella; but in the absence of explicit rejection by the narrator, or of perceptible irony on his part, one supposes that he assumes responsibility for it also; and indeed nothing suggests that the text as a whole (Wayne Booth's "implied author") is more critical than the narrator himself. So it is significant that "insouciante pétulance" (p. 91), caprice, and coquetterie are precisely what the narrator sees as the defining characteristics of Mme de Rochefide: even as their contract is sealed she speaks at one point "d'un air mutin," at another "avec une coquetterie désespérante":

Elle eut l'audace de valser avec un jeune aide de camp, et je restai tour à tour fâché, boudeur, admirant, aimant, jaloux.

—A demain, me dit-elle vers deux heures du matin, quand elle sortit du bal.

—Je n'irai pas, pensais-je, et je t'abandonne. Tu es plus capricieuse, plus fantasque mille fois peut-être . . . que mon imagination. (p. 92)

When she insists on hearing the story, she reveals perhaps one of those "troubles instinctifs . . . audaces sans cause" that Sarrasine sees in Zambinella, something equivalent to the impulse that led her—"sous le charme de cette craintive curiosité qui pousse les femmes à se procurer des émotions dangereuses" (p. 87)—to examine and even to touch—"avec cette hardiesse que les femmes puisent dans la violence de leurs désirs" (p. 89)—the decrepit old apparition in the Lanty salon. And when, having heard the story, she reacts so violently with despair and refusal, she displays something of the "peurs soudaines," and indeed the "caprices sans raison," that Sarrasine saw in Zambinella—and her reaction has its precise equivalent in her earlier panic retreat from the old man: "Ma compagne se jeta sur un divan, palpitant d'effroi, sans savoir où elle était. —Madame, vous êtes folle, lui dis-je" (p. 89). That such spontaneity of emotion and behavior is entirely characteristic of Mme de Rochefide, more fundamental than her renunciation of life and love at the end of "Sarrasine," is borne out, as Barthes points out,[3] in her subsequent behavior in other Balzac texts.

But there is a structural point here (the parallel, or equivalence, between Mme de Rochefide's hearing of the narrator's story and her examination of the elderly Zambinella) that is a more important clue than the coquetterie and spontaneity that *enable* her sudden reversal but do not of themselves account for it. The clue would reinforce Barthes's relatively laconic explanation of her reaction, which is couched in terms of the content of the narrator's story:

. . . le "contenu" même du Récit-Marchandise (une histoire de castration) empêchera le pacte de s'accomplir jusqu'au bout: la jeune femme, touchée par la castration *racontée,* se retirera de la transaction sans honorer son engagement.[4]

But what I wish to suggest is that what determines the reaction is not simply the content of the story told by the narrator (although that is a significant element) but the total impact of the *telling*— not the mere acquisition of a piece of information so much as a whole experience that is that of a work of art (in this case, the art of narration). Not so much "la castration *racontée*" as "une narration *castrée,*" for the narrator's art is as deceptive as—and is rhetorically analogous with—the charade Zambinella and his friends play for the benefit of Sarrasine. What the narrator believes to be the point of his narration (the obtaining of a night of love) turns out, then, not to have been the "real" point, which lies, ironically, in his having—involuntarily, as it were—produced an art tale, with an impact on the hearer totally undreamt of in his own scheme of things. Read in this light, "Sarrasine" turns out to be, if one will, "une histoire de castration," but also a story about the power of art and the problem of its reception.

In this connection, it is very significant that from the outset the real object of Mme de Rochefide's desire is not the narrator but a work of art. She is in love with the Adonis in the Lanty salon, as the narrator immediately realizes:

Oh! comme je ressentais alors les atteintes de cette jalousie à laquelle un poète avait vainement essayé de me faire croire! la jalousie des gravures, des tableaux, des statues, où les artistes exagèrent la beauté humaine, par suite de la doctrine qui les porte à tout idéaliser.

And:

J'eus la douleur de la voir abîmée dans la contemplation de cette figure. Elle s'assit en silence, je me mis auprès d'elle, et lui pris la main sans qu'elle s'en aperçût! Oublié pour un portrait! (p. 90)

Here, too, we find Zambinella as the object of her fascination, since the portrait is a copy, in male guise, of the statue of Zambinella as a woman that Sarrasine produces as an act of love. Not only does Mme de Rochefide's listening to the narrator's storytelling appear as a structural equivalent to her fascination with the old man, but her fascination with the old man now turns out to have as a pendant her fascination for a work of art—a representation (two, or really three,[5] steps removed from the original) of the self-same Zambinella in his youth. (This parallel is explicitly drawn at the end of the story by the narrator, who refers to "le portrait qui vous a montré Zambinella à vingt ans, un instant après l'avoir vu centenaire . . . ," p. 110). And like the young Zambinella himself, whom Sarrasine loved as a woman, the portrait that Mme de Rochefide desires is cruelly deceptive. Not only, as the narrator notes, does it draw its charm from the artistic propensity for idealization, which falsifies human beauty by exaggerating it; not only is it so far removed from its ultimate model as to constitute the model of an artistic type (that is, a falsification through generalization), but as a consequence it has more affinity with a family of works of art than with the reality it so distantly represents:

—Madame, le cardinal Cicognara se rendit maître de la statue de Zambinella et la fit exécuter en marbre, elle est aujourd'hui dans le musée Albani. C'est là qu'en 1791 la famille Lanty la retrouva, et pria Vien de la copier. Le portrait

. . . a servi plus tard pour l'*Endymion* de Girodet, vous avez pu en reconnaître le type dans l'Adonis. (p. 110)

And the ultimate "reality" itself, when one works one's way back along the chain to the point of departure, turns out to be what Barthes calls "castration" and I will refer to more generally as *lack*, or the *void*, that is, the crucial absence in Zambinella that makes possible his masquerade and engenders by extension the chain of works of art. Art, then, is ultimately baseless, and its beauty is fascinating but deceptive; the experience of art as an object of desire can only lead from the initial fascination to the disillusioning awareness of deception and of a central absence that is the condition of that deception and, hence, of the fascination. Such, at least, will be Mme de Rochefide's experience.

"Sarrasine," as a story within a story (a narrative act within a narrative act), is a well-recognized classic of self-reflexive art. But the inner story is itself self-reflexive, in that it is a miniature *Künstlerroman* concerning Sarrasine's artistic development and his encounter with, and fatal love for, a Muse (Zambinella) who represents the nature of the work of art itself. In Lucien Dällenbach's terms,[6] the inner and outer stories form a *mise en abyme de l'énonciation*, while the inner story, preoccupied with the nature of art and of the artist, constitutes a *mise en abyme du code*. Consequently, I will look first at the inner story, with a view to exploring more completely the characteristics of the work of art as it presents them, before examining the *Wirkung* of such characteristics, the impact of art as it is enacted, on the one hand, in the narrator's storytelling for Mme de Rochefide and, on the other, in the text of "Sarrasine" itself, perceived in turn as an act of narration.

From the Deceptive to the Significant

The story of Sarrasine's apprenticeship to art falls into two parts of unequal length and importance. France is the place where the talented young man explores the relationship of art to external authority and to society: the provincial world of his father, the religious world of the Jesuit college, the artistic tradition as it is represented by his substitute father, Bouchardon. Here, art is a matter of temperament (the "turbulence" displayed by Sarrasine as a child) and of work (which Bouchardon employs as a means of taming the "fougue extraordinaire" of the young "génie sauvage" and which Sarrasine feels is the only way to rival the geniuses of the past). Rome, on the other hand, represents the discovery of art as personal inspiration and the exploration of the relationship between artistic illusion and desire. The implication appears to be that, from the point of view of the artist as producer, the work of art stands at a point of convergence between temperament (which sets the artist against authority but also gains him social approval),[7] ambition (which leads to emulation within the artistic tradition), and personal vision (which stands as the expression of individual desire). And Sarrasine's tragedy derives from an undue preponderance of the passionate component in the stamp of his genius.

For desire can be destructive when it leads to despair, as it does in Sarrasine's encounter with Zambinella. I have discussed elsewhere[8] the theme of love for an actress in nineteenth-century literature as an exploration of the aesthetic and metaphysical implications of the arbitrariness of signs—their lack of anchorage in either so-called reality or some equally elusive transcendent principle. The work of art—as it is figured by the actress as muse—appears as an object of desire, but an illusory one, standing for an absolute object (or referent) that can only be elsewhere, or (more radically) irremediably absent. "Sarrasine," by virtue of its exploitation of the "castration" motif, which defines the object of the protagonist's quest as a void, is in this context one of the most radical texts, while the motif of transvestism, which adds an additional veil of illusion to the distance separating signs from their supposed referent, stresses no less dramatically the autonomy and ultimate baselessness of the signs that constitute the beautiful. Zambinella does not simply conform to the stereotype of the actress as *femme sans cœur* (although she[9] says this of herself: "Je n'ai pas de cœur!" p. 105); she is an illusory woman who is "really" a man—except that she is a man who is himself not "essentially" a man, and Sarrasine concludes bitterly, but understandably: "Tu n'es rien! Homme ou femme, je te tuerais, mais . . ." (p. 109). What then is the statue that itself represents this mirage? Sarrasine's despairing response: "C'est une illusion" (p. 109).

The despair is the more intense, not simply because of the convincingness of the initial illusion, but because of the contrast between what the illusion represented and the lack Sarrasine eventually discovers. Zambinella on stage is, to Sarrasine's eyes, an embodiment of the ideal: "Il admirait en ce moment la beauté idéale de laquelle il avait jusqu'alors cherché çà et là les perfections dans la nature . . ." (p. 96), which is as much as to say that, like the Adonis in the Lanty salon, she is more perfect than the real and that the reality to which she refers is of another world, the world of ideas. She is a work of art—"C'était plus qu'une femme, c'était un chef d'œuvre!" (p. 96)—but a work of art miraculously made living flesh: "Sarrasine dévorait des yeux la statue de Pygmalion, pour lui descendue de son piédestal" (p. 96). The text insists, of course, that this illusion is the product of skillful and harmonious composition, for in the real world, ideal perfection is attainable only "en demandant à un modèle, souvent ignoble, les rondeurs d'une jambe accomplie; à tel autre, les contours d'un sein . . ." (p. 96), and so forth; and Zambinella is herself described as an assemblage of parts:

L'artiste ne se lassait pas d'admirer la grâce inimitable avec laquelle les bras étaient attachés au buste, la rondeur prestigieuse du cou, les lignes harmonieusement décrites par les sourcils, par le nez, puis l'ovale parfaite du visage, la pureté de ses contours vifs, et l'effet de cils fournis, recourbés qui terminaient de larges et voluptueuses paupières. (p. 96)

In terms of my earlier essay, she is an automaton; for what is not explicitly stated, although it is implied by the logic of the whole situation, is that such an effect of composition is achievable only by artificial means—that is, by the manipulation of signs that consequently become deceptive in their apparent embodiment of an unreal referent.

It is to the harmony of the representation—not the deceptive means by which it is produced—that Sarrasine is attentive; and it is this harmony—doubled in the text by the voluptuous harmony of Italian music making—that awakens his senses ("lubrifiés par les accents de la sublime harmonie de Jomelli," p. 95), arouses his emotions ("l'artiste . . . sentit un foyer qui pétilla soudain dans . . . ce que nous nommons le cœur, faute de mot!" p. 96), and produces the orgasmic experience that is the soul's response to such perfection. Paradoxically, then, it is the illusion of beauty, predicated on a central void, that has the power to awaken in the artist the reality of his own inner life, a "soul" that has long lain dormant and unrecognized.

The illusory phenomenon that is the actress is the product of various sets of deceptive signs: disguise ("les prestiges d'une toilette qui . . . était assez engageante," pp. 95-96),[10] coquettishness ("elle s'avança par coquetterie sur le devant du théâtre, et salua le public avec une grâce infinie," p. 95), and finally the stage itself ("les lumières, l'enthousiasme de tout un peuple, l'illusion de la scène," p. 95)—that is, ultimately, it is a product of distance. When

Sarrasine emerges from his passive "âge d'or" of nightly adoration and begins to break down this theatrical distance—that is, to treat the work of art as if it were real—he is unwittingly committing himself to the path that will lead to his disillusionment. And it is in this that the parallel with Mme de Rochefide's experience is clearest, since his "Pygmalion complex" corresponds to her "Adonis complex": in desiring a portrait, she too commits the error (Proust would say the idolatry) of confusing art with reality, and she too will undergo a process of disillusionment as a result of her experience of the narrator's story. At the artists' orgy, Sarrasine is able to approach Zambinella, sit with her, and speak with her; at Frascati, they stroll together and talk again, more intimately. Her words are defensive, elusive, and disguised, but their intimation is clear: "Souvenez-vous, seigneur, que je ne vous aurai pas trompé . . . . Si je n'étais pas une femme? . . . Je n'ai pas de cœur!" (pp. 104-105). Stronger still, however, is her deceptive dress:

Elle avait quitté ses habits de théâtre, et portait un corps qui dessinait une taille svelte . . . . Sa poitrine, dont une dentelle dissimulait les trésors par un luxe de coquetterie, étincelait de blancheur. Coiffée à peu près comme se coiffait madame du Barry, sa figure, quoique surchargée d'un large bonnet, n'en paraissait que plus mignonne, et la poudre lui seyait bien. La voir ainsi, c'était l'adorer. (p. 101)

And above all, her—to Sarrasine—undeniably feminine behavior: her "expression si coquette, si voluptueuse," her "beauté capricieuse et pleine d'une certaine engageante" (p. 101), her fears, her "excessive sensibilité" (p. 102), "la coquetterie, la faiblesse, la mignardise de cette âme molle et sans énergie" (p. 106).

Over and beyond the male chauvinism, the concept of femininity displayed here is thematically relevant because feminine mutability, on the one hand, and languor, on the other, are imagined in the text as symptoms of the underlying lack; they embody the unreliability of signs divorced from substance, just as lack of inner "substance" makes changeability of personality inevitable and accounts for all forms of fear and weakness. To the very end, when Sarrasine has seen Zambinella in male garb at the ambassador's reception, when the theatrical customs of the Papal States have been explained to him, when the *enlèvement* has removed the last shred of distance between himself and the singer, the sculptor is still encouraged to cling to his illusion by the terror and lack of fiber Zambinella displays: "—Ah! tu es une femme, s'écria l'artiste en délire; car même un . . . . Il n'acheva pas. —Non, reprit-il, *il* n'aurait pas tant de bassesse"

(p. 108). Thus, the void that the deception conceals is the prime cause of the deceptiveness, and only the explicit confession of Zambinella ("Je n'ai consenti à vous tromper que pour plaire à mes camarades, qui voulaient rire," p. 109) finally breaks down Sarrasine's resistance and, sweeping away his last illusion, leaves him in the state of despair in which he is so willing to die.

But the text hints strongly that the deceptiveness of signs *need* not reduce the artist to despair. Certainly, Zambinella's fellow artists, the actors who by virtue of their profession exemplify the awareness of art as an illusion, do not view life in tragic colors: "Hommes et femmes, tous paraissaient habitués à cette vie étrange, à ces plaisirs continus, à cet entraînement d'artiste qui fait de la vie une fête perpétuelle où l'on rit sans arrière-pensées" (p. 104). Their motives in mounting their practical joke on Sarrasine appear to be affectionate rather than malicious (they greet him affectionately [p. 100]); and the part of the spoof that involves sending an ancient crone to guide the young sculptor through "un labyrinthe d'escaliers, de galeries et d'appartements" (p. 100) suggests that they have an initiatory purpose in mind—a purpose that can only be to cure Sarrasine of his "ignorance profonde sur les choses de la vie" (p. 94), to lead him to maturity, and to make him worthy of induction into their fellowship. In this context, to know life, for an artist, is to know the power and the deceptiveness of signs, and the plot mounted by the singers is in theory nicely calculated to bring about just such an awareness, while providing for the initial shock to be dispelled in a joyous "orgie d'artistes" (p. 100). That it misfires is no fault of theirs; the cause lies in the young man's ineradicable innocence, and even more in his excessive power of passion, which, once released, cannot be satisfied in a world of illusion. What would have made for Sarrasine's artistic greatness—his "génie sauvage," his "fougue extraordinaire"—is precisely what makes it impossible for him to accommodate to the deceptive conditions in which art *must* be practiced.

That his despair is paralleled by that of Mme de Rochefide when she has heard his story suggests that she, like him, has invested too much in, and undergone too powerfully, the erotic fascination of art to be able to bear with equanimity the inevitable disillusionment, the revelation of the void beyond the prestigious representation. The difference is that Mme de Rochefide is anything but ignorant of the "choses de la vie": *her* evolution is not from the practice of art as a matter of talent and craftsmanship to the practice of art as an expression of emotional intensity and personal desire but from a frivolous view of life and love to one of austere renunciation. But for both the creative artist (Sarrasine) and the receiver of art (Mme de Rochefide) the outcome of the encounter with artistic experience is strikingly similar. Their two outcries echo each other. Sarrasine:

Aimer, être aimé! sont désormais des mots vides de sens pour moi, comme pour toi. . . . Monstre! toi qui ne peux donner la vie à rien, tu m'as dépeuplé la terre de toutes ses femmes. . . . Plus d'amour! je suis mort à tout plaisir, à toutes les émotions humaines. (p. 109)

Mme de Rochefide, in her turn, generalizes the conclusion, drawing from art a lesson concerning desire in general and from that lesson a sense of metaphysical absurdity:

Vous m'avez dégoûtée de la vie et des passions pour longtemps. Au monstre près, tous les sentiments humains ne se dénouent-ils pas ainsi, par d'atroces déceptions? . . . Si l'avenir du chrétien est encore une illusion, au moins elle ne se détruit qu'après la mort. Laissez-moi seule. (p. 110)

But what is the meaning of this generalization? Structurally, it meshes the story of Sarrasine with the thematic concerns of the text as a whole, which involves the opposed visions of life as a *fête* and the world as a desert. Mme de Rochefide's role in this connection is for her character to evolve, through hearing the story, from that of a capricious and teasing woman, very much at home in the atmosphere of the Lanty ball, to the austere and "pensive" woman of the dénouement, intent on solitude. And it is the shift of scene from the Lanty's reception rooms to the setting of the storytelling—the intimate circumstances of the "petit salon" where she and the narrator sit by the fire in the silent night under the "clarté douce" of the lamp—that provides the mediating step in her conversion. The mood of coquetterie and irresponsibility has shifted here to one of involvement, attention, and closeness:

C'était une de ces soirées délicieuses à l'âme, un de ces moments qui ne s'oublient jamais, une de ces heures passées dans la paix et le désir et dont, plus tard, le charme est toujours un sujet de regrets, même quand nous nous trouvons plus heureux. Qui peut effacer la vive empreinte des premières sollicitations de l'amour? (p. 92)

This, then, is the situation, the context that gives point to the narrator's tale: it recalls the "joli boudoir" in which Mme de Rochefide discovers the Adonis painting, and thus underlines the parallel between her two experiences of art; but it is matched as well (although the roles are reversed)[11] by the one moment of intimacy between Sarrasine and Zambinella in the narrator's story, their conversation at Frascati. As such, the situation is a profoundly ambiguous one, based as it is on a double misunderstanding, for whereas the narrator believes it (like the deceived Sarrasine at Frascati) to be a situation of erotic promise, Mme de Rochefide is really heading (unbeknownst to her, but like Sarrasine in actuality) for disillusionment and the choice of the desert (which in him will produce a parallel, at the end, between the frustrated narrator and the despairing Sarrasine).

That Zambinella's evasive discourse in the Frascati scene is an embedded model of the narrator's own discourse in his story can be quite briefly demonstrated. Each is essentially deceptive, concealing an "affreuse vérité" (p. 107) that in each case is the same: the truth of Zambinella's identity as a castrato. Each is deeply ambiguous, hinting at a concealed secret, and hence producing a form of fascination in the hearer: the fascination of narrative suspense in Mme de Rochefide, the fascination, for Sarrasine, of a desire that is only heightened by the resistance, or reticence, it encounters: "Chaque parole était un aiguillon" (p. 105). The difference lies in the fact that Zambinella is anxious, without being able to speak openly, to hint at the real truth; her words are deceptive only in that they are too general for the real circumstances ("Je suis une créature maudite, condamnée à comprendre le bonheur, à le sentir, à le désirer, et comme tant d'autres, forcée à le voir me fuir à toute heure," p. 104) or else phrased according to modalities—the "universal" masculine of "Je puis être un ami dévoué pour vous" (p. 104), the "hypothetical" mode of "Si je n'étais pas une femme?" and the "metaphorical" quality of "Je n'ai pas de cœur!"—that make it possible for Sarrasine to misinterpret them in conformity with his own desire.

By contrast, the narrator's deceptive discourse deliberately conceals the truth, referring to Zambinella frequently as "*la* Zambinella," "cette femme," "sa maîtresse," "la cantatrice," and "l'Italienne" or enveloping the character in broad generalizations about women in general (the erotic appeal of their slippered feet, p. 101; their "organisation féminine," "la malice d'une jeune femme libre et amoureuse," "une modestie de jeune fille," p. 102; their gourmandise—"une grâce chez les femmes," p. 103—not to mention their supposedly tell-tale "mollesse," timorousness, capriciousness, and other weaknesses). The alibi is that the narrator is espousing the viewpoint of the deceived protagonist, Sarrasine, but the effect is also to deceive the narratee, be it Mme de Rochefide or the first-time reader. The function of such deceit is, of course, to maintain narrative suspense—but narrative suspense is also an alibi for the maintenance of the narrator's power over Mme de Rochefide, a power that compensates him for his humiliation at her sexual power ("elle toujours aussi fière, aussi rude, et moi toujours aussi ridicule en ce moment que toujours," p. 92) by putting her in thrall to him. The deception inherent in the narrator's discourse has as its purpose the production of a state of subjugation, intellectual and emotional—a state of intense involvement—in Mme de Rochefide. It is the discourse of seduction.

He is led, in other words, to adopt a *fictive* mode of narration in order to achieve ends to which he is prompted by desire. Were he indifferent to her, it would be a simple matter to reveal from the outset the secret he has to impart, filling in the details—if necessary —later on. But his adoption of the storytelling mode, with its maintenance of narrative authority through suspense, shows that his motives are more complex than the simple need to convey information. Indeed, there is a strong hint in the text that the narrator's discourse is not simply fictive in its rhetorical technique but that it is wholly fictional, in the sense that it produces not "true" information but a fabulation. How else can one interpret his angry musing as his beloved flounces coquettishly from the ball?

> —A demain, me dit-elle vers deux heures du matin, quand elle sortit du bal.
> —Je n'irai pas, pensais-je, et je t'abandonne. Tu es plus capricieuse, plus fantasque mille fois peut-être . . . que mon imagination. (p. 92)

The unexpected comparison, with its equivalence between her unpredictability and his imagination, can only suggest that the one is being used to match the other and that the narrator's claim to know the *truth* about the Lantys and to "révéle[r] ce mystère" (p. 91) is a cover for his intention to invent a story, and a fantastic one at that. He knows that she likes to "entendre raconter l'histoire de ces passions énergiques enfantées dans nos cœurs par les ravissantes femmes du Midi" (p. 91), and it seems that his intention is to relate a (perverse) variant of this recognized literary stereotype. But this is an intention that derives less from his anxiety to please her than it does from jealousy: he is jealous of her coquettish ways and proposes to focus her attention exclusively on him, for once; but he suffers also from the "jalousie à laquelle un poète avait essayé vainement de me faire croire" (p. 90), the jealousy of art works that Mme de Rochefide's fascination with the portrait has kindled in him. His effort, then, is to outdo the painter of the prestigious Adonis; his recourse to the artistic modality of narration is motivated by emulation and inspired by desire; and the type of discourse he opts for is that duplicitous form of art that presents fiction as truth.[12]

That his attempt works is indicated by Mme de Rochefide's first interruption (p. 98). Intrigued and puzzled, she interjects: "Mais . . . je ne vois encore ni Marianina ni son petit vieillard." The narrator's response is significant: "Vous ne voyez que lui, m'écriai-je impatienté comme un auteur auquel on fait manquer l'effet d'un coup de théâtre." It is significant for two reasons. He acknowledges his artistic intent ("comme un auteur") while identifying this with the theatrical production of suspense (and surprise). But at the same time, he inaugurates a new and more ambivalent technique of deception, his rejoinder—like Zambinella's responses to Sarrasine—being an anticipated revelation of the outcome that, however, the hearer (Mme de Rochefide or the reader) can understand only erroneously (taking the "lui" to refer to Sarrasine).

But Mme de Rochefide's second interruption, a page or two later, although it is more delicate to interpret, seems to show some distancing of her attention. One infers that, warming to his narration and encouraged by his success in subjugating her attention, the storyteller has gone a little to far in his narrative enthusiasm, and specifically in his enthusiasm for the erotic power of eighteenth-century women's footwear. Perhaps he has permitted himself to fondle her own feet? (We remember from p. 92 that, as he speaks, he is "sur des coussins, presque [aux] pieds [de Mme de Roche-fide].") Her apparently amused interjection ("Un peu! . . . vous n'avez donc rien lu?") functions in this context as a kind of distancing of the narrator, in response to his own earlier invitation ("Si je m'enthousiasme, vous me ferez taire," p. 92); and it has an unexpected brittleness that is perhaps a sign of Mme de Rochefide's embarrassment. The narrator's answering smile is both a recognition of Mme de Rochefide's worldliness (in itself encouraging to his intentions) and a graceful acknowledgment that he has overstepped a certain limit.

Certainly, from that point on, the narrative frees Mme de Rochefide (and the reader) from absolute subjugation to Sarrasine's point of view, and it thus begins, although suspense is maintained and even heightened, to prepare for the distancing and disillusioning surprise at the end. A part of the narrator's power is abdicated through the shift in narrative point of view, which is now able to notice (although

Sarrasine does not) the malicious smiles that accompany Vitagliani's equivocal remark: "Vous n'avez pas un seul rival à craindre ici" (p. 101), which points out that an involuntary start on Zambinella's part "fut *interprété par l'amoureux artiste comme* l'indice d'une excessive sensibilité" (p. 102) and draws attention to the "scène étrange" (p. 103) that the sculptor himself shrugs off. Thus, by the time the intimate conversation at Frascati is reached, both Mme de Rochefide and the reader are in a position to be aware of its ambivalence (as Sarrasine is not), to perceive Sarrasine's persistence in interpreting it in the light of his own desire-inspired illusions, and to *pressentir* another, and darker, secret. Consequently, when the final revelation does come, its effect on Mme de Rochefide (and the reader) is somewhat different from its effect on Sarrasine. Totally unprepared for the revelation of castration and the deceptiveness of signs, the latter lapses into a wild and self-destructive despair and accepts death eagerly. Prepared by the narration's more graduated presentation of its own deceptiveness, Mme de Rochefide's despair, while it repeats and resembles that of Sarrasine, takes on a more contemplative and philosophical hue:

Mères, des enfants nous assassinent ou par leur mauvaise conduite ou par leur froideur. Épouses, nous sommes trahies. Amantes, nous sommes délaissées, abandonnées. L'amitié! existe-t-elle? Demain je me ferais dévote si je ne savais pouvoir rester comme un roc inaccessible au milieu des orages de la vie. (p. 110)

Thus, her generalizing tone not only matches the thematic level of the tale as a whole; it also indicates that, situationally speaking, Mme de Rochefide has responded in the way that one responds to a work of art (whereas Sarrasine has responded to an event in his personal life—an event that *allegorizes* the experience of art). Unlike Sarrasine, who confuses art with reality to the end, she has learned, from both the content and the mode of the narrator's story, that such "idolatry" is an error.

To learn something new, as Bernard Shaw says somewhere, is to experience a painful sense of *loss,* and it is natural that Mme de Rochefide should turn her aggression not against herself for her error but against the agent of her disillusionment, the narrator: "—Ah! lui dis-je, vous savez punir. —Aurais-je tort?" (p. 110). And she *is* right, for the narrator has misused art in attempting to make his narration a means of subjugation; and his punishment fits the crime in that the narratee, Mme de Rochefide, has derived from it a philosophical vision, as is proper, instead of responding to it, improperly, as an act of seduction: "Et la marquise resta pensive"

(p. 111). Her pensiveness does result from disappointment: she has learned to overcome the artistic idolatry induced in her by the Adonis, but at the price of a certain disillusionment concerning the emptiness of artistic signs. However, this response of pensiveness to the work of art is also positively marked, and it functions structurally as a mediating element in the text as a whole. For Mme de Rochefide's evolution links her, on the one hand, with Sarrasine's idolatry and his desperate reaction to his own experience of art in the inner story, but, on the other hand, with the very much cooler reception that the whole narrative appears to assume on the part of its own reader. In short, the difference between Sarrasine's intensity of involvement, in the inner story, and the detachment required of its reader by the text as a whole is mediated by the evolution that Mme de Rochefide undergoes between her acceptance of the narrative pact with the narrator and her breaking it.

But the essential difference between the narrative situation of the inner story (with its intimate involvement of the narrator and Mme de Rochefide) and the much more controlled situation implied by the story as a whole can most clearly be seen when one examines the persona of the narrator himself. In his dealings with Mme de Rochefide, he is a slightly ludicrous figure, overeager at points, humiliated at others ("moi toujours aussi ridicule en ce moment que toujours," p. 92), and never so inadequate, perhaps, as at the point when, demoralized by Mme de Rochefide's final rejection, he struggles "avec une sorte de courage" to tack on to his drastically miscalculated tale, in extremis, a positive moral: ". . . je puis vous donner une haute idée des progrès faits par la civilisation actuelle. On n'y fait plus de ces malheureuses créatures" (p. 110). But the new narrative situation—in the story as a whole—is such that, with no erotic purpose or involvement now, the narrator is able to display much greater coolness and mastery; and he assumes a narratee who is as controlled and distanced as he. The past tense of the incipit, "J'étais plongé dans une de ces rêveries profondes . . .", suggests a first reason for this new confidence and control: the events related are now remote from the present in which the narration occurs; both the initial "rêverie" at the Lanty ball and the involvement with Mme de Rochefide are now over, and the "point" of relating them is entirely different from the point of the story the narrator told (also in the past tense—but situation makes meaning!) to Mme de Rochefide. Now they are being related, so to speak, for their own interest. So there are no embarrassed preliminaries or concluding "Eh! bien?"s; there is no deceptiveness and no attempt to subjugate the narratee's attention; indeed, the narrator's new-found confidence is most clearly manifest in the authority he now simply assumes, in his lack of attention to the effectiveness of a discourse whose interest he takes for granted. This means that the narratee is presumed to be, like the narrator, something of a philosopher: a man or woman of the world, capable of sharing the detachment with which the latter, from his vantage point between life and death, "sur la frontière de ces deux tableaux si disparates" (p. 80), not only was *once* able to view salon life and its participants (including its "observateurs" [p. 82] and its "philosophes" [p. 85]) but also *now* presents even himself in a somewhat self-deprecating light, both in his amorous role as unsuccessful suitor (as we have seen) and in his narratorial role as philosopher: "Je faisais une macédoine morale, moitié plaisante, moitié funèbre. Du pied gauche je marquais la mesure, et je croyais avoir l'autre dans le cercueil" (p. 80).

Humor, then, as much as wisdom (or as a form of wisdom) is this philosopher's stock-in-trade, and his narrative presupposes a narratee with his or her own sense of humor if it is to be rightly understood. His other outstanding characteristic—to which he himself draws attention—is his "folle imagination" (p. 85): that is, a faculty that comprehends the fictionalizing talent we saw him deploy in relating the story of Sarrasine but that also is now seen to include a broader interpretive power. This is the power that enables him to see in the contrast between a wintry garden and a warm ballroom the balanced principles of life and death, the *fête* and the desert (pp. 79-80), the power also to perceive the picture of Mme de Rochefide and the decrepit old Zambinella standing side by side as a realization of the same fancy: "la pensée en demi-deuil qui se roulait dans ma cervelle en était sortie, elle se trouvait devant moi . . ." (pp. 85-86).

Here, too, then, the narrative makes no claims to factual status. Indeed, in a French text of this period, the combination of humor and imagination in the narrator—especially as they serve as a foil for the entirely fantastic figure of the eerie old man, with his much more disquieting grin, his "rire implacable et goguenard, comme celui d'une tête de mort" (p. 88)—clearly connote a fictional category, *le genre hoffmannesque.* Hoffmann is not mentioned in the text (although the dedication to Charles de Bernard is a *signe de connivence* for those who know),[13] and I am not implying an influence, but an intertextual phenomenon: the tone is a hint to the reader, *une indication de lecture,* as to the mood in which the story should be approached—a mood in which both the everyday and the *insolite* (such things as a Paris ballroom and its ancient specter, or an Enlightenment sculptor's grotesque courtship of a castrato) are to be appreciated as vehicles of philosophical depth, capable of making a statement about life and its mysteries. Such a hint is supported by the two explicit intertextual references that frame the discussion of the enigmatic beauty of the Lanty family (that is, the *key* enigma that serves as pretext for, and hence as a paradigm of, the whole narration); the interest they arouse is like that produced by Gothic novels, specifically those of Ann Radcliffe; and like a poem by Byron, open to widely differing interpretation, they are "un chant obscur et sublime de strophe en strophe" (p. 82).

But here a new question surfaces, that of the *quality* of the interpretation to be placed on such a mystery, for it is insistently conveyed to the narratee that the *salonnards'* response to mystery—be it literary or social in character—is inadequate. The "intérêt de curiosité" aroused by Ann Radcliffe, the manner of reading Byron, "dont les difficultés étaient traduites d'une manière différente par chaque personne du beau monde" (p. 82), do not do justice to texts as deeply significant as those mentioned or to the strange text that is the Lanty family. As regards the latter, the narrator is relentless in his mockery, on the one hand, of the "contes . . . ridicules" put about by "gens amis du fantastique," the exotic stories invented by "des romanciers," the "fable spécieuse" subscribed to by "des banquiers plus positifs" (in short, by narrative explanations) (p. 83), and, on the other hand, of the superficial hypotheses of philosophers "qui, tout en prenant une glace, un sorbet, ou en posant sur une console leur verre de punch, se disaient: — Je ne serais pas étonné d'apprendre que ces gens-là sont des fripons . . ." (p. 85). These interpretive antimodels are manifestly provided so as to invite the reader of "Sarrasine" not to read *en mondain*—out of idle curiosity for some social enigma that can be solved by an anecdote or a classification—but with a sense of philosophical reverie and dreamy distance, the "folle imagination" that will look for a *significance* in life-and-death terms rather than some mere "solution," however apt.

The narratee is thereby warned, on the one hand, not to attach excessive significance to the narrator's claim to possession of the *true* solution to the mystery (it is, after all, yet another narrative or fable) and, on the other, not to be a dupe of the narrative technique of suspense, which consists of posing a question, then solving it. The true enigma is elsewhere, on a more philosophical plane; and if we are invited to take an interest in the more immediate problem this should clearly be what might be called *un intérêt d'interprétation* as opposed to a merely trivial "intérêt de curiosité." In this way, the narratee is specifically forearmed against the deceptiveness of the narrator's tale.

For it is clear that, just as Mme de Rochefide is deceived into believing Zambinella a woman, so too the narrator seduces us into sharing the *mondains'* illusory passion for the solution of a mystery. The questions are introduced with compelling force: what can the origins of the family be and what are the origins of their vast wealth? Then: what is the identity of the strange old man and what is his relationship with the family? In a sense, this deceptiveness is the opposite of that practiced by the narrator on Mme de Rochefide—since she is gulled by a false certainty (that Zambinella is a woman), whereas here we are deceived by a false uncertainty (the questions are not the true questions); but the end result is the same—the production of narrative suspense by a narrator who, in possession of the truth from the start, holds it back so as to keep the narratee's interest. In this respect, a warning to the reader is actually incorporated in the subplot—or second source of narrative suspense—of the main story, the narrator's courtship of Mme de Rochefide, which, by virtue of the parallel with Sarrasine's courtship of Zambinella in the inner story, may be read in turn as allegorizing an involved relationship with a work of art.[14] In each case, a similar thematics of fascination (based on desire) lays the ground for a deflationary dénouement (in which Mme de Rochefide's unexpected *dérobade* is equivalent to the discovery of Zambinella's sexual unavailability as a castrato). To allow oneself, as a reader, to be fascinated by narrative enigma and techniques of suspense is to fall victim to a form of "coquetterie"—that is, to artistic deception— and hence to court the same ultimate disillusionment.

But, forewarned by the textual invitation to be concerned with significance rather than solution, the reader of "Sarrasine" also receives quite early many hints that the true subject of the tale, and hence the true object of his or her interest, is not these deceptive enigmas but the wider mystery of art and its relationship with life. The beauty of the Lanty family, and especially of Marianina ("type de cette poésie secrète, lien commun de tous les arts et qui fuit toujours ceux qui la cherchent," p. 81), is a living exemplification of the unity of art and life, their common mystery, on the side of the ledger that is concerned with youth and splendor, and wealth— in short, the *fête.* On the side of the ledger that looks toward lack, and the desert of death, the decrepit old man appears as the same "création artificielle" that Sarrasine knew, and the continuity of the personage from youth to extreme old age is complete:

Les sourcils de son masque recevaient de la lumière un lustre qui révélait une peinture très bien exécutée. Heureusement pour la vue attristée de tant de ruines, son crâne cadavéreux était caché sous une perruque blonde dont les boucles innombrables trahissaient une prétention extraordinaire. Du reste, la coquetterie féminine de ce personnage fantasmagorique était assez énergiquement annoncée par les boucles d'or qui pendaient à ses oreilles, par les anneaux dont les admirables pierreries brillaient à ses doigts ossifiés, et par une chaîne de montre qui scintillait comme les chatons d'une rivière au cou d'une femme. (p. 88)

Readers sometimes fail to perceive—they have fallen victim to the narrative's deceptive questions—that the truly central enigma of the tale, the one that finally precipitates the narrator's offer to tell Mme de Rochefide Sarrasine's story, is in the question posed by the Marquise: what is the relationship between Marianina and the old man: "Qu'est-ce que cela veut dire? me demanda ma jeune partenaire. Est-ce son mari? Je crois rêver. Où suis-je?" (p. 91). The seeker after solutions will discover only that Marianina is Zambinella's great-niece. The seeker of significance who is prepared to enter the mood of the story as a manifestation of the interpretive imagination —a dream—will learn that at the symbolic level the two are indeed *married*, as beauty (with its deceptive splendor and its central void) weds life to death and as life itself places a figure like Mme de Rochefide beside an old death's head like Zambinella, "auprès de . . . débris humains, une jeune femme," forming "une arabesque imaginaire, une chimère hideuse à moitié": "—Il y a pourtant de ces mariages-là qui s'accomplissent assez souvent dans le monde, me dis-je" (p. 89).

Fiction Idealized

It was Walter Benjamin's insight that the relevant question to ask of the (preindustrial) story was "What is the moral of the tale?"— whereas the question appropriate to the novel is: "What is the meaning of life?"[15] Short as it is, "Sarrasine" belongs to the age of the novel: "Je crois rêver. Où suis-je?"—such utterances, occurring at the pivotal point of the text, acquire a significance beyond their superficial sense; but the "Qu'est-ce que cela veut dire?" is crucial. It signifies that "Sarrasine" is a text of philosophical import, which can be read appropriately only if the reading is an interpretation. This is not the place to attempt such a full-scale interpretation of "Sarrasine," but enough has been said for it to be clear why an appropriate starting point for such a global reading might be the sentence that defines the component elements in Zambinella's career, linking the world of art to the world of money under the joint sign of caprice:

Ce fut la première fois qu'il exerça cette tyrannie capricieuse qui plus tard ne le rendit pas moins célèbre que son talent et son immense fortune, due, dit-on, non moins à sa voix qu'à sa beauté. (p. 108)

Talent, wealth, and "tyrannie capricieuse" are equated (they are of the unstable order of signs, reposing on the basic void), and on such fragile grounds celebrity rests. But wealth appears additionally as representing the exchange value of "beauty" and "voice," which are, thus, themselves drawn into the network of deceptive phenomena. What is particularly germane to my present purposes, however, is the *equivalence* of beauty and voice that this final phrase suggests.

Voice, in this text, is what symbolizes the power of art, its impact on those who are subject to the effect (or effectiveness—the *Wirkung*) of beauty. It is Zambinella's voice that works on Sarrasine's soul to produce an orgasmic response:

Enfin cette voix agile, fraîche et d'un timbre argenté, souple comme un fil auquel le moindre souffle d'air donne une forme, qu'il roule et déroule, développe et disperse, cette voix attaquait si vivement son âme qu'il laissa plus d'une fois échapper de ces cris involontaires arrachés par les délices convulsives trop rarement données par les passions humaines. (p. 97)

Marianina's voice—with her beauty—is what makes her the living symbol of the element common to all the arts: "Marianina savait unir au même degré la pureté du son, la sensibilité, la justesse du mouvement et des intonations, l'âme et la science, la correction et le sentiment" (p. 81). Her voice not only exerts its drawing power on Zambinella himself, "échappé de sa chambre, comme un fou de sa loge" (p. 86) but its musicality, when she speaks the word *addio*, adding "sur la dernière syllabe une roulade admirablement bien exécutée, mais à voix basse, et comme pour peindre l'effusion de son cœur par une expression poétique," stirs in the old man— "frappé subitement par quelque souvenir" (p. 91)—what can only be a reminiscence of the power he himself once exercised through his own singing. Thus it provokes from him the gift of a precious ring— a relational gesture of exchange that also enacts the transmission of Zambinella's fortune to his descendants, the Lantys, while signifying at the interpretive level the exchange of wealth for art (signs for signs) and finally, of course, the symbolic marriage of Zambinella and Marianina.

The thematic centrality of the voice motif as a relational phenomenon is, then, what justifies textually my focus on the impact of art in "Sarrasine." In summary, the story analyzes the topic in terms of two essential questions: How is the voice of art used? How may one respond to it? There is a seductive use of art, illustrated by Zambinella's seduction of Sarrasine and the narrator's use of narrative in an attempt to win the favors of Mme de Rochefide. And there is a nonseductive use of art, which, like the general narrator's use of storytelling, aims to produce a reflective distance between the narratee and the story, and a philosophical evaluation of its fictions in terms of significance. Similarly, as far as possible responses go, the meditative, distanced approach to art contrasts with the passionate involvement displayed by Sarrasine in his encounter with Zambinella and by Mme de Rochefide in her fascination with the Adonis as well as in her initial subjugation to the narrator's storytelling—as well as by the narrator's own subjugation to the coquettishness of Mme de Rochefide. Such involvement, powered by the force of desire, derives from a fatal error of judgment, the confusion of artistic artifice with actual reality; and the text shows it to be an ultimately destructive approach to art—self-destructive in the case of Sarrasine but destructive, too, in the case of Mme de Rochefide, who turns her disillusionment and disappointment against the narrator, punishing him by withholding her sexual favors.

Roland Barthes anatomized "Sarrasine" with a view to answering the question of how a classical text ("texte lisible"), in spite of the infinite polyphony latent in textuality, succeeds in limiting the reader's interpretive freedom and in blocking semantic "drift." In my turn, I have attempted to put some of the larger parts back together so as to demonstrate another way in which the text seeks to restrict the reader's options, by indicating the appropriate narrative situation that will give it its "true" point. Structurally, "Sarrasine" may be said not to choose between the polarized options it presents: it displays them and mediates between them (through the evolution induced in Mme de Rochefide by the narrator's storytelling). But ideologically, it is clear that the text hierarchizes these experiences of art, implying a judgment both by its fictionalization of the seduction-involvement relationship as a destructive error and by the concentricity of the double *mise en abyme* that situates Sarrasine's complete involvement in relation to Mme de Rochefide's evolution toward a more interpretive stance, while in turn placing her evolution within the cooler, philosophical mood of the narrative situation assumed by the text as a whole.

Such a hierarchization (and the reading approach it recommends) represents an attempt to remove art from the sphere of desire through an idealization of aesthetic experience, a valorization of art as understanding over art as involvement. The major emblem of this valorization is the general narrator's initial posture, observing the dance of life from a vantage point at the window that looks out also onto the desert of death—a posture itself mirrored at the end by Mme de Rochefide's pensiveness.[16] Such idealization is an ideological stratagem to co-opt the intuition of the arbitrariness of signs by assigning it, yes, negative value in the world of "reality," but also positive value in the domain of "art," where fiction is *not false*, because it represents a higher truth. Art is *like* life in that it, too, incorporates the deceptive festival of signs and the deathly reality of their underlying void; but art, rightly understood and used (that is, recognized and interpreted as a symbolic statement, a fiction capable of producing meaning), is *unlike* life in that it brings about an emancipation from the conditions of reality into a world of thought, understanding, and significance. That is why it must be a denial of seduction.

This idealization of art by the ancestor of literary realism makes of "Sarrasine" one of the pilot texts of the French nineteenth century. Sarrasine's "Pygmalion complex"—his desire to embrace a "statue . . . descendue de son piédestal" (p. 96), that is, a work of art perceived as real—meshes with a problematics treated obsessively by Gautier[17] and Nerval,[18] the same problematics that Baudelaire examined decisively in *La Fanfarlo*. "La poésie avec des bras et des jambes":[19] in condemning Samuel Cramer's infatuation for the dancer who inspires this Pygmalionesque definition of the dance, the poet of the *Fleurs du Mal* emblematically sets the tone for the whole long lineage of Symbolism, with its essentially idealist aesthetic. But also the creator's love for his creation is structurally symmetrical with the "Adonis complex" displayed by Mme de Rochefide, the consumer of art; and, as has been mentioned, her attitude foreshadows the analysis in Proust of the form of error he calls "idolatry"—just as her evolution toward a more contemplative attitude foreshadows (distantly) the Proustian narrator's eventual discovery of an aesthetic miracle in a world of experience removed from the contingent. It is a distant prefiguration, because the idealization of art in "Sarrasine," although it forms the basic ideological assumption of the text, has not yet achieved the status of an explicit thesis and has not developed into a fully fledged sacralization of the aesthetic category; but it does permit us to see why it can be said that "Sarrasine," with its flight from the insertion of art into the real, the world of desire and of events, embodies attitudes that have been fundamental to modern experience. It is indeed only recently that we have begun to perceive such attitudes as a symptom of alienation and to face up squarely to the realization that art is real, its seductiveness legitimate, and the desires it arouses productive.

NOTES

1. Roland Barthes, *S/Z* (Paris: Éd. du Seuil, 1970), p. 95. Other discussions of "Sarrasine" include: P. Barbéris, "À propos du *S/Z* de Roland Barthes," *L'Année Balzacienne* (1971), 110-123; P. Citron, "Interprétation de *Sarrasine*," *L'Année Balzacienne* (1972), 81-95; Helen O. Borowitz, "Balzac's *Sarrasine*: The Sculptor as Narcissus," *Nineteenth Century French Studies*, 5 (1976-1977), 171-185; Barbara Johnson, "The Critical Difference," in *The Critical Difference: Essays in the Contempory Rhetoric of Reading* (Baltimore: Johns Hopkins University Press, 1980), 3-12; F. Flahault, "Sur *S/Z* et l'analyse des récits," *Poétique*, 47 (septembre 1981), 303-314.

2. All quotations are from H. de Balzac, *La comédie humaine*, 6 (Paris: Bibliothèque de la Pléiade, 1965). Page numbers in parentheses refer to this edition.

3. *S/Z*, 216-217: "Elle n'en fera pas moins trois ans plus tard une fugue en Italie avec le ténor Conti, aura une aventure célèbre avec Calyxte du Guénic pour faire enrager son amie et rivale Félicité des Touches, sera encore la maîtresse de la Palférine, ..." But see Barbéris, "A propos du *S/Z* de Roland Barthes," p. 113, for a reminder that, in the original (1830) version, this character is perforce unrelated to Béatrix de Rochefide and *La comédie humaine*.

The coquettishness of Mme de Rochefide, linked as it is to the "mignardise" of Zambinella, means that the story is producing a parallel between Sarrasine's fascination with Zambinella and the narrator's fascination with Mme de Rochefide. In each case, the feminine figure signifies the arbitrariness of signs and hence the lack that exists at the heart of the object of desire. Compare my analysis of the coquette in *L'Ange et l'automate: Variations sur le mythe de l'actrice, de Nerval à Proust* (Paris: Minard, 1971) and also later in this discussion; see too (for Zambinella as a deconstruction of the classical "readerly" conception of literature), Barbara Johnson, "The Critical Difference" in *The Critical Difference*: what is said of Zambinella is applicable, *mutatis mutandis*, to Mme de Rochefide.

4. *S/Z*, p. 96. In deconstructing Barthes, Barbara Johnson, in "The Critical Difference" in *The Critical Difference*, also relies specifically on the content of the story: "It is obvious that the key to this failure of the bargain lies in the content of the story used to fulfill it," p. 7.

She is right to stress the fact that the text requires one to distance oneself from Sarrasine's "reading" of Zambinella. On the other hand, her point that Barthes "erects castration into *the* meaning of the text" (p. 11), echoing Derrida's criticism of Lacan on "The Purloined Letter" ("le manque a sa place"), and her insistence that Zambinella is thus deprived of his power, as a figure of the "fragmented, unnatural and sexually undecidable" (p. 8), to signify "writerly" values and hence to deconstruct a "readerly" reading such as Sarrasine's, or Barthes's, are convincing only to the extent that one is prepared to admit an ahistorical reading of the text. If our contemporary (post-Nietzschean) sensibility is able to celebrate the arbitrariness of signs as a liberation, it is clear that in pre-Nietzschean contexts, the arbitrariness is difficult to dissociate from a sense of absence, loss, lack, and emptiness. The absence of the word *castrat* from Balzac's text—which for Barthes is evidence of a taboo, for Johnson a way of withholding ultimate meaning as an "unequivocal answer to the text's enigma" (p. 11)—does not, of itself, prove anything. It is interpretable also as a textual mimesis of Zambinella's condition, a gapping of the discourse that reproduces the lack in the character, and hence is subject to as many variable interpretations as the figure of Zambinella himself.

5. It depends whether one regards Sarrasine's clay statue and the marble derived from it as one work or two.

6. See *Le récit spéculaire* (Paris: Éd. du Seuil, 1977).

7. Sarrasine is at first disapproved of by his father and the Jesuits; but later, supported by "l'autorité du sculpteur célèbre" Bouchardon (p. 94), he regains his father's approval and that of "Besançon tout entier."

8. *L'Ange et l'automate.*

9. I follow the convention of using the feminine or the masculine pronoun for Zambinella as the context requires.

10. For a look at women's clothing as a metaphor for text, see my "Pour une poétique de vêtement," *Michigan Romance Studies,* 1 (1980), 18-46.

11. I mean the roles of courter and courted: the narrator is seducing Mme de Rochefide with his discourse, whereas it is Zambinella who with *his* discourse is deceiving Sarrasine. But the use of discourse as a form of deception remains constant.

12. It might be objected that the story of Sarrasine, being "assez connue en Italie" (p. 110), cannot be an invention of the narrator's. But if such is the case, how is it that only he—out of the whole population of Paris—is in possession of the Lantys's secret? It is more likely that the assertion is one of those devices by which the authors of fictions attempt to boost the credibility of their discourse.

13. Balzac had corresponded with Charles de Bernard concerning the influence of Hoffmann on *La peau de chagrin,* and the epigraph to the original version of "Sarrasine" read: "Croyez-vous que l'Allemagne ait seule le privilège d'être absurde et fantastique?" See Helen O. Borowitz, "Balzac's *Sarrasine,*" and Lucie Wanuffel, "Présence d'Hoffmann dans les œuvres de Balzac (1829-1835)," *L'Année Balzacienne* (1970), 45-56.

14. Cf. note 3.

15. See "The Storyteller," in H. Arendt, ed., *Illuminations* (New York: Schocken Books, 1969), 83-109.

16. My argument thus converges, from a different angle, with that of Peter Brooks concerning the relationship of (melodramatic) "representation" to "signification" in Balzac. See *The Melodramatic Imagination* (New Haven, Conn.: Yale University Press, 1976), p. 151: "Fiction, in Balzac's conception, exists to make us 'pensive,' exists to make us reflect on the substance of life and its principles."

17. See my "Gautier et le complexe de Pygmalion," *Revue d'Histoire Littéraire de la France,* 72, 4 (1972), 641-658.

18. See Michel Jeanneret, *La lettre perdue: Écriture et folie dans l'œuvre de Nerval* (Paris: Flammarion, 1978).

19. Charles Baudelaire, *Œuvres complètes,* I (Paris: Bibliothèque de la Pléiade, 1975), p. 573.

Chapter Five
Seduction Renounced:
"Sylvie" as Narrative Act

From the *Romanesque* to *Bricolage*

It has become customary, in the criticism of Nerval's "Sylvie," to distinguish between the two narrative instances covered by the same first-person pronoun, "I" ("je").[1] There is a hero "I," the subject of the act of "folly" recounted in the text (its *narré*): his voyage to the Valois in verification of the intuition that past and present are identical and that Aurélie, the actress he loves *de lonh*, is "the same" as the aristocratic young girl Adrienne, now a nun, with whom he fell in love as a child, betraying his first love, the peasant girl Sylvie. And there is a narrator "I," the subject of the *narration*, who has lost Adrienne (she is dead), lost Aurélie (she refused him when at last he courted her openly), and all but lost Sylvie (she is married to another but remains his affectionate friend): he now tells the story of his past adventures and of the loss of his illusions. As in a *Bildungsroman* or an autobiography, it is the hero's experiences that have made him, in the course of time, a narrator (one who knows) capable of evaluating them judiciously; so there is, as well as continuity, a measurable distance between the narration and the greater part of what is being narrated, the gap gradually closing as the story develops. Since there is no hint of "unreliability" on the part of the narrator, nothing to suggest that the text itself does not espouse the mature perspective of its narration, the reader is led to assume that the narrator's act of

97

narration is identifiable with the text's own narrative stance and so espouses in turn this perspective of "maturity."

However, twice in the text, the hero "I" is led to take on a narrator's role and to become the subject of a narrative act; and in each case, it is his own life that furnishes the subject matter of his narration, the goal being not only to obtain sympathetic understanding from the woman who is his narratee but also—and more especially— to obtain from her his *salvation*. Walking home from the dance with Sylvie, on the occasion of his impulsive return to the Valois, he confides in her his secret obsession (the "fatal" resemblance he perceives between Aurélie and Adrienne):

Tout à coup je pensai à l'image vaine qui m'avait égaré si longtemps.
"Sylvie," dis-je, arrêtons-nous ici, voulez-vous?"
Je me jetai à ses pieds; je confessai en pleurant à chaudes larmes mes irrésolutions, mes caprices; j'évoquai le spectre funeste qui traversait ma vie.
"Sauvez-moi! ajoutai-je, je reviens à vous pour toujours." Elle tourna vers moi ses regards attendris . . . . (p. 259)[2]

But here there is an interruption (Sylvie's brother suddenly appears from the bushes), and the narrative is not picked up again until the end of the day, when they are again walking, this time near the ruins of Châalis, where the hero's manipulations suggest that—far from wishing to escape the "image" that pursues him—he hopes to see the "salvation" he pursues arise from some miraculous identity between all three women, Adrienne-Aurélie, of course, but also now Adrienne-Sylvie:

Alors, j'eus le malheur de raconter l'apparition de Châalis, restée dans mes souvenirs. Je menai Sylvie dans la salle même du château ou j'avais entendu chanter Adrienne. "Oh! que je vous entende! lui dis-je" . . . .

La route était déserte; j'essayai de parler des choses que j'avais dans le cœur, mais je ne sais pourquoi, je ne trouvais que des expressions vulgaires, ou bien tout à coup quelque phrase pompeuse de roman—que Sylvie pouvait avoir lue. Je m'arrêtais alors avec un goût tout classique. . . . (pp. 265-266)

So the story is again interrupted, and nothing is resolved: soon the hero returns to Paris, where he undertakes a new seduction, this time of Aurélie. Once again, it takes the form of an act of confession, but now the mode is not so much that of romance (the *romanesque*) as it is theatrical or dramatic. The word *comic* (picking up the implied reference to Scarron's *Roman comique*) catches the generic solidarity of the two attempts, for the hero "I" courts Aurélie, first by letters (in the romance style) and then by means of a drama that he resolves to write for her.

A travers mes courses et mes loisirs, j'avais entrepris de fixer dans une action poétique les amours du peintre Colonna pour la belle Laura, que ses parents firent religieuse, et qu'il aima jusqu'à la mort. Quelque chose dans ce sujet se rapportait à mes préoccupations constantes. . . .

Aurélie avait accepté le rôle principal dans le drame que je rapportais d'Allemagne. Je n'oublierai jamais le jour où elle me permit de lui lire la pièce. Les scènes d'amour étaient préparées à son intention. Je crois bien que je les dis avec âme, mais surtout avec enthousiasme. (pp. 269-270)

Once again, it is clear that the hero "I" 's main intention is to bring about an identification (of Aurélie with Adrienne, the nun), but he is attempting also to bring into contact the "poetic action" and his own life, through an identification of the historical Laura-Colonna couple (in the past) with the couple he forms (or wishes to form) in the present with Aurélie. Given Aurélie's affectionate diagnosis of his "madness" ("Vous êtes bien fou," p. 270), the reader thinks of his ancestor in Scarron, the "petit fou" Ragotin, poet, lover of actresses, and confuser of the planes of the theatrical and the real; for the hero "I," like Ragotin, accompanies Aurélie's troupe, with the anachronistic and perhaps self-proclaimed title of "seigneur-poète," on its tour of the Valois. But it is here that reality and dream are definitively severed, and once again as the outcome of an act of narration on the part of the hero:

Alors je lui racontai tout; je lui dis la source de cet amour entrevu dans les nuits, rêvé plus tard, réalisé en elle. Elle m'écoutait sérieusement et me dit: "Vous ne m'aimez pas! vous attendez que je vous dise: La comédienne est la même que la religieuse; vous cherchez un drame, voilà tout, et le dénoûment vous échappe. Allez, je ne vous crois plus." (p. 271)

What is common to "romance" and the "comic" as modes of narration, then, is that each attempts to bring about an *ending* ("dénoûment") by bringing off, miraculously, an impossible identification, both of past and present (Adrienne-Aurélie) and of reality (the world of Sylvie) and dream (the theatrical world of Aurélie). The interruptions in one case, the refusal in the other to admit the possibility of the desired ending, consequently act as signals to the hero that he is on the wrong track, whether on the plane of lived experience (where he has been persisting in an impossible illusion) or on the plane of art (where the model of the seductive narrative, producing a "happy ending," has been proved inoperative because not true to lived reality).

Cette parole fut un éclair. Ces enthousiasmes bizarres que j'avais ressentis si longtemps, ces rêves, ces pleurs, ces désespoirs et ces tendresses . . . ce n'était donc pas l'amour? Mais où donc est-il? (p. 271)

The personage who shows the *benefit* of this experience on the hero's part is the narrator "I": on the occasion of his own returns to the Valois, his behavior reflects resignation to the realities of experience, and the confession-narrative he himself undertakes—the text of "Sylvie"—is evidence that he has renounced the narrative of seduction. Narration for him, as we will see, has become not an appeal for salvation through a miracle of love but an attempt to understand himself and to obtain the understanding of others. The rejected narrative model figures most clearly in his text, perhaps, in its references to the Rousseau of the *Nouvelle Héloïse,* which is here taken as the seductive novel par excellence. "Te voilà, petit Parisien," says Père Dodu (a folksy disciple of the *philosopher* Rousseau) when on his trip to the Valois the hero meets him, "tu viens pour débaucher nos filles?" (p. 267). It is a crude but not inaccurate accusation: Sylvie, that same day, has mentioned that, during the hero's absence, she had imprudently read the *Nouvelle Héloïse* (with its epigraphic warning against the seductiveness of romances) and that, at that time, she might well have been sensitive herself—with all her common sense—to the delusions of identification:

Vous m'avez parlé autrefois de *la Nouvelle Héloïse,* je l'ai lue, et j'ai frémi en tombant d'abord sur cette phrase: "Toute jeune fille qui lira ce livre est perdue." . . . Les gravures du livre présentaient aussi les amoureux sous de vieux costumes du temps passé, de sorte que pour moi vous étiez Saint-Preux, et je me retrouvais dans Julie. Ah, que n'êtes-vous revenu alors! (p. 259)

But it is now *too late* for the seductive approach to be operative.

Since the narrator needs to adopt, then, a quite different model of narration than that of the *romanesque,* it is significant that such a model does already exist in his own experience—not in the stories he *told* as hero but in those that, as a child, he *heard.* These were the stories told him, for example, by his uncle, the old rake whose opinion about actresses left such a mark upon the hero:

. . . il m'avait raconté tant d'histoires de ses illusions, de ses déceptions, et montré tant de portraits sur ivoire, médaillons charmants qu'il utilisait depuis à parer des tabatières, tant de billets jaunis, tant de faveurs fanées, en m'en faisant l'histoire et le compte définitif, que je m'étais habitué à penser mal de toutes sans tenir compte de l'ordre des temps. (p. 242)

These were not stories designed to seduce: in taking for their subject matter a romance-filled past, as the narrator "I" 's story must also do, they were attempting to teach a lesson, to convey what the narrator will later refer to, in his own case, as the "fruit" of his abandoned illusions, his "experience." They did it, it is true—and in this also they are models for the future narrator of "Sylvie"—in an ambivalent way, due to their indulgence in the poetics of nostalgia, the supposedly salutary memories being attached to reliquiae of the past that are lovingly preserved and whose charm derives from their "faded," "yellowed," old-fashioned quality. But there was, in addition, a more complex, and more fundamental, lesson to be drawn from the uncle's storytelling. On the one hand, by his practice of accumulating anecdotes that are so similar that one loses track of the difference between them, the uncle furnishes a structural model for the future narrator "I" of "Sylvie," which is composed of a series of superimposed accounts of his past loves and his many returns to the Valois. But on the other hand, in order to become the narrator, this "I" had first to overcome a mental disposition induced, precisely, by listening to his uncle's stories. As an adept of what Queneau might call *les temps mêlés*, he had learned to leave out of account "l'ordre des temps," and it is this that he must unlearn in order to escape the illusions of identity that have made him "fou"; whereas the narrator "I," on the other hand, displays in constructing his story an absolute mastery over time and hence invites his own readership to maintain their own lucidity, taking care not to confuse chronologically distinct episodes and to maintain careful distinctions between the various female objects of love in order the better to understand and to evaluate the errors and confusions of the hero's childhood and youth.

But there is another old man in the text, also remembered from childhood, who figures as a model of storytelling in the experience of the future narrator: he, too—more clearly than the ambivalent uncle—is a master of time. I am referring to Père Dodu, whom the hero encounters, as a figure out of his distant past, during the last stages of his crucial trip back to the Valois:

Je reconnus tout de suite un vieux bûcheron, le père Dodu, qui racontait jadis aux veillées des histoires si comiques ou si terribles. Tour à tour berger, messager, garde-chasse, pêcheur, braconnier même, le père Dodu fabriquait à ses moments perdus des coucous et des tourne-broches. (p. 267)

Like the homely stories of the uncle, Père Dodu's folksy tales stand in contrast with the novels and drama that furnish the hero with false narrative models. In this, they are like yet another set of models in "Sylvie," the folk songs (embeddings both of the *énoncé* and of the *énonciation*). As a legendary personage in his own right (if only by virtue of his fairy-tale occupation as a woodcutter), Père Dodu's person imprints on his tales a legendary character: they are not seductive but "comiques ou . . . terribles," funny or scary. It is true that, as a *philosophe*—having been converted from his old superstitious practices as the local *guérisseur* through the influences of "les conversations de Jean-Jacques"—he has followed an itinerary leading toward rationality, much as the future narrator must do; but Père Dodu remains faithful to, and acts as spokesperson for, a certain sense of the marvelous that is firmly ingrained in the traditions of the region. In a not dissimilar way, the narrator "I" will also display a certain fidelity to his former illusions and errors, even as he philosophically and rationalistically classifies them, and judges them —denies them—as "illusions" and "errors."

However, what makes Père Dodu a prime model for the narrator "I" is his status as jack-of-all-trades, a status that makes of him a socially marginal individual, a sort of "bricoleur"—one, that is, who has no real trade or profession at all. But he *is* a genuine "bricoleur," and what he puts together "à ses moments perdus" is cuckoo clocks and turnspits. Storytelling, for the narrator "I," will also be a *bricolage*: he talks of "trying" to give permanence ("fixer"), "sans beaucoup d'ordre," to the illusions, the "chimaera" of his youth (p. 271) —and indeed, one may wonder also what exactly is his own social station, since, having renounced his former marginality as a poet enclosed in his ivory tower (p. 242), having renounced the *romanesque* and the dramatic, he now seems to have no conventional artistic function, and no other profession either. Storytelling is his social identity, as it is Père Dodu's, an identity inseparable from the form of "pottering about" called *bricolage*. But neither his nor Père Dodu's *bricolage* is undirected: it takes as its essential function a certain way of dealing with time. The one makes cuckoo clocks and turnspits; he deals with clockwork; and the other will find in him the model for a narrative that is respectful both of illusions and of philosophy, that is, in terms of regional culture, strongly localized but that above all is meticulous in its ordering of time.

After having, as a child, "drownded" ("nayé") his watch and become the young man who owns a beautiful Renaissance clock but never winds it, the future narrator's discovery in rediscovering Père

Dodu, with his "coucous" and "tourne-broches," is the discovery of time. In "Sylvie," the clock is the fundamental model (or figural embedding[3]) of the narrative, and the narrator "I" is, in imitation of Père Dodu, a master of time, for the clock signifies respect for linear time. And indeed the text of "Sylvie" is scrupulous in registering historical time, whether it be the chronology of the Valois past and its continuing evolution in the present or the description of the "époque étrange" when the main events of the story take place; or again, in the personal time span of the hero/narrator's life, the chronological ordering of his memories and his different trips back to the Valois; or finally, in the narrative time of the tale itself, the ordering of events occupying the reverie-filled night, the wanderings of the following day, and their subsequent outcome.

But the time of clocks and watches—marked out by the revolving hands—is not only a linear time; it is also a circular time, a time that appears to inscribe, within the linear flow of historical time, another, cyclic time, which produces continuity, sameness, repetition, similarities, and identity, a time that is therefore a sort of "hors-temps," an extratemporal time. There is no need to invoke here the famous sonnet, "Artémis," that incorporates this conception of time: "La Treizième revient . . . C'est encor la première;/ Et c'est toujours la seule . . . ." Circular time is also inscribed in the narrative of "Sylvie" through the association of cuckoo clocks with the circular movement of turnspits. What is remarkable about the cuckoo clock, precisely, is its way of marking the ever-returning hours by the regular reappearance, in some cases of the bird famous as an unwanted visitor to the nest (like the hero in his returns to the Valois), in others of tiny human figures, slightly old-fashioned and countrified like the villagers in the story, who are *always the same.* This is not the place to insist (it has formed the subject matter of many critical analyses) on the repetitive character of "Sylvie"'s structures and themes or on the central importance to its thematics of the motif of resemblance.

What might more profitably be stressed is that in clockwork the smooth movement of the hands (espousing both the circularity of repetitive time and the linearity of history) is produced by a precise and complex mechanism, a meticulous combination of cogwheels and springs, in which it is very easy to see a metaphoric equivalent of the "grammar" of narrative, or more generally, all the *work* of writing that constitutes the text. Leaving aside Père Dodu, the theme of work, in "Sylvie," centers exclusively on the eponymous heroine, the peasant girl who, after presumably starting life at the spinning wheel, becomes a lacemaker and then a glovemaker, as the story develops. In their different ways, it is clear how these different manual trades can stand as figures of the production, through writing, of text. But it is worth noting also that the progression of Sylvie's occupations reflects not only her personal advancement in social status but also the growing mechanization of cottage industry in the increasingly industrialized France of the period. The needles Sylvie uses in lacemaking click "avec un doux bruit sur le carreau vert" (p. 252), like the ticktock of a clock; she makes gloves with the help of an iron instrument significantly called "une mécanique" (p. 263). But the point of recording Sylvie's upward social mobility is to stress the increasing distance between herself and the hero "I." "Vous avez vos affaires de Paris; j'ai *mon travail*" (p. 266) (my emphasis), she says when she finally dismisses him. And it is true that the young hero is not separated from her only by his bookish culture (a distance that *diminishes* in the course of the story, with a significance we have yet to explore); the more cogent aspects of their growing apart are the young man's idleness as a frequenter of theatres and clubs and his idealism as a poet, indulging within the safety of his ivory tower in "l'amour, hélas! des formes vagues, des teintes roses et bleues" (p. 242), by contrast with the heroine's practical common sense and her busy hands.

Consequently, the fact of becoming a narrator, with clockwork as his model, means a reconciliation on his part not only with time but also with the world of work (albeit the amateurish work of *bricolage*), and one that makes him worthy of Sylvie, the "fée industrieuse," as she is called at one point (p. 264). But the irony is that it takes the shock of losing Sylvie, combined with that of the loss of Aurélie, to bring about his conversion and divert him from the love of "teintes roses et bleues" toward becoming the *bricoleur*-clockmaker-narrator who is worthy of her affections. In this, too, he is *too late,* for meanwhile she, for her part, will have become not only the wife of another but the wife of a pastry cook (a trade it is difficult to see as a figuration of narrative). She is now a town dweller and a shopkeeper: her marriage to *le grand frisé* (the narrator's foster brother and "double") represents not only the culmination of her social ascent but also a choice of bourgeois standing that sets her apart from the narrator's artistic practice as artisan-*bricoleur,* much as previously her identification with the cottage industry of the countryside had separated her from the hero's citified artistic stance, his poetic but unproductive "enthusiasm."

The Narration of Madness

Why, then, does the narrator produce the narrative act that is "Sylvie"? "Si j'écrivais un roman," he says (and we know that it is precisely *not* a romance he is writing), "jamais je ne pourrais faire accepter l'histoire d'un coeur épris de deux amours simultanés" (p. 269). This means that, in the antiromance he does give us, the purpose is not to resolve differences and contradictions by means of seductive discourse but to make sense of something that is, on the face of it, implausible, or more accurately, to have this implausibility "accepted"—by means of a narrative act that might be called, not seductive, but therapeutic. In this way, although from a slightly unexpected angle, "Sylvie" demonstrates a certain similarity with *Aurélia*: in both texts, the problem is the narration of a form of madness, an experience of doubleness which common judgment might regard as unlikely. To have others accept this story, for the narrator, is a way of having them accept *himself,* by making believable for them what he himself considers strange or aberrant: here, the fact of being capable of "deux amours simultanés." As a first step toward having others accept him, he must presumably, therefore, begin by achieving an understanding of himself—and the narrative does offer certain characteristics of a self-analysis (whose primary *destinataire* is identical with its *destinateur*). But it is also clear that, for the narrator, self-understanding and self-acceptance are insufficient and that acceptance of self needs to be validated by the acceptance of others. An implication of this is that the narration of "Sylvie" will be carried out by an "I" who is attempting to understand what is incomprehensible in his own existence but in a framework of concern for the values and perspectives of a readership that is assumed to be, by definition, unsympathetic to the madness represented by a heart capable of double love, and hence to the narrator's basic program. So, the problem of acceptance resolves partly into that of rendering the actual sensation of double love (i.e., making it acceptable as a possibility in lived experience) and partly into that of obtaining some positive evaluation of this madness (i.e., making it acceptable in ethical or social terms).

This, in turn, implies a rhetorical tactic—or more accurately a double rhetoric—designed, on the one hand, to obtain the reader's involvement in the adventure and, on the other, to elicit his or her understanding judgment. Let us begin with the latter. The double-loving heart is in love, first, with a twofold image (Adrienne-Aurélie) representing the mirage of cyclical extratemporality and second, with a real figure (Sylvie) who embodies the linear temporality of history and change. A "therapeutic" account of their double love must then incorporate, and make acceptable, both the desire that has Adrienne-Aurélie as its object and the desire that concerns Sylvie (and we will see that this is indeed what happens). But part of the rhetorical tactic consists of an initial displacement of the idea of madness, which comes to refer only to the love of Adrienne-Aurélie (i.e., "simultaneous" love): "Aimer une religieuse sous la forme d'une actrice! . . . et si c'était la même!—Il y a de quoi devenir fou! . . . Reprenons pied sur le réel" (p. 247). In this context, the lover of Sylvie, whose desire has a real object, tends to appear as the ancestor of the narrator himself, since the latter inherits the experience of the former and incorporates into his narration the disenchanted view of "illusions" and "chimères" that, precisely, we see Sylvie's lover acquiring. For this narrator, the way to make the hero's capacity for "deux amours simultanés" acceptable is to classify as madness the attractive notion of simultaneity (along with the conception of time it applies) while projecting as sensible only respect for the linear time he associates with "la douce réalité." That this involves a certain betrayal is indisputable—he is betraying both the hero's heart, with its double love, and his own narrative program, since in order to bring about acceptance of his double-loving heart he is obliged to deny half of his desire.

However, these are the terms in which, referring apparently to his love for Aurélie, he is led to conclude: "Telles sont les chimères qui charment et égarent au matin de la vie" (p. 271). The act of deixis —relegating the narré, slightly disdainfully, to a distanced status that clearly separates it from the moment of narration, and hence from the narrating "I," is eloquent in its implications. "J'ai essayé de les fixer . . . ," the text continues: here the narrating "I" appears ("je"), but taking responsibility only for the récit, having no other task than to stabilize through writing the chimeras of the past. (In which, it is true, he displays a certain fidelity to that past, since to "fix" a chimera is to reinforce its principal charm, its resistance to linear time). What follows, however, continues to insist on the distance between the time for illusions and the time for narration: "J'ai essayé de les fixer sans beaucoup d'ordre, mais bien des cœurs me comprendront." To "fix" a chimera "sans beaucoup d'ordre" is to compromise what is essentially order by transposing it into the world in which entropy is the master—the world of time;

it is an essentially unfaithful way of being faithful to it, since it subordinates fixity to the lack of order characteristic of the universe of temporal flow and change. "Mais"—this "but" is a crucial one[4] — such is the very condition of gaining the acceptance of others: "bien des cœurs me comprendront," for it is not in spite of the disorder of presentation that the chimeras are now comprehensible but because of the narrative disorder, which functions as a sign of the narrator's allegiance to the world of time. In this way—the chimeras becoming acceptable *as illusions*, precisely—"bien des cœurs *me* comprendront."

This means that the narrator "I," having distanced himself from youthful illusions, is appealing for understanding, not of them, but for himself. And appropriately, he follows up immediately with a passage in praise of experience (the recognition of linear time) that, separating him from his illusions, has made him what he is. "Les illusions tombent l'une après l'autre, comme les écorces d'un fruit, et le fruit c'est l'expérience." It is as if the writing "I" of the narrator —"qu'on me pardonne ce style vieilli," he says a few lines later, displaying his awareness of being a writer (and a writer addressing an audience assumed to be out of tune with the charms of nostalgia) —is defining himself in opposition to the desiring "I" he once was, since his erstwhile double desire has now split into "chimères" on the one hand and on the other "expérience," that is, renunciation. It is ironic, then, that the understanding he needs as the subject of a strange desire can only be obtained by presenting himself as a (now reformed) writing "I."

Throughout the story, the narrator presents to the implied reader (the "hearts" who are entrusted with "understanding" him) this reassuring persona. The "I" who speaks in the text speaks *in place of,* not on behalf of, the "I" he once was; and to do so he uses language that distinguishes him carefully from his former dream-ridden self. This is a language of philosophical wisdom and cultured serenity, the language of one who has learned to "take things as they may be." What he calls "le monde des rêveries" (p. 258) is duly gratified with his comprehension, and he shows himself a most judicious analyst of psychological phenomena and states of semiconsciousness, about which he produces considered observations: "Cet état, où l'esprit résiste encore aux bizarres combinaisons du songe, permet souvent de voir se presser en quelques minutes les tableaux les plus saillants d'une longue période de vie" (p. 242). For the main value to which he now subscribes is the thirst for knowledge, the "soif de connaître" he attributes to humankind as its only eternal characteristic, a desire of the mind replacing the desire of the heart as "mobile de toute force et de toute activité" (p. 262). And the tradition in which he now seems to situate himself in order to judge and understand matters of the heart is the tradition of the philosophers, from Lucretius and Virgil, as he says, to Montaigne, Descartes, and Rousseau.

But this same distance that intervenes, by the nature of his philosophical investigation, between himself and the manifestations of his erotic desire (such as memory and dreams), can be seen also when the narrator concerns himself, as a folklorist and historian (that is, a Parisian) with the area of experience of which Sylvie is an embodiment, the folk culture of the Valois. The peasants, who are "peu étymologistes de leur nature" (p. 265), as he says, are ignorant of what he, the narrator, knows, that is, the historical dimension of the customs, monuments, and manner of speech of the region. Once, as a child, he had shared their unawareness: ". . . nous formions le cortège . . .—sans savoir que nous ne faisions que répéter d'âge en âge une fête druidique, survivant aux monarchies et aux religions nouvelles" (p. 244). But soon—having been sent away to school, having lived in Paris, having traveled abroad—the young man who was initially indistinguishable from the peasant population began to return among them with forms of knowledge (historical, archaeological, geographical, literary) that set him apart. The story of his alienation from Sylvie does not involve only the changes on her side, setting the hardworking and practical girl apart from an idle and chimerical poet; it results also from the hero's increasingly "Parisian" culture that gives him a stranger's viewpoint on Valois life, whether he is evaluating the continuity of its traditions in his role as historian or whether, in his poetic moments, he is nostalgically lamenting the changes that take place there.

The alienation that comes to separate the hero "I" from Sylvie clearly foreshadows the narrator "I" 's alienation from "himself." In this respect, the narrative voice can be seen in the final analysis as being almost equally removed from the part of the hero's heart that loved Sylvie as it is from the part of his heart that is now judged to have been a victim of illusion in the form of "simultaneous" loves. The *only* continuity connecting the speaker with the personage on whose behalf he speaks is "experience"—but "experience" is the experience of loss, it is a principle of discontinuity in that it is disillusioning, separating one not only from what one calls "chimères" but from the *whole* of one's past—from the love of Sylvie as well as from the love of Adrienne-Aurélie. The upshot is that, in the way the connotational field of "madness" ("folie") was initially restricted, for tactical reasons, so as to cover not both of the hero's loves in their incompatibility but only the love of Adrienne-Aurélie as love of the simultaneous, now the term "chimères," in the summing-up phrase that introduces the *Dernier Feuillet,* comes in a compensatory way to acquire a broadened range of significance, referring both to the disillusioning courtship of Sylvie and to the hopeless love for Aurélie(-Adrienne), and consequently distancing the whole of the hero "I" 's adventure.

But what this means is that, in rejecting both sides of his double love as "chimères," the narrator is also recognizing their solidarity. And this is the solidarity that can now be found—but with a positive valorization—if one looks again at the formulation of the narrator "I" 's program in the phrase "J'ai essayé de les fixer sans beaucoup d'ordre." A new reading is possible, which corresponds to the other half of the rhetorical tactic (the part that consists of obtaining the reader's adherence to, or involvement with, the lived experience of double love). In this reading, instead of seeing in the oxymoronic "fixer"/"sans beaucoup d'ordre" the sign of a deliberate distancing, it is perceived as a paradoxical collocation indexing a narrative project no less strange than the hero's own double love, since it attempts to be no less respectful of the continuity characteristic of "chimères" than of the discontinuity recognized by disenchantment and experience. There is no incompatibility here—as we will see in due course—with the narrator "I" who espouses the stance of philosophical wisdom; but this statement of his narrative program can be seen as an *échangeur,* a switching device, which allows the definition of a distanced mode of narration to reverse itself into an invitation, or appeal, for a sympathetic, and indeed empathetic (nondistanced), mode of reading. The narrator who is so anxious to distinguish himself from the hero he once was is also no less anxious for his narrative to be read as the faithful reflection of the double postulation that once occupied the hero's heart—the postulation he now wishes to have "accepted" by those "hearts" that are capable of "understanding." His success, which depends partly on *distancing the narrative act* from the narrative content, depends equally on a second and absolutely complementary tactic, which aims to achieve the *reader's adherence* to the self-same narrative content.

Hence, the presence in the story of a series of *models for reading* that function as indices of the narrative code, models of order and disorder none of which is individually capable of being applied to the narrative in its full extent but that cumulatively form a complex that covers the whole. These models, logically speaking, are opposed to each other; yet they are simultaneously valid; in this way, they call for a reading of what is perhaps an impossible totality, but a totality that would, if one could achieve it, transcend the opposed categories, the logical oppositions in the text. Thanks to this, the reader's "heart" would be the place where understanding might take place of the double loves that the mind can accept only as "chimères," as "folie." The reader would now apprehend the text *simultaneously* in the mode of order and permanence and in the mode of disorder and change; such a reader's heart would become, in relation to the text, "épris d'un double amour."[5]

Festivity, Theatre, Ruins

The first reading model is that of festivity (*la fête*) as a celebration of cultural continuity and repetition, as in the "fête de l'arc," which, we have already seen, recurs "d'âge en âge . . . survivant aux monarchies et aux religions nouvelles" (p. 244), surviving—that is—the course of history itself. The emblem of the *fête* is the procession ("cortège"), itself an image of repetition within continuity, whether it be the "cortège de l'arc" or the girls' round dance on the lawn or the "gracieuse *théorie* renouvelée des jours antiques," which turns a later "fête de l'arc" into what is at once a reproduction of Watteau's *Voyage à Cythère* and an "image des galantes solennités d'autrefois" (p. 249). Once more, I do not intend to underscore here, after so much criticism, from the Proust of *Contre Sainte-Beuve* to Sarah Kofman, the ways in which the text of "Sylvie" lends itself to a reading that focuses on its repetitive structures, its thematics of similarity, its temporal minglings and confusions of period with period. This has been the classic reading of the *nouvelle.*

I will note instead that festivities, in the tale, are subject to a kind of degenerative trend, as a result of which their significance as a mere "image," a "*mirage* de la gloire et de la beauté" (p. 246) (my emphasis), gradually comes to predominate. Even of the round dance on the lawn it is said, symptomatically, that "nous *pensions* être en paradis" (p. 245) (my emphasis); but it is the scene of the pseudowedding at the home of the aunt—with its disguised participants, their consciousness of their own disguise as Greuzean "accordés de village," the many allusions to the passing of time and the brevity of happiness—that most clearly illustrates the fragility of the *fête,* its theatrical quality. One might think also of the village dance that is going on in chapters III through VII while the hero, his mind alive with memory, makes his nocturnal dash through the Valois countryside toward Loisy: it symbolizes memory as the *fête* of the mind, on the one hand, but, on the other, it prepares for the morning-after-the-night-before mood of the following day, with its overcast ("maussade") weather, its sleepy villagers, and the hero's own sense of fatigue, growing disenchantment, and final abandonment of the Valois and everything for which it has, up to that point, stood. In this respect, the supper party with Père Dodu, a modest festivity whose subdued mood is specifically attributed to the fact that it follows the livelier *fête* of the night before, is symptomatic: it typifies a mood that prevails in a narrative that itself "comes after" and is a festivity "de lendemain de fête" (p. 267). The festive character of "Sylvie" derives from the *memories* of previous festivities rather than from any direct or immediate rendering of what are contrastingly described as "les fêtes *naïves* de notre jeunesse" (p. 244) (my emphasis).

So, there is a mental component in the festivity model, and a consequent vulnerability with respect to everyday reality, that invite comparison with the theatre, the place of illusions.[6] The opening words of "Sylvie" ("Je sortais d'un théâtre où tous les soirs je paraissais aux avant-scènes en grande tenue de soupirant") teach us that the whole text can be read as the story of an *emergence from the theatre* into cold daylight. In point of fact, things are more complex, since part of the narrative is devoted also to the story of the hero's *entry* into the world of the theatre, that is, to an account of how he came to the point of appearing every evening "en grande tenue de soupirant," as the lover of Aurélie, and this narrative is conducted in tandem with that of the events (the exciting night of memories, the disenchanting day in the Valois, the courtship of Aurélie) that cured him of his addiction to a *romanesque* and theatrical conception of love and thus brought him out of this world of inauthenticity. "Ce n'était donc pas l'amour," he says at the culminating point of this process "Mais où donc est-il?" If the *fête* figures what is genuinely comforting in the phenomenon of memory, then the theatre figures the false hold memory can exert, the fascination it has for a mind caught up in love of an "image" and unable or unwilling to disturb the "magic mirror" of simultaneity that has him in its thrall. In the theatre, there is no real continuity of past and present, only a resemblance that masks their actual discontinuity; and although the actress may *remind* one of the nun, the two are not identical. To believe in their identity, therefore, is to be subject to an illusion, a "chimère," and indeed only the distance the hero is so careful to maintain between himself and the actress makes it possible for him to protect the "image" for which he longs.

From the very start, then, there is a hint of the vulnerability of the theatrical experience when it enters into contact with the real, and this is confirmed by the gradual degeneration of the theatrical theme as the story develops. Thus, in the episode of the "wedding" at the home of the old aunt, the reference is to the fairy plays of the Théâtre des Funambules, with their magical, but palpably false, dénouements. With respect to Châalis, where he recalls the performance of a "mystère des anciens temps" in which Adrienne appeared, "transfigurée par son costume," the narrator finds he can no longer be certain whether the details, as he says, are "real" or whether he has "dreamed" them (p. 257); and this *mental* theatre will soon become the initiatory *hell* in which, courting Aurélie, as a latter-day figuration of the redemptive goddess Isis, the hero passes "par tous les cercles de ces lieux d'épreuves qu'on appelle théâtres" (p. 270). In this way, the theatre as a place of initiation becomes retrospectively identified with the Parisian club ("cercle") in which the young men of the time, the hero among them, indulged in "rêves renouvelés d'Alexandrie" (p. 243) and "l'homme matériel aspirait au bouquet de roses qui devait le regénérer par les mains de la belle Isis" (p. 242)—a club that, as the narrator knows, was an ivory tower. "Vue de près, la femme réelle révoltait notre ingénuité; il fallait qu'elle apparût reine ou déesse, et surtout n'en pas approcher" (p. 242). The theatrical theme has brought us back full circle, then, to the narrator in his "grande tenue de soupirant"—but it is this whole dreamworld "renouvelé d'Alexandrie" that is destined to collapse when once it comes, at last, into contact with reality. The travels with Aurélie's company, the hero's declaration of love to her, "au château, près d'Orry, sur la même place verte où pour la première fois j'avais vu Adrienne" (p. 271), and her refusal of his hand are a structural repetition and thematic confirmation of the disenchantment brought about already by the return to the Valois in the night of memories, followed by the disillusioning wanderings of the day and the collapse of the hero's aspirations at Père Dodu's supper party, with the announcement of Sylvie's forthcoming marriage.

As a self-acknowledged inheritor of the Enlightenment, and a reader of the Abbé Terrasson in particular, Nerval quite naturally associated the idea of the theatre as a place of initiatory ordeal with that of *artifice*. Everywhere in the text, the magical illusion is deflated by reference to the material means that produce it—the footlights that shine on Aurélie from below, the twisting sun of the

Funambules stage, the gilt cardboard producing a "cercle de lumière" about the head of Adrienne (p. 257)—so that what is mediated for the hero is not a passage from the profane to the sacred but from illusion to reality, a process of disenchantment that is also a discovery of the real. Here there is doubtless a lesson for the reader who is first invited to share the hero's fascination with an art of illusion and then to join him in discovering the theatrical machinery, the "clockwork" that underlies it, and, hence, in renouncing it. One should not be content to read "Sylvie" in submission to the "charm" of a narrative constructed according to the theatrical principle of resemblance; one must also conceive one's reading as an initiation into the artifices of the tale, the seductive secrets of its "miroir magique," and hence as an *emergence* out of this fascinating but deceptive world into the real. For, in "Sylvie," alongside the *fête* (whose patron is Adrienne) and the theatre (presided over by Aurélie), there is also a whole art of lucidity, of the "après-fête," of the daylight world of time. This art has, of course, as its representative the figure of Sylvie.

Sylvie is the one who remains, who survives in the world of time. Present like Adrienne in the hero's childhood and like Aurélie in his young manhood, she is the only one of the three to remain present in his life at the end, in other words, the only one who participates in his life as *narrator*. But in this way and for this reason, she is associated with the whole idea of *aftermath*: after the nocturnal *fêtes* (dominated by Adrienne), Sylvie is there the next day, ready to walk with the hero (although she sometimes disappears on account of fatigue, leaving him significantly alone); after the breakup with the theatrical Aurélie who then fades from the hero's life, Sylvie is still there, with her husband and children, unavailable as an object of love but always willing to welcome him as a friend and a visitor. She is the patron of an art of the *residual*—which both signifies the power of entropy and yet resists its force—and she invites us to read "Sylvie" in terms of "making do" with what is "left over" (another name for which is *bricolage*).

Hence, the persistent motif of "bric-à-brac" in the tale. It is a manifestation of the dispersion, destruction, and disorder produced by the passing of time; but it is evidence also of a human need to preserve these residual objects so as to use them as a point of departure for memory, and even to collect them—"sans beaucoup d'ordre"—into a more or less harmonious blend that might serve as a monument in the present to the past. "Au milieu de toutes les splendeurs du bric-à-brac qu'il était d'usage de réunir à cette époque"

(p. 247), what stands out in the hero's fashionably decorated apartment is a Renaissance clock that, demonstrating his airy ignorance of temporality, he never winds. But his later visit to his dead uncle's house—with its antique furniture, its engravings, the stuffed dog "que j'avais connu vivant" and the parrot "qui vit toujours" (p. 260) —can only inspire a more complex attitude to time, and one more respectful of its power. Yet, at the end, when the narrator returns to his room in a Valois inn, "dernier retour vers le bric-à-brac, auquel j'ai depuis longtemps renoncé" (p. 272) (a very Nervalian phrase in its quiet enunciation of paradox), he rediscovers the objects (an eiderdown, an old tapestry, the "trumeau") that in his last visit as hero to Sylvie's room he had missed (p. 263); and as well he notes yet again the permanent characteristic of the village cottages, the trail of creeper and roses around the window frame. Here we see, then, the persistence of this particular reading model, since the narrator remains faithful to his *taste* for "bric-à-brac" (and to the possibilities of temporal survival it represents) even while announcing that he has "long since" renounced the passing *fashion* of his youth, with its too ambitious aspirations (cf. "toutes les *splendeurs* du bric-à-brac," "pour *restaurer* dans sa couleur locale un appartement d'autrefois," p. 247). Like Sylvie herself, then, but unlike the *fête* and the theatre, "bric-à-brac" provides a reading model for which the narrator himself continues to stand guarantee.

Alongside "bric-à-brac," ruins offer a more noble version of what an art of leftovers might be; and this, too, is a model to which the narrator remains faithful to the end, since on the last page we find him walking with Sylvie's family near the "débris des vieilles tours de brique" of the château of Dammartin (p. 273). But the special relevance of ruins to the narrator's art is demonstrated by the gardens of Ermenonville, with their reminders of the eighteenth-century vogue for *constructing* ruins. One such reminder is the temple to Urania, a "ruine moderne" in which the festivities of the "fête de l'arc" take place (p. 249); but more important is the temple to Philosophy, "que son fondateur n'a pas eu le bonheur de terminer . . . . Cet édifice inachevé n'est déjà plus qu'une ruine" (p. 261). Here ruins appear simultaneously as what survives the destructiveness of time and as a symbol of what an art that is respectful of the conditions of reality can nevertheless construct.

And it is in this respect that they symbolize also the type of "philosophy" that the narrator achieves at the end of his adventure, a philosophy whose components are renunciation but also a certain ineradicable aspiration. What must be renounced is, of course, the need for a "dénoûment," and the unfinished state of the temple to Philosophy stands for the very conditions of temporal life to which the narrator must submit: his narrative is indeed characterized by a certain failure to end, by a sense of the ongoing quality of life. But the very existence of the temple, evidence as it is in its half-finished state of the power of time, is also a manifestation of a powerful human principle that the text sees as escaping from time, because it is eternal, a principle that—far from seeking illusory satisfaction in endings, derives from the eternal *absence* of satisfaction and indeed *relies* on this lack in its confident proclamation of the permanence of a certain form of desire, the desire to comprehend.

Rerum cognoscere causas: —Oui, ce temple tombe comme tant d'autres, les hommes, oublieux ou fatigués, se détourneront de ses abords, la nature indifférente reprendra le terrain que l'art lui disputait; mais la soif de connaître restera éternelle, mobile de toute force et de toute activité! (p. 262)

In this need to understand we recognize, of course, the narrator "I" who so carefully distinguishes himself from the hero "I" as a victim of erotic desire, the folly of double love; or, to put it more accurately, this is the point at which we see the narrator "I" constitute himself by the reversal of values in which the desire to know and to understand comes to replace erotic desire. At this point, too, we realize that the reading models of the text can be classified in terms of their relevance, on the one hand, to a reading of the text as *énoncé* (its structures, intimately tied up as they are with the adventure of the hero as lover) and, on the other, to the apprehension of the text as *énonciation* (its function as narrative act, which is no less intimately tied to the narrator's project as philosopher). To read "Sylvie" as *énoncé* is to read it as a *fête* through attention to the paradigmatic equivalences, the repetitions and resemblances that constitute the text. To read it as *énonciation* is to read in terms of "bric-à-brac" and ruins, to be sensitive to the way in which someone is reconstructing his past out of the vestiges of the present —reconstructing it the better to comprehend it, and to make it comprehensible. These are not two opposed modes of reading; they are not mutually exclusive, but complementary.

And what mediates them is the theatrical reading, which is also a reading of structures, but of the syntagmatic structures of the *énoncé*, those that convey the story of an evolution, a change. This reading makes of the reader himself or herself an initiate, following in the path traced by the hero in his *emergence from the theatre*, his transformation into the narrator. The reader passes from a certain dazzled reception of the text as *fête,* a magical illusion, to awareness of the presence of a narrator (philosopher, *bricoleur*), and hence of the narrative act, with its necessary clockwork of narrative artifice. This *informed* reader will now focus on the narrative act as an art of making do with leftovers, of constructing from them a temple, not to love, but to wisdom—an ongoing and never completed activity. And like the narrator, this reader will take as motto the Lucretian *rerum cognoscere causas,* a phrase that for the narrator "I" signifies his need to understand the whys and wherefores of his youthful errors and of his emergence out of them into the philosophical wisdom he now professes. For the reader, it signifies the need to understand the narration, in "Sylvie," through identification with the narrator—an identification that takes the form of *experiencing the narration as the narrator has experienced his life,* that is, as an initiation into wisdom.

"Bien des cœurs me comprendront"—it is now easier to see why the narrator is so confident in this affirmation. He is relying on the reading of the text itself to convert them, that is, by imposing on them the itinerary he himself has followed, through festivity, entry into the theatre and emergence from it, into exploration of the real and the discovery of "philosophy." The two halves of his rhetorical tactic—the distancing of the narrator from the narrated, the involvement of the reader in the narrated—come together here, since the outcome of the reader's involvement with the hero's adventure is identification with the distanced attitude that has become that of the narrator. What they define, however, is a curiously solipsistic narrative, in which the subject of enunciation can envision being understood only by an addressee who has been shaped by the narrative in his own image. And the renunciation of seduction, which in the narrative content makes the narrator out of the hero, appears finally as a seductive device in its own right, since it functions to lead the reader imperceptibly along (*sub-ducere* is the source of "to seduce" and "to subdue"), through the power of the narrative *act,* into union with the narrator "I."

Residues

When one looks in "Sylvie" for explicit thematization of the act of reading, one quickly sees that it is connected with the theme of the residual, whose significance is not exhausted by the "philosophical" interpretation we have just explored. For the narrator, "recompos(er) les souvenirs" (p. 248) also means reconstituting a lost capital, and the "economic" significance both of the hero's adventure and of the narrator's activity needs some examination. At the point when his adventure begins, the hero—addicted to the theatre and a denizen of the "tour d'ivoire des poètes, où nous montions toujours plus haut pour nous isoler de la foule" (p. 242)—is also financially *ruined.* An opportunity then presents itself to make good the vestiges ("débris") of his fortune:

Dans les débris de mon opulence se trouvait une somme assez forte en titres étrangers. Le bruit avait couru que, négligés longtemps, ils allaient être reconnus; ce qui venait d'avoir lieu à la suite d'un changement de ministère. Les fonds se trouvaient déjà cotés très haut; je redevenais riche. (p. 243)

How then to exploit this sudden wealth? Should he buy Aurélie with gold? The young hero cannot stomach such materialism: it would mean "toucher du doigt mon idéal"—and, as he says, "ce n'est pas à mon âge que l'on tue l'amour avec de l'or" (p. 244). His plunge into the world of dreams and illusions is, then, a turning away from the option of reaping gain from his wealth: "Mon regard parcourait vaguement le journal que je tenais encore, et j'y lus ces deux lignes: *Fête du Bouquet provincial . . .*" (p. 244). The journey back to the Valois begins here.

We now know that it is an error. With his platonic ideals, his "amour, hélas! des formes vagues, des teintes roses et bleues, des fantômes métaphysiques" (p. 242), the young poet is involving himself in an adventure whose only outcome can be disenchantment. He emerges, as we have seen, as the narrator of "Sylvie," a philosopher now reconciled with the world of work to the extent that he himself practices an art of narration inspired by a workmanlike trade, that of the clockmaker, even though, more modestly, his own practice of it appears as a *bricolage* with *bric-à-brac.* In this sense, he has returned to the initial question of the appropriate manner of exploiting his leftover wealth: the Aurélie option has been disposed of (through his refusal to buy her and his failure to realize his double love in the Valois), and he proposes now to construct from his *residuals* (which Sylvie continues to represent) something positive, corresponding to the human "soif de connaître." It seems, then, that the correct response to the sudden possibility of fortune the hero was vouchsafed lay not in the latter's impulsive adventure but in the narrator's assumption of the work of narration, of which "Sylvie" is the outcome and embodiment.

So, it is not irrelevant that, at the moment the chance of fortune is offered him, the hero figures as a reader. "En sortant, je passai par la salle de lecture, et machinalement je regardai un journal. C'était, je crois, *pour y voir le cours de la Bourse*" (p. 243) (my emphasis). But instead of this reading, in the economic-productive mode, his eye falls accidentally on "ces deux lignes: *Fête du Bouquet provincial,*" and he is off on his madcap adventure in the Valois. It is as if he has missed his chance: instead of reading the market rates, he slips into a world of dreams and "chimères." He will not read again until at the end of the text we find the narrator "I" giving an account of his quiet pursuits when now he visits the Valois to see Sylvie. He walks with Sylvie near the "débris des vieilles tours de briques du château," and: "Tandis que ces petits s'exercent, au tir des compagnons de l'arc, à ficher dans la paille les flèches paternelles, nous lisons quelques poésies ou quelques pages de ces livres si courts qu'on ne fait plus guère" (p. 273). The reference to the still vital tradition of the archers' festival (the *fête du Bouquet*), together with the allusion to the theme of residue, underscores the positional equivalence (at the beginning of the adventure, at the end of the narrative) of these two reading episodes, the reading of the newspaper and the reading of one of "ces livres si courts qu'on ne fait plus guère." But the differences are important. The lonely newspaper reader was too much of a "poet" to grasp his chance; but here he is now reading in company, and in the company of the beloved woman whom, previously, the "poet" had let slip through his fingers. The narrator's mode of reading seems a compensation for the false mode of reading into which the hero allowed himself to slip.

The intertext of this final passage quite clearly includes the Paolo and Francesca episode in Dante, another and very famous reading situation. But the Dantean model is what is being denied here, since reading together is not a prelude to passion in this case, but the sign that an affair is over, a reward for renunciation. Sylvie and the narrator are reading together because they are *no longer* lovers, because they have changed: having renounced the "chimères" of love, the narrator now discovers a form of compensatory happiness in a relationship *mediated by a literary text.* It is the happiness of communication, taking the place of the impossible happiness of the "fantômes métaphysiques"—for it is difficult not to see this picture of the narrator and Sylvie reading together as the representation of two "hearts" that *understand* each other through the mediation of a shared text, that is, as a figure of the realization of the narrator's narrative program.

What, then, is the book they are reading? The words "quelques pages de ces livres si courts qu'on ne fait plus guère" read like a reference to "Sylvie" itself, with its unfinished, fragmentary quality ("quelques pages . . .") and its old-fashioned mode (cf. "qu'on me pardonne ce style vieilli" and "ces livres qu'on ne fait plus guère"), not to mention its brevity. The more explicit reference is, of course, to *Werther,* which is alluded to in the opening sentence of the same paragraph: "Je l'appelle quelquefois Lolotte, et elle me trouve un peu de ressemblance avec Werther, moins les pistolets, qui ne sont plus de mode." But this sentence itself serves to define "Sylvie" as an aftermath, belonging to a literary genre once popular but now outdated, one of "ces livres . . . *qu'on ne fait plus guère,"* a leftover. It is a late-coming, and passion-free, version of *Werther.* So, the scene in which the narrator "I" and Sylvie bend their heads together over the fragment of a residual and short text can only be an embedding of the relationship that the text of "Sylvie" as narrative act seeks to create between its narrator and its understanding narratee, between "I" and the many "hearts" that may be assumed to comprehend . . . . And the slightly ironic distinction the characters themselves make between their own relationship and that of Goethe's characters—a distinction that distributes the two situations on either side of the dividing line between "romance" and non-romance—not only confirms "Sylvie" 's belonging to the afterstage of a literary tradition that has undergone significant evolution but it also underlines the appeal being made to an understanding readership—one, that is, that, like the narrator, has *transcended* the stage of "romance."

For, in the course of the story, Sylvie's own taste as reader has been formed precisely by the influence of the future narrator. Her original inclination was for the sentimental romances of Auguste Lafontaine (p. 253), and it was the future narrator who first mentioned to her the *Nouvelle Héloïse.* Her reading of this seductive romance consequently represents in her own evolution something like the theatrical ordeal the hero undergoes (and the reader of "Sylvie" with him) in his own brush with *le romanesque:* "Vous m'avez parlé autrefois de la *Nouvelle Héloïse,* je l'ai lue, et j'ai frémi d'abord en tombant sur cette phrase: 'Toute jeune fille qui lira ce livre est perdue.' Cependant j'ai passé outre, me fiant sur ma raison" (p. 259). We have already noted how narrowly Sylvie escaped the illusions of identification: the ordeal that she has survived in this way, thanks to her natural good sense ("raison"), is precisely the ordeal that qualifies her as the appropriate reader for a text like "Sylvie," which needs a reader who is both attuned to the seduction of illusion (able to "understand" it) and aware of the superior claims of philosophical sense, or wisdom. Her experience, her initiation into reading at the future narrator's hands, is consequently an exact model for the initiatory experience that the implied reader of "Sylvie" is led to undergo in his or her own passage through the ordeal of the *fête* and the theatre—the experience that constitutes such a reader as fit to "understand" the narrator "I."

It was pointed out earlier that, in discovering the virtues of narrative work, the narrator "I" becomes worthy of hardworking Sylvie at precisely the moment when he learns that she is no longer available. She cannot provide a model for the work of narration because she is about to become, as a *pâtissière,* the opposite of what she has been heretofore: a town dweller, a shopkeeper, and, in short, a *bourgeoise.* And so it is Père Dodu, the clockmaker-*bricoleur,* who provides the narrative model. But what can now be perceived is that Sylvie eluded the hero at that point only as a possible wife (on the plane of the "chimères" of love) and that in becoming a *bourgeoise* she constitutes herself on a new plane as the ideal partner for the narrator "I"—the appropriate reader for his "philosophical" enterprise of narration. As a reader, one may assume that she is realistic and serious-minded, but also a tad sentimental, her taste having been formed by her reading of novelists such as Scott, Rousseau, and Goethe, but being informed also by her own "solid" values—the very values that the narrator presupposes in the "hearts" he expects to understand him. In short, it was not on the plane of emotional relationships but on the plane of literary communication that Sylvie and the narrator were destined to form a couple.

The hovering presence of the husband in the reading scene at the end—he fixes lunch while they read—and that of the children, sending their pre-Freudian arrows with a thud into the targets, certainly suggest that the reading couple is a compensation, and a sublimation, for another coupling. But it is true that the narrator "I" has regained, in his own terms, what the hero "I" lost in the world of erotic illusion. And what he has regained is something solid, for, economically speaking, it is clear that, where the hero failed, the narrator has succeeded in making good the vestiges of his lost fortune. What, indeed, is an artist's capital unless it be the "débris," the residue of life that is called experience? Is experience not the "fruit"—the profit—one derives from one's existential losses? "Les illusions tombent l'une après l'autre, comme les écorces d'un fruit, et le fruit, c'est l'expérience" (p. 271). The contrast is clear with "l'amère tristesse que laisse un songe évanoui" (p. 243), the only type of profit that can be hoped for by a poet such as the hero, with his love of "teintes roses et bleues" and his proclivity for the ivory tower. In the final analysis, "Sylvie" appears as a text that thinks of itself in terms of a commercial conception of literature, renouncing values like the *romanesque,* enthusiasm, the dream, and madness as *unprofitable* and turning toward a public whose values, embodied in the character of Sylvie, are those of a petty shopkeeper.

What does this mean? Has Nerval capitulated, abandoned the values of poetry, of lyricism, of "folie"? It is essential to distinguish the narrator "I" of Sylvie from the historical Nerval who more or less contemporaneously was introducing into a parallel text, *Aurélia,* a narrator who is diametrically opposed, as a spokesperson for madness, to the narrator of "Sylvie." But it is difficult not to postulate that "Sylvie" does represent an attempt on Nerval's part, per medium of his narrator, to overcome a sense of personal alienation and to regain a place in the bourgeois society that had marginalized him, both as "poet" and as "madman." In light of Nerval's biography — Gérard Labrunie was the son of a doctor and the heir to a fortune he rapidly squandered—this appeal to middle-class values makes sense. Baudelaire, too, was obsessed throughout his life by the memory of a squandered fortune, his consequent infantilization (his remaining wealth was placed in trust), and the urgency of compensating for this disastrous loss through artistic work. Nerval, even more than Baudelaire, is one to whom *all* the senses of the word *alienation* apply: small wonder if the practice of art came to seem to him a means of struggling for "acceptance."

At the same time, there is something *rusé* in the narrative program of "Sylvie." The reader who experiences the reading of the text as an *emergence from the theatre* must first of all enter into it, enter— in other words—into the experience of the hero's "madness." Even if such a reader does come eventually to share the narrator "I" 's carefully distanced situation, he or she can no longer maintain watertight divisions between such categories as folly and wisdom, reason and dream. In "Sylvie"—much as in *Aurélia,* there is "épanche-ment du songe dans la vie réelle"—such divisions are thoroughly permeable; and, for a "philosophical" reader, there is some risk in "accepting"—in Rimbaud's phrase—"l'histoire d'une de mes folies." Between *Aurélia* and "Sylvie," there is certainly a very different distribution of functions between hero and narrator (madness and writing), but the two texts do combine as parts of a common project. Indeed, to the (very considerable) extent that *Aurélia* itself displays a measurable gap between the adventure and its narration, one can see in it the same cleavage as in "Sylvie" between faithfulness to experience and desire for rehabilitation. The social diagnosis in each case must, then, be the same.[7]

NOTES

1. I introduced the distinction in the chapter on "Sylvie" of my book, *Gérard de Nerval et la poétique du voyage* (Paris: Corti, 1969). My understanding of "Sylvie" owes much to the following critical work: G. Poulet, "*Sylvie* ou la pensée de Nerval," in *Trois essais de mythologie romantique* (Paris: Corti, 1966), 13-81; A. Fairlie, "An Approach to Nerval," in *Studies in Modern French Literature Presented to P. Mansell Jones* (Manchester: Manchester University Press, 1961), 87-103; R. Jean, *Nerval par lui-même* (Paris: Éd. du Seuil, 1964) ("Le temps délivré"); L. Cellier, *De "Sylvie" à "Aurélia"* (Paris: Minard, 1971); H. Bonnet, *"Sylvie" de Nerval* (Paris: Hachette, 1975); U. Eisenzweig, *L'Espace imaginaire d'un récit: "Sylvie" de Gérard de Nerval* (Neuchâtel: La Baconnière, 1976); G. Schaeffer, *Une double lecture de Nerval: "Les Illuminés" et "Les Filles du Feu,"* (Neuchâtel: La Baconnière, 1977); M. Jeanneret, *La lettre perdue: Écriture et folie dans l'œuvre de Nerval* (Paris: Flammarion, 1978). At the time of writing, I had not yet read three other relevant essays: S. Kofman, *Nerval: Le charme de la répétition* (Lausanne: L'Âge d'Homme, 1979); J. Geninasca, "De la fête à l'anti-fête," *Versants*, 1 (1981), 93-108; R. B. Gordon, "Dentelle: Métaphore du texte dans *Sylvie*," *Romanic Review*, 73, 1 (January 1982), 45-66.

2. Quotations are from G. de Nerval, *Œuvres*, I (Paris: Bibliothèque de la Pléiade, 1966), and all page references in parentheses refer to this edition.

3. For this term, see chapter 2.

4. "Mais," in Oswald Ducrot's analysis, refers not to a preceding (explicit) statement but to the implications the statement may be taken to have, the conclusions an addressee may mistakenly derive from it. So, here it means: "contrary to my apparent implication of narrative incompetence, I am in fact claiming narrative competence, in that many hearts will understand me." See O. Ducrot et al., *Les mots du discours* (Paris: Éd. de Minuit, 1980).

5. For a rhetorical analysis of textual means of arousing and maintaining the reader's desire, see Michel Charles, *Rhétorique de la lecture* (Paris: Éd. du Seuil, 1977).

6. On the complex relationship of *fête* and theatre, see also Henri Bonnet, "Nerval et la fête continue," *Cahiers de l'Herne*, 37 (1980), 139-155; and Geninasca, "De la fête à l'anti-fête."

7. On *Aurélia*, see particularly Shoshana Felman's masterly analysis in *La folie et la chose littéraire* (Paris: Éd. du Seuil, 1979), 61-77 ("De Foucault à Nerval: *Aurélia* ou le livre infaisable").

Chapter Six
An Invitation to Love: Simplicity of Heart and Textual Duplicity in "Un Cœur Simple"

Félicité and Théodore

"Elle avait eu, comme une autre, son histoire d'amour" (p. 592).[1] Innocuous as this sentence may seem, its vocabulary is pointed: Félicité's "love story" with Théodore is embedded in the "love story" that is her life, and we must ask in what way it is a narrational model of the text. At the level of *mise en abyme de l'énoncé,* the answer is relatively simple: by contrast. The commonness ("comme une autre") of the story of Félicité's seduction by Théodore points up the relative uniqueness of her true love story, the self-abnegation she displays throughout her life for others—for Mme Aubain and her children, her own kinsfolk, the population of Poland, Père Colmiche, Loulou the parrot, and, last but not least, God. Inversely, Théodore's pusillanimity in loving and leaving her for a woman who can buy him out of the draft points up her own generosity and simpleness of heart, her ability to love without return. But—still on the plane of the *énoncé*—this means that the episode functions also as a completely straightforward (I do not want to say "positive") model for the story of Félicité's life, which will consist of a long series of such episodes in which she gives herself wholeheartedly to those who, far from reciprocating her love, exploit it in their own interests. Even simple gratitude, although she sometimes encounters it, is a rarity in her existence; and there is a strong hint, since Théodore means "God's gift," that God himself accepts her love and abandons her.

But, given that embedded stories of seduction (or of storytelling as seduction) together with denials, or renunciations, of seduction in the embedding narratives have proved highly relevant in the situational analysis of texts such as "Sarrasine" and "Sylvie,"[2] it is worth asking whether Théodore's seduction of Félicité should not be examined also as a *mise en abyme de l'énonciation.* What, in other words, is the relationship of "Un cœur simple" to the tactics and procedures of seduction? We have seen that in "Sylvie" the renunciation of seduction proved to be a seductive device on the part of the narration as a whole—and, since "Sarrasine" makes a similar appeal to the values of "understanding," it would not be difficult to show that the Balzac text's "philosophical" stance similarly incorporates a subtle seductive thrust, contrasting with the more heavy-handed operation in the "inner" narrative. To seduce and to subdue are related activities:[3] it could easily be demonstrated (it is almost a tautology) that narratives that are most concerned, in "readerly" fashion, with guiding the reader's interpretation are those that, at the same time, have the greatest stake in seducing that reader into a proper "understanding" of their functions and purposes. Curiously, the two stories in question are both "self-designating" narratives: it seems, then, that their relative "openness" about their status as *narrative* is matched by a kind of duplicity relating to the *situational point* of the storytelling: a "pretense" of being antiseductive masks "genuinely" seductive aims (according to a well-recognized technique known to every Don Juan).

"Un cœur simple," on the other hand, is "duplicitous" narrative, in the sense adopted in this book from the outset: it is a story that "tells itself," without foregrounding its status as story. But in examining "The Purloined Letter,"[4] I was led to distinguish two forms of duplicitous narrative, which I labeled *mimetic* and *textual,* respectively. Mimetic narrative is duplicitous in the way that the Minister, in the Poe story, is duplicitous: behind the openness with which he displays his "letter" lies a concealed power ploy. As "realist" art, "Un cœur simple" qualifies almost automatically for this form of duplicity: in its apparently "objective" representation of real life lurks narratorial manipulation (a point to which we will return). Textual duplicity is, however, the duplicity of Dupin, who unlike the Minister advances masked and uses a "smoke screen" of discourse to conceal—nothing. The fact of concealing that there is nothing behind one's discourse can become, when it is "seen through," an art of displaying discourse for its own brilliant sake (the nothingness behind it then becoming the productive principle enabling the ongoing production of discursive "smoke"). I mentioned Baudelaire, Mallarmé, and Valéry in connection with this curious form of duplicity that resolves, in fact, into an ostentatious simplicity, the simplicity of *écriture*. But Flaubert also, although a prose writer—but one haunted, as we know, by the idea of a "livre sur rien"—belongs also to the "Dupin" tradition; and part of the purpose of this essay is to show that "Un cœur simple" invites us to read it—through the figural embedding of the character Félicité—in the light of a kind of "duplicity" (in quotation marks) that derives from textual simplicity. This new "duplicity" is a phenomenon that now has little to do, directly, with the covert procedures of Dupin.

What, then, is the relationship between the *mimetic* and the *textual* writing, which appear to operate together in Flaubert's tale? Are they, too, in duplicitous relationship, and if so, does this duplicity betray a seductive purpose? The question is relevant because, whereas self-designating narratives produce a duplicitous (seductive) narrative situation, there is a sense in which the duplicitous narrative, covert as it is about its status as narrative, conversely produces a narrative situation of genuine simplicity. Rather than seducing the reader actively, it is simply "there," waiting or asking to be "loved." It renounces seductive maneuvering out of a certain faith in the reader's own capacity to bring to the act of reading the necessary "heart," or "understanding." In this, such a narrative is not unlike Félicité, in "Un cœur simple," who does not seduce but loves and waits to be loved. A love story that would contrast most markedly with the story of her seduction by Théodore, and that would make her truly unique (as opposed to "comme une autre," for in the long run the self-abnegating and exploited Félicité is a type, her seduction by Théodore a common story), would be the story of her encounter with a genuinely loving individual who would return her love, with the same simplicity she herself displays. And—since she never meets such a person in the *narré* of the text—can it be that this person, whom her existence seems to imply, is a function not of the *narré* but of the *narration*? If Félicité can be seen as a figure of the text in its narrative simplicity, as I hope to show, then perhaps the narrative act being performed by the text is best analyzed not as an attempted (or even successful) seduction but as an *invitation to be loved* (an invitation to which the text itself teaches us to respond in an appropriate manner by its own exploration of the virtues of "simpleness of heart").

Such an analysis would apply quite well to the text in its "writerly" simplicity. But mimetic duplicity is another matter, if only because it involves the covert, and manipulative presence, of a narrative "instance," making the events meaningful: there is some subduing here of the reader's initiative. And the combination of "writerly" simplicity with mimetic duplicity in the text can, therefore, only make for a certain ambiguity. My suggestion is that, if Félicité is the figure of *simplicity* in the text, Théodore is the figure, not of duplicity, but of a certain *ambiguity* between seductive duplicity and straightforwardness. With the crudity of his seductive techniques, and the obviousness of his peasant cunning, he is not the smooth Don Juan of fable but a *village Don Juan,* that is, the very embodiment of simplicity and duplicity combined. Who can tell? The narrator of "Un cœur simple" cannot himself sort out Théodore's *arrière-pensées* from the straightforwardness of his courtship and quite understandably takes refuge in an "objective," noncommittal account of the affair. In this respect, Théodore's proposal of marriage (and the text's narration thereof) are entirely characteristic: "Cette résistance [i.e., Félicité's "raison" and "instinct de l'honneur"] exaspéra l'amour de Théodore, si bien que *pour le satisfaire (ou naïvement peut-être)* il proposa de l'épouser" (p. 594) (my emphasis). Is the proposal genuine ("simple") or seductive ("duplicitous")? The ambiguity is characteristic, not only of Théodore, but also of the text's own situational stance, which makes a "proposal" both simple and duplicitous. Passive in its simplicity, like Félicité, it is also seductive in the manner of Théodore, that is, in its combination of "mimetic" manipulation and "textual" simplicity. So, Félicité's love story is a narrational embedding of "Un cœur simple" because it is not Félicité's love story alone: it is also the story of Théodore, of a relationship between Théodore and Félicité. In speaking of the story's "invitation to love," I am attempting to characterize a narrative move that lies halfway between, and combines, the simple stance of Félicité (placing all the onus on the reader) with a residually seductive thrust, that of its mimetic duplicity (with the manipulation this implies). Like many a proposal of marriage, it is both genuinely simple and, under analysis, infinitely duplicitous.

It becomes important, then, to look more closely, before proceeding, at some of the implications, both of mimetic duplicity and of textual "duplicity." Flaubert wrote to Mme Roger des Genettes, on June 19, 1876—while he was working on "Un cœur simple"—as follows:

L'Histoire d'un cœur simple est tout bonnement le récit d'une vie obscure, celle d'une pauvre fille de campagne, dévote mais mystique, dévouée sans exaltation et tendre comme du pain frais. Elle aime successivement un homme, les enfants de sa maîtresse, un neveu, un vieillard qu'elle soigne, puis son perroquet; quand le perroquet est mort, elle le fait empailler et, en mourant à son tour, elle confond le perroquet avec le Saint-Esprit. Cela n'est nullement ironique comme vous le supposez, mais au contraire très sérieux et très triste. Je veux apitoyer, faire pleurer les âmes sensibles, en étant une moi-même.[5]

I quote this famous passage not as evidence of the author's intentions but to illustrate what—"tout bonnement"—"Un cœur simple" is *not*. It is certainly true that Raymonde Debray-Genette has demonstrated the accuracy of Flaubert's analysis of the story's narrative structure ("Elle aime successivement . . .") and thematic composition ("pauvre fille de campagne, dévote mais mystique . . . . Elle confond le perroquet et le Saint-Esprit").[6] But the description of the *narré* is surrounded by statements concerning the text as *narration*: the admission that the text is a story (in the redundancy of "*L'Histoire d'un cœur simple* est tout bonnement le récit . . ."), and the announcement of a performative program ("Cela n'est nullement ironique . . . mais au contraire très sérieux et très triste. Je veux apitoyer . . .") implying illocutory understanding between the *destinataires* ("apitoyer, faire pleurer les âmes sensibles") and the *destinateur* ("en étant une moi-même").

Whereas, in the text itself, the equivalent of all this performative apparatus is missing, the suppression from the title of the word *histoire* eliminates generic self-reference, and in the body of the text the writing strives to conceal both the existence of a narrative "grammar" and the presence of indices that might point too clearly to the act of narration. The story, as I have said, appears to be "telling itself"—it presents as the simple mimesis of a life that is being reported neutrally, without authorial intervention and in an order of parataxic succession that counts as a sort of zero degree of "narrativity," innocent of any structuration that might give it "meaning":

Puis des années s'écoulèrent, toutes pareilles et sans autres épisodes que le retour des grandes fêtes: Pâques, l'Assomption, la Toussaint. Des événements intérieurs faisaient une date, où l'on se reportait plus tard. Ainsi, en 1825, deux vitriers badigeonnèrent le vestibule; en 1827, une portion du toit, tombant dans la cour, faillit tuer un homme. L'été de 1828, ce fut à Madame d'offrir le pain bénit; Bourais, vers cette époque, s'absenta mystérieusement; et les anciennes connaissances peu à peu s'en allèrent: Guyot, Liébard, Mme Lechaptois, Robelin, l'oncle Gremanville, paralysé depuis longtemps. (p. 610)

Here, then, is a narrative simplicity that "matches" the simplicity of its subject matter: the heart of Félicité and her life.

But this observation shows that such narrative simplicity is in fact an illusion. It is axiomatic that there is no narrative that is not oriented by the mode of its telling, and this rule transforms the simplicity of "Un cœur simple" into an *effect of simplicity* produced (in accordance with some purpose) by the narration. For example, we have just admired the equivalence of characterological simplicity and narrative straightforwardness: this amounts to perceiving the text as an artistic phenomenon (according to a certain conception of art) and hence, to seeing in the match up the sign of a scriptorial *performance.* And indeed, careful reading does show that in "Un cœur simple" the admirable simplicity of the narrative is pointed up by a *contrast* with the very discreet, but discernible, presence of a narratorial persona who displays attitudes of some sophistication. Flaubert criticism has not failed to pose the question: Who is speaking here? And this is a matter I will return to in more detail. But my purpose in doing so will be to show that this form of narrative duplicity—in which the perception of artistry on the part of the narrator implies the covert presence, "behind" the representation, of a figure making meaning through "style" and "point of view"[7]—relates to a conception of literary communication that can be called classical in that it conceives discourse as emanating from a *subject* whose personality has determining force.[8] In this light, a third-person text such as "Un cœur simple" is not *radically* different from a first-person text, since, in both, an "I" (who may be present in a more or less obvious way) controls the narrative operation. For this reason, the conventional semiotic scheme for communication, in which a *destinateur* emits a "message" in the form of discourse for a *destinataire,* is entirely adequate for the analysis of *mimetic,* or "realist" duplicity, which (contrary to the airs of "objectivity" such writing gives itself) is inseparable from an ideology of the subject.

On the other hand, *textual,* or "writerly," "duplicity" is here referred to in quotes because it is in no sense deceptive, even for a moment: it is duplicity as doubleness. It does not proceed from a distinction between textual discourse and an emitter (author or narrator); it is inscribed in the discourse itself and appears as a "polyphony" attributable, not to any controlling narrative instance, but to the actual writing ("écriture") of the text, its "textuality." We are dealing, to be sure, with a minimal form of polyphony (reduced to a duality), but it is sufficient to make it possible to say that the Flaubert text, for instance, foreshadows the power to multiply meaning endlessly that characterizes those more "modern" texts Barthes would call "writerly." Or, to put this more accurately, the Flaubert text displays an affinity, in one way, with the "reader-ly" (in that it *contains* the proliferation of meaning by reducing it to a duality) while demonstrating in another way its kinship with the "writerly." The textual "duplicity" of the tale does arise out of what is the essential characteristic of "writerly" texts, that is, not simply the fact that they resist efforts to *hierarchize* the meanings produced by the text but also that they disallow all *division* into textual "levels." "Duplicity" in this sense does not need to be "seen through" because there is no point, in the "writerly" text, in distinguishing, for example, the *narré* from the *narration* (e.g., Félicité's simplicity versus the alleged simplicity, or duplicity, of the narrative act) any more than there is in distinguishing between "apparent" and "real" meanings of the text (e.g., the story of Félicité's life versus the more or less implicit judgment being pronounced on her and her social milieu). There is no deceit, however short-lived; no *ars celandi artem.* There *are,* however, in "Un cœur simple," two possible readings of the character's simplicity, readings that simultaneously produce equally valid meanings, even though one projects a "positive" and the other a "negative" interpretation of the character. And here it is useless to seek out some narrative "I," however skillfully con-cealed, who might stand guarantee for one or the other of the possi-ble interpretations of the *narré.* The choice of either or both of the interpretive options is left up to the reader, who must read Félicité's simplicity as his or her own reading situation may dictate.

Félicité is a figure of the text, then, because such textual "duplici-ty" is the mark of the text's own simplicity. Like the character who is "all heart," the text presents itself as being indivisible, all of a piece. All of a piece, but polyphonic (or, to be pedantic, biphonic)— polyphonic because all of a piece. All distinctions having disappeared between "apparent" and "real," between narrative "content" and "meaning" derived from narration, and the "I" subject responsible for these distinctions having also faded out of the picture, there is nothing left to "guide" or control interpretations except the textual *datum*—what can be called, with a nod to current fashion, the text as "signifier"—which takes on the same potential for meaning as Félicité herself. Without paradox, then, it is possible to say that what makes the character of the unfulfilled old maid an embedded figure of the text is the simplicity that lies *at the heart* of all textual "duplicity," while it is the lack of fulfillment of her "heart" that requires, on the reader's part, an act of love in return.

Mimetic Duplicity

"Pour de pareilles âmes, le surnaturel est tout simple" (p. 609): here, for once, the text's tendency to *orient* our reading is out in the open. Not only does the sentence constitute deictic commentary, situating the fictional character with respect to a certain experience of the real world (an experience claimed by the narrator and presumed in the narratee), but the thematic "clue" (referring back to the word *simple* in the title and relating it to the thematics of the transcendant) also proposes a reading that, this time, relates the character to the internal structuring of the text. In other words, the text here constructs itself as "discourse," in the narratological sense of the term. Although the explicitness of this particular narratorial intervention makes it a relatively rare case, it is exemplary because it obliges the reader to decipher the text in terms of a "story" on one hand and "discourse" on the other (where "discourse" is interpretive commentary revealing the presence of a textual subject, an "I" distinguishable from the referential object).[9] This, we know, is the distinction that founds the "realist" text and defines its duplicity. In other places, the presence of the narrating instance may need some construing on the reader's part; but it is quite discernible, for instance, in judgments such as the mention of M. Bourais's "beau sourire de cuistre" (p. 606), in tense shifts such as the suddenly appearing present in the description of the farm at Geffosses ("La cour *est* en pente . . . ," p. 596 [my emphasis]), and even, of course, in the hesitation as to appropriate interpretation in the comment about Théodore's proposal: "(ou naïvement peut-être)."

But this presence of a narratorial "I" also implies an I-thou relationship, that is, the reader's participation as narratee. Certain ironies, for instance, are imputable to a narrator who is without doubt setting himself apart from his character but is doing so in such a way as to recruit the reader's sympathy for a specific way of understanding the character's situation. This is the case when the gift of a parrot to Mme Aubain is described as "un grand bonheur" for Félicité, for both the naïveté of the character and her deprivation are to be read into the comment; similar implications (of sensory deprivation and poverty of experience) are in the *tout de suite* that marks her arrival at a village fair: "Tout de suite elle fut étourdie." Other ironies, relating to characters other than Félicité, are less charitable (the story of Théodore's *lâcheté*, the manifestations of *bêtise* in the townsfolk of Pont-l'Évêque . . .), but they all imply a certain complicity and constitute a sort of knowing wink from narrator to narratee.

Stylistic effects betray narrative "voice" more subtly still. This is the voice whose marked distinction (by contrast with characters who say *salle* for "salon" — as Mme Aubain does (p. 591) — or declare themselves "minée" and ask permission to "se dissiper" (p. 603), like Félicité) gives elegance to the narrative, with its slightly affected *"et" de clausule* and its carefully crafted, expressive sentence structure (such as in the opening sentence, with its final focus on the words "sa bonne Félicité," or in the last sentence of all, which manages to summarize her life in a description of her death). Here, too, then, in the "manner" of the writing, a form of commentary can be discerned, again setting the narrator off from his characters but involving the reader in a certain way of understanding the events. Once this kind of distinction has been established between the narrative instance and the characters, it becomes possible, for example, for the narration to espouse the psychological vision of Félicité, secure in the knowledge that the narratee can distinguish, in the terms clarified by G. Genette,[10] between "who sees" and "who speaks." Thus, when news comes that Virginie has pneumonia, the text reads: "La nuit allait venir. Il faisait très froid." The reader who has been alerted to the duplicity of the narrative will most probably attribute this perception, with its premonitory overtones, to Félicité, for it is somehow too *obvious* to derive from the narrator (whose language nevertheless incorporates it). Similarly, when Félicité, having just learned of Victor's death, goes to the river with the laundry, "Les prairies étaient vides, le vent agitait la rivière; au fond, de grandes herbes s'y penchaient, comme des chevelures de cadavres flottant dans l'eau" (p. 607), we are again invited to divide up the responsibilities, between the character's vision and the textual diction, so that the sympathy we achieve for the character in her grief is at least partly a function of the narrative vehicle, that is, of a certain understanding shared with the narratorial voice.

Flaubert criticism has explored these devices thoroughly, and they need no further exposition. The point is that, in all these ways ("discourse" versus "story," narrative style versus character's speech, characters' vision versus textual diction), the text both presupposes and requires a double reading, concerned on one hand with what happens in the *narré* and on the other with the *narration* itself, that is, the illocutionary relationship of narrator and narratee on which the narration depends. Even in its silences the narration is an active agent—for the narrative contains skillful ellipses (Wolfgang Iser might say "gaps"[11] if they did not direct attention to themselves quite so distinctly) that are not there so as to "leave out" a portion of the *narré* but to draw attention to the fact of the narration and to recruit the reader as an active participant in the construction of meaning. On Félicité's homeward walk with Théodore, we encounter this sentence: "Il l'embrassa encore une fois," and going back in the narrative in search of the first kiss, we find only this: ". . . il se ralentirent. Le vent était mou, les étoiles brillaient, l'énorme char-retée de foin oscillait devant eux; et les quatre chevaux, en traînant leurs pas, soulevaient de la poussière" (p. 593). The effect, of course, is partly to lead the reader to draw some implications (for example, about Félicité's susceptibility to sensory experience, once more) but partly also to teach him or her a more general lesson about how the text asks to be read, the sensitivity it requires to the unsaid, to an art of suggestion and insinuation that expects the narratee to join the narrator in implicit understanding of the sense of what is going on, over the heads of the characters themselves. So, if mimetic duplicity functions very frequently in such a way as to generate sympathy for Félicité, despite the apparent objectivity of the story, this is its secondary or derived function, the first and fundamental one being to produce complicity between reader and narrator. For all its stance of neutrality, the "realist" text thus produces in the reader a *double* state of involvement, since adherence to the world of the *narré* (Félicité's world) depends on adherence to a more or less concealed "discourse" element that calmly presupposes a certain understanding of the characters, their actions and interactions—and beyond that, a basic agreement (ideological, psychological, aesthetic, etc.) with the perspectives the narration itself adopts. To the extent that this involvement is produced without conscious awareness, on the reader's part, of the orientation of his or her perceptions and the mobilization of his or her emotions, there is here a kind of seduction, a "subduing" of any possible urge to produce rival interpretations of the events.

Yet . . . . There is in the story an episode, a narrative situation that provides a *mise en abyme,* and hence an opportunity for exam-ination, of "realist" narrative, with its major characteristics (the distinction of "story" and "discourse"; the involvement of the reader in both *narré* and *narration*). In the course of the vacation trip to Trouville, Liébard, Mme Aubain's share farmer, is led to become a storyteller:

La jument de Liébard, à de certains endroits, s'arrêtait tout à coup. Il atten-
dait patiemment qu'elle se remît en marche; et il parlait des personnes dont les
propriétés bordaient la route, ajoutant à leur histoire des réflexions morales.
Ainsi, au milieu de Toucques, comme on passait sous des fenêtres entourées de
capucines, il dit, avec un haussement d'épaules:
— "En voilà une, Mme Lehoussais, qui au lieu de prendre un jeune homme
. . . ." Félicité n'entendit pas le reste . . . . (p. 598)

Here we have a clear *mise en abyme de l'énoncé*—the episode picks
up the *topos* of the voyage of life: Mme Aubain makes preparations
"comme pour un long voyage" (p. 597), and the characters are
heading toward the void of their "vacances" in a place called Trouville (*trou* means "hole"). A parallel is foreshadowed, also, with
Félicité's more lonely voyage to Honfleur with Loulou's corpse
(p. 616), an episode whose symbolic force is more frequently com-
mented on. But as an *énonciation* within this narrative situation,
Liébard's storytelling serves as a way of signifying the place and role
of storytelling—of artistic activity generally, perhaps—in the "voyage of life." It is a diversion, serving to fill in the gaps and the forced
halts in the movement of events toward death. It takes as its object,
so to speak, life itself, that is, the story of the narrator's and narratee's *fellows*—those people whose properties "border the road"
along which the voyage continues as the narrative flows. Between
"story" as *énonciation* and "history" (the subject of the *énoncé*),
there is, then, here, a clear affinity.

One might say, indeed, that the storyteller and his hearers, like the
subjects of the storytelling, are all involved in history as they are
involved in the story itself. Some distinctions must be made, doubtless: the "propriétaires" are partly out of history (on the edge of
the road) and enjoy relative stability, as householders, compared
with the voyagers who are also—it is not a coincidence—the participants (*destinateur* and *destinataires*) in the narrative act. These
last are truly involved in the story as they are involved in history—
for everything in Liébard's storytelling makes for such adherence.
Even if there is a sense in which storytelling (talking of "others" in
an existential "halt") appears as a way of placing oneself outside of
history, the attempt fails, for what Félicité hears (of another, Mme
Lehoussais) is what she knows already, of herself, the story of her
own life. Not only does Mme Lehoussais's "love story" dovetail
biographically with Félicité's, but it is also the story of another—
the same—betrayal by the seducer, Théodore. And so, encouraged
by Liébard's moralizing comments (which imply emotional involve-

ment in the events on his own part as well as inviting his hearers' participation in judging them), Félicité cannot avoid complete self-identification, both with the tale and with the telling. Even though she does not "hear the rest," she is now completely fused, as the story continues, with an experience of movement and travel: ". . . les chevaux trottaient, l'âne galopait; tous enfilèrent un sentier; une barrière tourna, deux garçons parurent, et l'on descendit devant le purin, sur le seuil même de la porte" (p. 598). For Félicité, all distance has disappeared, through the phenomenon of involvement, between story and history; and so, at the end of a narrative that is now indistinguishable from the voyage itself, she comes out "devant le purin, sur le seuil même de la porte"—that is (manure being the end product of the process of entropic disintegration),[12] face to face with death.

Flaubert is quite clearly taking aim at the sentimental and moralizing literature that is exemplified in "Un cœur simple" by the *only* explicit intertextual reference, to *Paul et Virginie* (a novel Mme Aubain must once have "devoured"—identified with her life—since it is the source of her children's names). It is difficult to designate more clearly the antimodel. By their equality as hearers of Liébard's moralizing stories, Mme Aubain and Félicité display a commonality of taste, to which I will return in another context. Liébard, on the other hand, if he shares with Bernardin de Saint-Pierre a taste for moralizing, also has something in common, more surprisingly, with the narrator of "Un cœur simple," for what is this narrator's social situation? "Pendant un demi-siècle, les bourgeoises de Pont-l'Évêque envièrent à Mme Aubain sa servante Félicité . . . ." He has knowledge of the citizens of Pont-l'Évêque as if he shared their life, but he speaks of them deictically, as if he himself were not a fellow towns-person. Liébard, as a share farmer, is not a "propriétaire," yet occupies the soil as if he were and knows the lives of the "personnes dont les propriétés bordaient la route." He knows what goes on behind the flower-framed windows of Mme Lehoussais's house as intimately as the narrator knows the details of life in Mme Aubain's household. Add to this common status as privileged observer (and gossip) the fact of a similar "style" of narration (narrative in one case, narratorial in the other, perhaps—that is the difference between them[13]). Each likes to accompany his story with interpretive "discourse," more subtle in the narrator's case, more openly didactic in Liébard's (perhaps he even *knows* the relevance of what he is saying to Félicité); but both given also, in the end, to a distanced stance (Liébard's "haussement d'épaules," the narrator's ironies). Furthermore, it happens that the only one of Liébard's "réflexions morales" that is directly quoted in the text has something in common with the "discourse" of "Un cœur simple": the fact of its being elliptical and of signifying only by implication. "En voilà une, Mme Lehoussais, qui au lieu de prendre un jeune homme . . . ." The reason Félicité *does not hear the rest* is that she does not need to, she *knows* it—and in this she is like the narratee of "Un cœur simple" who knows what the narrator only hints at and, thanks to shared presuppositions deriving from a common experience of life, understands him *à demi-mot.* It is Félicité's own "experience of life" that makes it unnecessary for her to "hear the rest."

This parallel has an important implication. It means that the reader's involvement in the narrative, and narration, of "Un cœur simple" must be interpreted, in the light of Félicité's involvement in Liébard's story, as an involvement with history, and a kind of giving of oneself to death: stories of this kind bring you out "devant le purin." And, in this light, the difference between moralizing literature à la Liébard or Abbé de Saint-Pierre (the antimodel) and the "realist" text itself, with its mimetic duplicity, is not a difference of kind, but only one of degree. Each exercises a form of seduction that uses the reader's experience of existence to involve him or her, per medium of narration, in . . . "life," that is, history and death. If this is so, then one does not need to invoke Flaubert's well-known aestheticism to suspect that what is being implied in the Liébard episode is a radical criticism of the very form of textuality to which "Un cœur simple," as a "realist" text using the devices of mimetic duplicity, nevertheless quite clearly belongs. And the question arises as to whether there may not be another form of textuality that would be different in *kind* from the "realist" text, one that might be less involved itself with the entropic processes of history and less likely, therefore, to involve both narrator and narratee-reader in the mire.

Textual "Duplicity"

Readers of Oswald Ducrot[14] are aware that *all* discourse is polyphonic and that to reduce the act of enunciation to the emitter-message-receiver model is overly schematic. "Le locuteur de l'énonciation peut être distinct de l'énonciateur de l'assertion," as the distinction *puisque/car* clearly shows ("Sortons puisqu'il fait beau" incorporates a quoted assertion, "Sortons car il faut beau" does not). More subtly, negation can be analyzed as the performance of two illocutory acts: "l'un est l'affirmation de *p* par un énonciateur E1 s'adressant à un destinataire D1, l'autre est le rejet de cette affirmation, rejet attribué à un énonciateur E2 s'adressant à D2"—an analysis valid for English but supported in French by the difference between the two possible affirmative responses to a negation: *si,* which affirms the assertion ("Si, Pierre est là"), and *oui,* which confirms the negation ("Oui, Pierre n'est pas là"). We do not need Ducrot's complex apparatus of *destinateurs, énonciateurs, locuteurs, destinataires,* and *allocutaires,* for I am interested only in the suggestiveness of a conclusion such as this, that "il est propre à la négation que l'on déchiffre en elle l'assertion de ce qu'elle nie," and I do not propose these observations as a model but only as a leaping-off point for an analysis of the textual "duplicity" of "Un cœur simple." The coexistence of an affirmation and a negation in the same sentence is an example of a form of "duplicity" proper to language alone, independently of distinctions such as those between emitter and message, or *narré* and *narration,* story and discourse.

Clearly, a literary text is different from the simple statements analyzed grammatically by Ducrot, if only because at the level of supraphrastic grammar there is no equivalent formal indicator of negation ("not" or "ne . . . pas"). And negation is, in fact, not quite what is at issue in "Un cœur simple." It is rather that a value in the text, such as simplicity, can be simultaneously marked in terms, not of affirmative and negative, but of negative and positive. If one grants, as the title suggests, an equivalence between the character of Félicité and the simplicity of her heart, on the one hand, and, on the other, between the simple-hearted character and the text that produces her, then it can be said that the figure of Félicité permits both a positive and a negative valorization of the quality of simplicity. Furthermore, it can be said that, far from being assertions, à la Ducrot, of different enunciating instances in the text, both the positive and the negative valorizations are produced simultaneously by the same narrative discourse. There is no point in examining the text for a group of favorable statements emanating from an E1 and addressed to a D1, and a group of unfavorable statements from an E2 to a D2; there is simply textual "polyphony"—or "duplicity"—the two valorizations resulting from the same text as it is actualized by the reader, but without it being possible to hierarchize the two different interpretations. Consequently, the meaning of the text does not depend here on the *presence* of a narrator, but rather it emerges from the *absence* of any instance that might be appealed to in support of one or other of the two opposed meanings, between which the text does not "hesitate," for it simply assumes them, simultaneously and undramatically.

However, in this we have not left behind a "realist" aesthetic (as certain "writerly" texts of modernism and postmodernism do), for in "Un cœur simple," the double possibility of reading derives from the mimesis of the servant as a social being (and hence from the mimetic duplicity inherent in realist representation). It is to the precise extent that Félicité's simplicity is simultaneously *shared* with her milieu while *separating* her from it that the text calls for a negative and a positive valorization of the character. The oppositional relationship between Félicité and her milieu is, of course, obvious in even the most hasty reading of the text: whereas the bourgeois characters are notably egocentric (Mme Aubain), caddish (M. Bourais), exploitive and indifferent; whereas the proletarian characters are distinguished by cowardice (Théodore), opportunism (Félicité's sister), brutality and *bêtise,* Félicité—surrounded by this cold and sterile milieu—appears as the only character who has *heart,* that is, a form of simplicity (or straightforwardness) that manifests itself as devotion, affection, and generosity, but also as an almost unfailing courage in the face of the innumerable defeats inflicted on her by life, and as a form of spontaneous mysticism that contrasts with the conventional religious observance of the other characters. This is the Félicité of the letter to Mme des Genettes, "dévote mais mystique, dévouée sans exaltation et tendre comme du pain frais," for whom Flaubert wishes to obtain the reader's sympathy and "faire pleurer les âmes sensibles." It is impossible not to identify with her, since it is precisely the function of the text's "realist" apparatus to point up the contrast between the moral and spiritual aridity of Félicité's milieu and the unrecognized worth of the character. Félicité's simplicity, her affective spontaneity, is in this case an entirely positive value, and it results from any average perceptive reading of the mimetic duplicity of the text. It is indeed the traditional or standard reading of "Un cœur simple" and does not need to be more fully elaborated here, although we will have to return to the qualities that make Félicité differ from her milieu.

Less frequently noted is the fact that the character's simplicity— in the sense, now, of a certain absence of sophistication, but still a function of the goodness of her heart—brings her into a relationship of similarity with other characters. We have seen her listening with Mme Aubain to Liébard's stories, and brought into illocutory relationship with the storyteller through identification, while sharing with her mistress equal status—implying a similarity of taste between them—as receivers of the same moralizing tale. Let us now explore a little more the relationship of Félicité and Mme Aubain, who for a half-century share the same dwelling, before Félicité appropriates it to herself, on the latter's death, and makes it her own. The progressive disintegration of Mme Aubain's house parallels the increasing decrepitude of the servant. Félicité's love for Mme Aubain's children is no less maternal than is their natural mother's, and in the absence of M. Aubain both women find themselves sharing a life of similar solitude. Loulou is a gift to Mme Aubain before becoming Félicité's property, and it is the mistress who advises the servant to have him stuffed. Grief for Virginie brings the two women together in an equalizing embrace (p. 611), and on Mme Aubain's death, Félicité weeps for her "comme on ne pleure pas les maîtres" (p. 618). So, it is certainly not coincidental that Félicité should share with her mistress and her mistress's house the honors of description in chapter 1. But, through Mme Aubain, she is also linked with the whole group of the "bourgeoises de Pont-l'Évêque," who share with the mistress and the servant the honors of the memorable first sentence.

What then is common to Félicité and the bourgeoises of the town? It is not, obviously, the ownership of property, but rather a related phenomenon, a certain cult of objects that, in association with a certain form of pious religiosity, becomes a kind of fetishism.[15] There is a pointed description of Félicité's bedroom as a place having "l'air à la fois d'une chapelle et d'un bazar, tant il contenait d'objets religieux et de choses hétéroclites" (p. 617), a description that associates Félicité's habit of collecting "junk" with the accumulative traits of a middle class whose primary attributes are piety (the "chapelle") and mercantilism (the "bazar"). To the extent that Félicité's cult of objects is a demonstration of materialism (which it partially is), her simplicity links her with the property-holding class and takes on negative connotations, for this fetishistic taste for objects that she shares with her milieu is evidence of deep complicity (we are back now listening to Liébard and coming out "devant le purin") with the entropic processes of time. The reason why the first chapter is divided between a synoptic view of the lives of the two women and an overall description of their shared dwelling is that the house gives rich evidence of a certain cult of *souvenirs* and as a corollary, of the phenomenon of heterogeneous accumulation this gives rise to. Madame's bedroom is dominated by the "portrait de 'Monsieur' en costume de muscadin"; the paneling in the library is indiscernible behind an accumulation of drawings, engravings, and gouaches, "souvenirs d'un temps meilleur et d'un luxe évanoui"; finally, "un vieux piano supportait, sous un baromètre, un tas pyramidal de boîtes et de cartons" (p. 591). The property at Toucques also has its collection of miscellaneous items— "Un dressoir en chêne supportait toutes sortes d'ustensiles, des brocs, des assiettes, des écuelles d'étain, des pièges à loup, des forces pour les moutons; une seringue énorme fit rire les enfants" (p. 598) —and Mme Aubain displays a characteristically procrastinating attitude toward the decaying state of the farm: "Les toits de paille . . . résistaient aux plus fortes bourrasques. Cependant la charreterie tombait en ruine. Mme Aubain dit qu'elle aviserait . . ." (p. 598). (And, of course, we never hear later of repairs being done.)

For the unpropertied Félicité to join in and become an active object fetishist herself, sharing the complicity toward time and death it signifies, takes—precisely—the death of Virginie, from whom she first "inherits" objects. Her first manifestation of the fetish is the taking of a lock of Virginie's hair; the second, her acquisition of the plush hat. Indeed, the whole scene in which she and her mistress go through Virginie's effects brings out, not only the connection between object fetishism and entropy, but also the commonality of feeling between the two women (Félicité is here very much "comme une autre") with respect to the significance of "souvenirs": "Elles retrouvèrent un petit chapeau de peluche . . . ; mais il était tout mangé de vermine. Félicité le réclama pour elle-même. Leurs yeux se fixèrent l'une sur l'autre, s'emplirent de larmes . . ." (p. 611). Once the habit is established, however, Félicité's fetishism goes well beyond Mme Aubain's. She even relays her mistress, taking into her room an old frock coat of Monsieur's, and in general "toutes les vieilleries dont ne voulait plus Mme Aubain" (p. 617). To her collecting she brings a religious intensity that finally dissolves the distinction between conventional piety and a true cult:

On voyait contre les murs: des chapelets, des médailles, plusieurs bonnes Vierges, un bénitier en noix de coco; sur la commode, couverte d'un drap comme un autel, la boîte en coquillages que lui avait donnée Victor; puis . . . ; et au clou du miroir, accroché par ses rubans, le petit chapeau de peluche! (p. 617)

The object on which the double thematics of fetishism and decay finally converges is, of course, the parrot. As a souvenir of the once-living Loulou and an object of an "idolatrous" cult, it calls to mind the plush hat, "tout mangé de vermine": "Bien qu'il ne fût pas un cadavre, les vers le dévoraient; une de ses ailes était cassée, l'étoupe lui sortait du ventre" (p. 620). But, unlike the hat, which like the rest of the household junk merely stands witness to the common collecting instinct of Félicité and Mme Aubain, Loulou is clearly, and quite specifically, a figure of the *objet d'art,* that is, of art as an object. Even when he was alive, Loulou figured art through his prestigious power of speech, associated by Félicité with the voice of God: "Le Père, pour s'énoncer, n'avait pu choisir une colombe, puisque ces bêtes-là n'ont pas de voix, mais plutôt un des ancêtres de Loulou" (p. 618). But what his voice does is to represent everyday human language; his is a mimetic art: "Elle entreprit de l'instruire: bientôt il répéta: 'Charmant garçon! Serviteur, monsieur! Je vous salue, Marie!' " (p. 613). After Félicité has become deaf, Loulou also represents for Félicité the sounds of the surrounding world that has become so distant from her: "Comme pour la distraire, il reproduisait le tic-tac du tournebroche, l'appel aigu d'un vendeur de poisson, la scie du menuisier qui logeait en face; et, aux coups de la sonnette, imitait Mme Aubain, — 'Félicité! la porte! la porte!' " (p. 615). He is a figure, then, of "realist" mimesis, here seen as the representation of what is repeated (in time), using a language that is itself repetitive, a language of *clichés,*[16] an automatic, clockwork language reproducing an existence that is itself automatic, an existence like that of Félicité, who "toujours silencieuse, la taille droite et les gestes mesurés, semblait une femme en bois, fonctionnant d'une manière automatique" (p. 592) and whose life is but a succession of episodes, repeating time and time again exactly the same data of character and situation. Loulou in life, then, figures the aesthetic of "Un cœur simple," to the extent that, as a mimesis of Félicité's existence, it is a realist text. (But we should note straightaway the specification that she only *appeared* to be a "femme en bois," which allows for a counteraesthetic corresponding to the real, flesh-and-blood heart within the automaton.)

Once dead and stuffed, however, Loulou represents less the mimesis of everyday life and speech in repetitive time and more the perils of identification, the product of mimetic duplicity. Identification here appears as a confusion of art, as a realistic reproduction of life, with the object itself, subject as it is to entropy. The result of the taxidermist's labors is to transform the living Loulou into a piece of "artwork," an *objet d'art* that Félicité can now store, and worship, with the other objects in her collection.

Enfin il arriva, — et, splendide, droit sur une branche d'arbre, qui se vissait dans un socle d'acajou, une patte en l'air, la tête oblique, et mordant une noix, que l'empailleur par amour du grandiose avait dorée.

Elle l'enferma dans sa chambre (p. 617).

What is striking here is not simply the bad taste of this monument to "l'amour du grandiose," it is the fixed and motionless quality that has been given to a creature who was once mobile, elusive, and difficult to interpret. "*Étrange* obstination de Loulou, ne parlant plus du moment qu'on le regardait!" (p. 613); "enfin, il se perdit . . . . *Que diable avait-il fait?*" (p. 614) (my emphases). By reducing to motionlessness what had once been an active, unfixed creature, the taxidermist has rendered possible the operation whereby, in making him a cult object, Félicité now gives him a single, fixed meaning. Before he becomes confused with the Holy Ghost (a transformation to which we will return), Loulou is, for Félicité, a relic of himself; that is, just as she and her mistress make fetishes of other objects, he is a cult object in the worship of memory (a "souvenir"), and as such is identified with time and history. "Chaque matin, en s'éveillant, elle l'apercevait à la clarté de l'aube, et se rappelait alors les jours disparus, et d'insignifiantes actions jusque dans leurs moindres détails, sans douleur, pleine de tranquillité" (p. 617). We may conclude that, through Loulou, realist art is defined as a mimesis of time-bound, cliché-ridden reality, and one with a double disadvantage, since through mimetic duplicity it reduces the multiplicity and elusiveness of "life" to a fixed meaning, and it involves one in the death-bound processes of entropy. Such a form of art thus has a clear affinity with the cult of objects that characterizes bourgeois materialism.

It is significant that, as a fetish among fetishes, Loulou's presence provides the link between the two major descriptions of heterogeneity and disorder in the text: the account of Félicité's room, with its "air à la fois d'une chapelle et d'un bazar," and that of the Corpus Christi *reposoir*. In both passages, he occupies an equivalent position, in terms of the rhetoric of description, the culminating one, although in the bedroom he is seen enthroned in full splendor while on the *reposoir* there is such a pile of precious objects that he has virtually disappeared: "caché sous des roses," he shows only his "front bleu, pareil à une plaque de lapis" (p. 622)—a reversal that reflects, of course, Félicité's own humble position in her society. But, as an expression of collective taste, it is significant that the *reposoir* betrays the same conception of beauty as Félicité's bedroom. Here, too, there is a heaped display of variegated objects: relics, orange-blossoms, silver candelabra, vases and flowers, forming "un monceau de couleurs éclatantes" in which "des choses rares tir[ent] les yeux." "Un sucrier de vermeil avait une couronne de violettes, des pendeloques en pierres d'Alençon brillaient sur de la mousse, des écrans chinois montraient leurs paysages" (p. 612). The whole is no less a mixture of chapel and bazaar than Félicité's room, so that, at the very moment when, through death (and mystic vision), the servant at last escapes this world of objects, her taste continues to link her with the community whose worship she shares. In this way, the end of the tale confirms the beginning, where Félicité also appeared in her relationship with the good, middle-class society of Pont-l'Évêque; and thus is rounded off the negative reading of the character's simplicity.

Negatively marked as attachment to the entropic world of objects, Félicité's simple-hearted devotion contrasts, then, with the positively marked simplicity of heart that sets her apart from her fellow citizens. This textual ambivalence as to the evaluation of simplicity is the sign of its "duplicity." But the analysis of Félicité's taste functions also, more specifically, as a condemnation of the "realist" aesthetic and hence as a condemnation of the text of "Un cœur simple" in its mimetic duplicity as a representation of the world of clockwork time and automatic existence that functions so as to involve the reader in its materialism, temporality, increasing disorder, and death. Yet this is the very type of reading on which, not only the positive interpretation of Félicité's simplicity (as opposed to social egotism and indifference) depends, but also without which one could not achieve the negative valorization of her simplicity (tied up with the bourgeois cult of objects) that amounts to a condemnation of "realist," mimetic art. There is no escape from the circularity of these two opposed readings that mutually imply each other—the "realist" reading leading to a condemnation of the "realist" aesthetic as Félicité's simplicity implies both negative and positive evaluation of the character—unless one can achieve a sense of the underlying textual simplicity that makes such "duplicity" possible. And this, in turn, involves the abandonment of a *social* reading of the character and a necessary breakthrough toward that in her—her "heart," her "mystic" potential—which makes her radically unique.

Simplicity of Heart

That Félicité is not the automaton, the "femme en bois" she appears but the possessor of a heart is yet another example of mimetic duplicity in the text, because—apart from its presence in the title— the heart figures as an unstated, but constantly adverted to, "meaning" that underlies the clockwork of the character's actions, perceptions, and words. It exists only as a function of certain characterological manifestations, or, in other words, as a *quality* of Félicité's behavior, the quality of "simplicity" (affective spontaneity, existential courage, generosity, devotion, etc.). But, as such, the heart itself is a hypothesis of the text, a motivation assumed to be real but "internal," and therefore unknowable, in the mimetic perspective, apart from its "external" manifestations. It is consequently strongly associated with Félicité's impassibility and indeed the strand of secrecy in her character: the "femme en bois" is also a woman who has a private domain, and the bedroom "où elle admettait peu de monde" (p. 617) is the figure of this deep personal recess, just as the house itself stands for the slowly disintegrating body she inhabits. Protected by a wall of silence, Félicité's heart makes her, in this sense, a figure of mimetic duplicity: it is the sign of a central presence in the text, real but inaccessible to analysis or discourse, from which its meaning emanates.

The title, then, is metonymic: the "cœur simple" is the deepest part of Félicité, her essential core, standing for the whole. But there is a sense, also, in which it is metaphoric, the heart being equivalent to the person; for Félicité is "all heart," all simplicity; there is nothing she does, thinks, or says that does not demonstrate heart. In short, she is *nothing but heart*, and if this is a secret it is an open one, which does not need to be deciphered but can easily be read in her every action. In the tradition whereby the sense of the arbitrariness of signs and the freedom of the signifier are figured by actresses, coquettish beauties, castrati, and in short *femmes sans cœur*,[17] a *woman with a heart* might be expected to signify the motivated quality of signs—and that is indeed Félicité's function as a figure of the text in its mimetic duplicity. But what is most striking about Félicité is that, as a woman who is all heart, she belongs to the same tradition of semiotic awareness as the *femme sans cœur*, except that she turns its intuitions on their heads, figuring the textuality of the signifier in entirely positive terms, not as a function of an absence but as a superabundant plenitude. The simplicity of her heart is the sign of a certain transparency of text, a readability of the signifier in its literal dimension; instead of figuring textuality as inconsistent and deceptive because devoid of substance, it manifests faith in the substantiality of text, and a wholly positive attitude toward the play of signifiers. Heart is not in this sense a center that organizes meaning but the very presence of text to itself. Such a text signifies of itself, qua text, not as the fragile substitute or facsimile for an irremediably absent meaning.

As a figure both of a "realist" reading of the text's mimetic duplicity and of "writerly" or textual simplicity, what Félicité signifies finally is a doubleness, an ambivalence, yet another form of *duplicity*, then, in the text of "Un cœur simple," which leads one, in realist fashion, to seek her (its) central heart but to discover, in textual fashion, her (its) all-pervading simplicity. This is the reading mimed in the structure of the present essay: we have been led by a "mimetic" perception of the text to discover its textual "duplicity," which, in turn, led us to seek a central simplicity, only to discover, as we are now doing, that the simplicity is not "central" but general. Since the negative reading of Félicité's simplicity in its social context led us only, in circular fashion, to a condemnation of realist, mimetic duplicity, it is via the positive reading of the simplicity of her heart, as a personage of spontaneous feeling at odds with a world of indifference, exploitation, and cruelty, and hence subject to the frustrations, wounds, and grief she stores quietly within her, that we can reach her central core, the warmth of devotion and generosity she protects within the sanctity of her chamber. But it is only when we abandon this perception of the servant as a social being that it becomes possible to perceive, in what constitutes her as a unique individual, the sign, on the one hand, of a reading of text in its "writerly" simplicity and, on the other, of a textuality freed of its social significance (as an imitation of human existence in time).

The cult of objects that Félicité shares with the bourgeoisie is connected also with a form of naïveté in her that links her, rather, with the popular classes and separates her from her betters. If she has something in common with Mme Aubain, she also shares with Liébard a quite essential characteristic, which is her inability to read. (When Liébard brings the letter with news of Victor's death, they are both forced to have recourse to Mme Aubain to find out what it says.) But in Félicité's case, her illiteracy translates into a kind of generalized semiotic incapacity, a form of *literalism* that appears to be very much her own. Bourais is able to feel superior to her because the lines of his atlas only confuse her: "ce réseau de lignes coloriées fatiguait sa vue, sans lui rien apprendre" (p. 606). She has no sense of the metaphoric or the symbolic:

Elle avait peine à imaginer sa personne [that of the Holy Ghost] ; car il n'était pas seulement oiseau, mais encore un feu, et d'autres fois un souffle. C'est peut-être sa lumière qui voltige la nuit aux bords des marécages, son haleine qui pousse les nuées, sa voix qui rend les cloches harmonieuses . . . . (p. 601)

Her "idolatrous" worship (p. 619) of the object Loulou derives from this radical inability to distinguish signifier and signified, parrot and Paraclete: "Quelquefois, le soleil entrant par la lucarne frappait son oeil de verre, et en faisait jaillir un grand rayon lumineux qui la mettait en extase" (p. 619).

But what this means is that, if Félicité's cult of objects has something in common with the middle class (its materialism) and something in common with the uneducated classes (her literalism), from this combination of materialism and literalism there arises finally something that distinguishes her from both; and that is a certain mystic aptitude for ecstacy. Is it a material, or a spiritual ecstasy? The question has little meaning for her: ". . . et, quand elle exhala son dernier souffle, elle crut voir, dans les cieux entrouverts, un perroquet gigantesque, planant au-dessus de sa tête." The parting heavens and the giant parrot are of exactly equal weight here, the spread wings of the huge bird being scarcely distinguishable from the opening of the skies, just as for Félicité the vehicle and tenor of a metaphor, the signifier and the signified, are *one*.

It seems to follow that, in "Un cœur simple," the inability to read can be interpreted in two ways. The inability Félicité shares with Liébard is a sign of aesthetic incompetence: it makes her (like Mme Aubain, who *can* read but whose aesthetic taste is no less dubious) a victim of mimetic duplicity. The trio formed by the group as *destinateur* and *destinataires* of Liébard's storytelling is thus a homogeneous one. But semiotic naïveté can also be a model of competence for a type of reading that does not look beyond the signifier for an intended meaning, a signified, but is content to read the *meaning of the signifier* itself. Félicité, who cannot make sense of signs, is capable of giving meaning to the objects of reality; or, as Françoise Gaillard would perhaps say, she has the gift of "ensignement," of making reality into sign.[18] This gift actually derives from the inability to distinguish the signifier and the signified in signs, for it is this that makes it possible to treat objects as signs (and signs as objects). And it is this gift that qualifies Félicité as a model for the "textual" or "writerly" reading of text, whose meaning can be grasped only if it is not decomposed into a signifier (say, "story" or *narré*) and signified (say, "discourse" or *narration*). The price Félicité pays for her semiotic literalism is the scorn of a middle-class character such as Bourais who knows how to read, but her reward is the mystic vision in which the open heavens and the huge parrot combine, a vision clearly unavailable to the educated characters in the text. Similarly, the reward of a "writerly" reading of "Un cœur simple" will derive from a vision of the indivisible text, in which there is no distinction between what is said and what is meant, so that two opposed meanings, such as the two contrary evaluations of Félicité's simplicity, can be available at the same time. But to earn this reward, one must approach the text with the same simplicity as Félicité herself.

One might say, then, that whereas the episode of Liébard's story-telling is, with respect to "Un cœur simple," a *mise en abyme de l'énonciation* as one that implies a situation of duplicity, Félicité, as a figure of "textual" reading, embeds not enunciation (if this word implies a distinction between emitter and message) but *code*. Code is a paradoxical concept that brackets out the notion of situation, implying not only the identity of text and message but also the absence of an intentional instance, or emitter. I am using it, in other words, to imply a communicational situation of absolute simplicity, or transparency, as opposed to the duplicitous circumstances inherent in the mimetic textual mode. But this does not help us to grasp all the implications of "en-signement" as a model for producing textual meaning.

What confirms the isolation of Félicité from the other characters, and the interpretation of her as a reading model for the text in its simplicity, is the fact that, although she cannot read or decipher an atlas, she does acquire, thanks to Paul's explanations of geographical illustrations, a kind of "éducation littéraire" (p. 596). "Ce fut même toute son éducation littéraire," as the text says: that is, as literary educations go, it is not really one at all. The readability of colored engravings ("estampes"), as opposed to the impenetrable duplicity of signs such as those of the atlas, here stands for the power to "en-sign" the real, and it is this that at last gives us some idea of what might be understood by the meaning of the text as signifier. Thanks to her imaginative spontaneity (yet another manifestation of simplicity), Félicité learns to use the illustrations as a basis for dreams and rêverie: later—thanks to this education—she will *imagine* Havana, "à cause des cigares" (the signifier), as a smoke-filled place with Negroes walking around in it. Her interpretations of the iconography of the church and her eventual identification of Loulou with the Holy Ghost are similar in spirit. The implication is that a "textual" reading of "Un cœur simple" is one that would consist, so to speak, of imagining one's way through the literality of the signs as the servant dreams Loulou into the Holy Ghost. For this, one needs a "literary education" like Félicité's, one that is distinct from the education of those who have been initiated into the duplicity of signs while distinguishing one from those who have had no literary apprenticeship at all. And such an education—the equivalent of Paul's nurturing of Félicité's imagination—is available only in the text of "Un cœur simple" itself, from the example of Félicité herself. It is clear, however, that textual simplicity, in Flaubert, cannot be too closely identified with the contemporary ideology of "écriture." In historical terms, Flaubert (like Mallarmé) occupies a middle position between the aesthetics of the signified (the aesthetic that perceives the freedom of the signifier as a *femme sans cœur*) and the contemporary aesthetics of the signifier as a wholehearted embracing of the materiality of the sign. His text is antirealistic in its double condemnation of focus on the signified—that is, the *referential* signified (a material world of entropy and death) and the *illocutionary* signified (what is "meant" as opposed to what is said, implying an instance of narration separable from the *narré*). But for him focus on the signifier does not have the same significance that a contemporary might give it, for the signifier as textual simplicity, if Félicité's example is to be believed, produces *another* meaning, a signified of its own, albeit of another order. Loulou opens up to Félicité a spiritual vision of "cieux entrouverts" that appears as an *alternative reading* of the object-sign, "rongé de vers," and leading back to the material universe, the world of time in which the rotting parrot signifies memories.[19]

Far from subscribing to a materialism of the signifier, it seems, then, that Flaubert conceives the signifier, in idealist fashion, as a means of eliminating from art its reference to the real and of substituting another, alternative, signified, conceived as an *absolute*—situated, that is, outside of time—and in opposition to all that is implied by memory, entropy, and history. Such idealism, which replaces the worship of objects by its own *religion du beau*, gives the Flaubertian ideology of text its clearest affinity with the context of nineteenth-century literary culture (the thought, for example, of Gautier, Baudelaire, and Mallarmé). With Flaubert, it is not the idea of "meaning" that disappears; rather there is a rivalry between the material meaning of things and the immaterial meaning that artistic writing can have when it is divorced from the material and flies on its own wings, like some Loulou with outspread pinions, freed at last from the world of worms and lost stuffing.

This, of course, is the self-same conflict that is perceptible in the text's situational apparatus, since we have seen that it requires to be read in realist terms—as mimetic duplicity—so as to reach the level at which it is no longer duplicitous but textually simple. The mediating stage is that of textual "duplicity," where the realist reading produces a doubleness of meaning that can be transcended only at the level of "writerly" simplicity. The upshot is that the text is both seductive (it leads one into involvement with its concerns as Félicité adheres to Liébard's story of Mme Lehoussais) and non-seductive (it invites a reading modeled on the simple power of Félicité's heart to love, a reading that, isolating her from the social environment in which her love is not reciprocated, places her in a textual environment in which it can be returned in the act of reading). Like Théodore in his proposal of marriage, the text is duplicitous and simple. But it is also like Félicité herself, whose heart is at the same time concealed at the center of, and beneath, the surface apparatus of the "femme en bois" and identical with a whole woman who is "all heart" and nothing but heart. Like the title, which is at once metonymic and metaphoric, the text here reveals its own ultimate duplicity: a *doubleness* (a reliance on the resources of both mimetic duplicity and textual simplicity) that is *duplicitousness* (since it is a seductive act of narration leading to a critique of that act and, concurrently, to a simple, "straightforward" invitation to love).

So long as texts rely on their own seductive power, the question of readership is less urgent to them than it becomes when the invitation they issue is more general. "Sylvie" and "Sarrasine" carefully define an appropriate readership and program the reading act. "Un cœur simple" must rely rather more on there being, "somewhere out there," a reader capable of simple-hearted love—a reader, furthermore, whose existence is excluded by the social thematics of the text but posited by its aesthetic situation. Relying on a not dissimilar distinction between the social (or general) context of reading and the aesthetic (or specialized) situation, but reversing the values in Flaubert, "The Figure in the Carpet" will be of interest to us because of its focus on this question of readership as an act of love. But "The Dead" even more radically turns the concerns of "Un cœur simple" like a glove, since there *acceptance* (not refusal) of cosmic disorder as the appropriate "referent" of art, and hence of a *materialism* of the signifier in its irrational freedom, leads in situational terms to a conception of text, not as an invitation, but as a *refusal* of love. Not a reciprocal love affair, but the exacerbation of desire becomes its model of the reader-text relationship.[20]

NOTES

1. Page numbers in parentheses refer to Gustave Flaubert, *Œuvres*, II (Paris: Bibliothèque de la Pléiade, 1952).

2. See chapters 4 and 5, respectively.

3. Etymologically, the two words have a common root (*sub-ducere*).

4. See chapter 3.

5. G. Flaubert, *Correspondance* (Paris: Charpentier et Fasquelle, 1893), IV, 233-234.

6. "Les figures du récit dans *Un cœur simple*," *Poétique*, 3 (1970), 348-364. Work on this much-discussed text that has been helpful to me includes: V. Brombert, *The Novels of Flaubert* (Princeton, N.J.: Princeton University Press, 1966), 233-245, and *Flaubert par lui-même* (Paris: Éd. de Seuil, 1971), 153-159; K. Uitti, "Figures and Fiction: Linguistic Deformation and the Novel," *Kentucky Romance Quarterly*, 17, 2 (1970), 149-169; R. T. Denommé, "Félicité's View of Reality and the Nature of Flaubert's Irony in 'Un cœur simple,' " *Studies in Short Fiction*, 7 (1970), 573-581; R. Debray-Genette, "Du mode narratif dans les *Trois Contes*," *Littérature*, 2 (mai 1971), 39-62, and "La technique romanesque de Flaubert dans 'Un cœur simple': Étude de genèse," in M. Issacharoff, ed., *Langages de Flaubert: Actes du Colloque de London* (Paris: Minard, 1976), 95-114; J. Culler, *Flaubert: The Uses of Uncertainty* (London: Paul Elek, 1974), 208-211; F. Gaillard, "L'ensignement de réel, ou la nécessaire écriture de la répétition," in Cl. Gothot-Meersch, éd., *La production du sens chez Flaubert: Colloque de Cerisy* (Paris: U.G.E. [10/18], 1975), 197-226; M. Issacharoff, *L'Espace et la nouvelle* (Paris: Corti, 1976), 31-33, 48-51; M. Bertrand, "Parole et silence dans les *Trois contes* de Flaubert," *Stanford French Review*, 1, 2 (fall 1977), 191-203; S. Felman, *La folie et la chose littéraire* (Paris: Éd. du Seuil, 1979), 159-169; A. Fairlie, "La contradiction créatrice: Quelques remarques sur la genèse d'*Un cœur simple*," in C. Carlut, éd., *Essais sur Flaubert en l'honneur de Don Demorest* (Paris: Nizet, 1979), 203-231, reprinted in *Imagination and Language* (Cambridge: Cambridge University Press, 1981), 337-360; J. O'Connor, "Flaubert: *Trois contes* and the Figure of the Double Cone," *PMLA*, 95, 5 (October 1980), 812-826. See also note 7.

7. On "Un cœur simple," see B. Stolzfus, "Point of view in *Un cœur simple*," *French Review*, 35, 1 (October 1961), 19-25; V. Brombert, *The Novels of Flaubert* and *Flaubert par lui-même*; B. Wagner, *Innenbereich und Äusserung: Flaubertsche Formen indirekter Darstellung und Grundtypen der erlebten Rede* (München: Fink, 1972), Kap. 4. For point of view in Flaubert generally, see also J. Rousset, *Forme et signification* (Paris: Corti, 1964), 109-133 ("*Madame Bovary*, ou le livre sur rien"); R. J. Sherrington, *Three Novels by Flaubert* (Oxford: Clarendon Press, 1970); and H. Weinberg, "Notes on Irony and style indirect libre in *Madame Bovary*," *Travaux deu cercle méthodologique* (Toronto: Department of French, University of Toronto), 7 (1979). Finally, on point of view in general, see P. Lubbock, *The Craft of Fiction* (London: Jonathan Cape, 1957); Wayne C. Booth, *The Rhetoric of Fiction* (Chicago: University of Chicago Press, 1961), and *A Rhetoric of Irony* (Chicago: University of Chicago Press, 1974); and G. Genette, *Figures*, III (Paris: Éd. du Seuil, 1979). Highly pertinent to my argument here is Susan S. Lanser, *The Narrative Act: Point of View in Prose Fiction* (Princeton, N.J.: Princeton University Press, 1981), which appeared too late for me to make use of it.

8. In opposition to the "ontology of voice" inherent in this critical tradition, Claude Perruchot, in "Le style indirect libre et la question du sujet dans *Madame Bovary*," in Cl. Gothot-Meersch, éd., *La production du sens chez Flaubert*, 253-285, proposes to read Flaubert's use of *style indirect libre* not as a function of the question "Who speaks?" but as

a manifestation of a "Cela écrit" (writing is going on), which, of course, radicalizes the whole question of point of view. It is quite true that this style is a function of writing and it does, notably in undecidable cases, deconstruct the notion of subject—but only if one begins by reading it in the first place as manifesting the divisibility of the text into *narré* and *narration,* "object" and "subject" of discourse. Hence, my decision to reserve the term "writerly" for a form of "duplicity" deriving from textual indivisibility and hence completely short-circuiting these traditional assumptions.

9. I am referring to the distinction, first made by Émile Benveniste, *Problèmes de linguistique générale,* I and II (Paris: Gallimard, 1966 and 1974), and which is enshrined in Seymour Chatman's title, *Story and Discourse.*

10. See *Figures,* III.

11. See *The Implied Reader* (Baltimore: Johns Hopkins University Press, 1974) and *The Act of Reading: A Theory of Aesthetic Response* (Baltimore: Johns Hopkins University Press, 1978).

12. For the awareness of thermodynamics in nineteenth-century literature, see Michel Serres, *Hermès, IV: La distribution* (Paris: Éd. de Minuit, 1977) and (on Zola) *Feux et signaux de brume* (Paris: Grasset, 1975). On Flaubert, see also Eugenio Donato, "The Museum's Furnace: Notes towards a Contextual Study of *Bouvard et Pécuchet,*" in Josué Harari, ed., *Textual Strategies* (Ithaca, N.Y.: Cornell University Press, 1979), 213-238.

13. My reference is to the distinction made in the opening paragraphs of chapter 3.

14. See O. Ducrot et al., *Les mots du discours* (Paris: Éd. de Minuit, 1980). Quotations from pp. 49, 50, and 53.

15. Cf. R. Debray-Genette, "Les figures du récit," p. 362.

16. For more detailed analysis of the implications of *cliché,* see F. Gaillard, "L'ensignement du réel," and S. Felman, *La folie et la chose littéraire.*

17. See chapter 2, note 29, for some references.

18. "L'en-signement du réel."

19. The irony discernible in the grotesqueness of Félicité's vision and the use of a verb ("elle crut voir") that puts its reality in doubt clearly subvert such idealism—but they do it as "discourse" commenting on the "story" and thus reintroduce the realist optic. The text does not thereby escape its ideological givens but, by reproducing the antagonism of materialist realism and "writerly" idealism, dramatizes and intensifies at its conclusion the aporia (here, between the vision as authentic and the vision as illusory) that produces the overall doubleness of the text.

20. On "The Figure in the Carpet" and "The Dead," see chapters 7 and 8, respectively.

Chapter Seven
Not for the Vulgar?
The Question of Readership
in "The Figure in the Carpet"

Art deals with what we see. . . . There is the story
of one's hero, and then, thanks to the intimate
connection of things, the story of one's story itself.

H. James, Preface to *The Ambassadors*

Critic, Text, and Audience

If I had had one of his books at hand I'd have repeated my recent act of faith—
I'd have spent half the night with him. At three o'clock in the morning, not
sleeping, remembering moreover how indispensable he was to Lady Jane, I stole
down to the library with a candle. There wasn't, so far as I could discover, a
line of his writing in the house. (p. 235)[1]

This passage opens various paths of entry into "The Figure in the
Carpet." The Jamesian identification of text with author (reading the
Vereker text is equivalent to intercourse with Vereker) produces an
image of reading as interpersonal intimacy that is central to the tale
and, of course, highly pertinent to the concerns of this book. No less
central is the narrator's failure, here in his quest for the book, and
elsewhere in his search for the elusive secret of Vereker's work (a
"quest for the book" in another sense)—the theme, then, of his
impotence and of his exclusion from the intimacy of reading. But
what is perhaps most obviously dramatized in the passage is one of
the most salient features of the tale: the discovery that Lady Jane
does not read Vereker (although she says she does) points up the
fact that, in this text, no one reads unless a member of a small
coterie of literati, highly self-conscious authors (like Hugh Vereker)
or "little demons of subtlety" (p. 232) (like the critics). Reading is
closely bound with writing. Authors, like Vereker or Gwendolen

Erme, write; and they read—Vereker reads criticism, albeit under protest, and Gwendolen pores over Vereker's work in search of its secret. Critics read: they read Vereker's work in order to write about it, or they read Gwendolen Erme in case there is a hint of the Vereker secret in her text; and finally they read each other's writing and gauge its "cleverness." The model of literary communication in "The Figure in the Carpet," and hence the text's own self-contextualization as literature, obviously involves a closed world in which "the few persons, abnormal or not, with whom my anecdote is concerned" engage in a fascinating game—"we sat around the green board as intently as the gamblers at Monte Carlo" (p. 250). But this "game" takes place also in the closed world of professionalism in which the text-reader relationship is at the center of a network of rivalries and ambitions, and critical "mastery" of a text is seen (in the event, rather falsely) as the key to reputation and authority—in short, a career.

Are we to take this representation of the world of the literary as a model or as an antimodel of the text's own presupposed communicational situation? Does it project itself as a consciously elusive piece of writing addressed as a kind of test to the perspicacity of critics, in the way that Vereker challenges the narrator to "lay him bare"? If so, the long line of critics who have responded with speculation about the Vereker secret as the key to the figure in the tale's own carpet are essentially right; or, at least, they are conforming to the text's own self-contextualization. But can it be, more problematically, that the tale is addressed to a readership whose existence is virtually unacknowledged in the tale, that is, to those readers outside of the profession of literature or those able to distance themselves from it, who do not participate in the game and whose careers are not at stake? Such readers are in a position to see the game, and the professional maneuvering, for something less heady, not "literature" but only the behavior patterns of the literati—that is, an aspect, albeit ludic and marginal, of "life." The intimacy of the critical relationship, so assiduously insisted upon in the text and pointed up in so many ways, perhaps implies, as its counterpart, a more distanced and ironic mode of reading; and the "*un*critical" involvement of the players in the game might then call for an attitude of some "critical" detachment on the part of those who are in a position to see it as something of a game of dupes. Or, finally, may it not be that both of these responses are valid? There is, after all, no contradiction in seeing the text as positioning itself, on the one hand, in the literary game while, on the other, maintaining that grace of irony, and more particularly of self-irony, that saves it from its own self-absorption.

Following the tradition of Balzac's *Illusions Perdues,* nineteenth-century literature is mainly aware of the phenomenon of criticism as a branch of journalism, that is, of writing about books for informational and promotional purposes. It is to this tradition that James seems obliquely to refer when in his Preface of 1909 he identifies as the "lively impulse" behind the writing of "The Figure in the Carpet" the desire to reinstate "analytic appreciation . . . in its virtually forfeited rights and dignities."[2] What flowed from this is the major historical originality of the tale: the depiction of the critical milieu as emerging from the journalistic practice of "reviewing" into something much more serious. Criticism is seen here, on the one hand, as a profession in its own right and, on the other, as one that is in symbiotic relationship with the profession of writing, such that each presupposes the other. Criticism cannot function without an object, the original "work," but equally the work, in this text, is in need of a mediator, or an explicator: "But you talk about the initiated," says the narrator to Vereker. "There must therefore, you see, *be* initiation." "What else in heaven's name is criticism supposed to be?" (p. 231) and: "Besides, the critic just *isn't* a plain man: if he were, pray, what would he be doing in his neighbour's garden?" (p. 232). So, criticism is not a mere parasite on literature but forms part of the literary garden itself. Although today the critical profession is centered in the institutions of liberal education and less dependent on the periodical press, it is impossible not to recognize here the presuppositions on which our own contemporary practice of criticism is posited. Literature is in need of interpretation, or "analytic appreciation"; the critic exists to supply that need and is thus a kind of collaborator with the creative artist.

But it follows from this that, although the garden of "literature" may be confined to authors and critics, the critical relationship itself must be a double one. It is a relationship to the text, but it is also a relationship to the audience, which, in turn, is to be "initiated" into that text—an audience that, by definition, is outside of literature, the audience of Lady Janes and plain men. What is striking, then, is that, in James's depiction, the audience for criticism turns out to be composed essentially of other critics (and authors). Lady Jane does read the narrator's early article in *The Middle*; she even marks its "brightest patches" and is anxious to read it aloud to her guests (p. 225). But even if this text were not, as Vereker judges it, "the usual twaddle" (p. 226), it is clear that the narrator has not written it for her. "The only effect I cared about was the one it would have on Vereker up there by his bedroom fire" (p. 225). More generally, it is evident that the opinions the narrator values are those of his colleagues: of George Corvick, who sides with Vereker ("The thing Vereker had mentioned to me was exactly the thing he, Corvick, had wanted me to speak of in my review," p. 237), of the anonymous group that—in spite of his failure in the case of Vereker —provides the "reputation for acuteness" that "was rapidly overtaking me" (p. 256). In short, the narrator's criticism is addressed, not outside of the small world of literature, but within it.

In discussions of "The Figure in the Carpet," and indeed in theoretical discussions of criticism generally, the relevant or primary critical relationship is usually taken to be that of critic to text; this is the relationship that is seen as constituting the problematics of criticism. The second relationship, that of critic to audience, is much less frequently analyzed, be it in general terms or in connection with James's tale, even though from the critic's point of view it is the essential one. In practical terms, success in the profession is a matter of one's colleagues' estimation of one's "cleverness"—a "cleverness" that, as the case of the narrator's success suggests, may or may not have much to do with the justness of one's relationship to text. And, whether in journalism or in the academic world, it is on reputation in this sense—on the estimation of one's professional colleagues and rivals—that monetary reward depends. If texts need the mediating effort of the interpretive critic in order to "initiate" a wider audience into them but if the critic's professional career depends rather on his addressing those who have already a foot in the literary garden, there is a basic and self-defeating contradiction in the conditions under which professional criticism is exercised. It is possible to suggest that James's tale is simultaneously posing the critical relationship to *text* as the appropriate model of literary communication to which it subscribes ("analytic appreciation" instead of "the usual twaddle") while propounding a critical relationship to *audience* that differs from that to which the small circle of characters, blindly and uncritically, conform. How else could one account for the evolution of the narrator, who learns from Vereker the problematic relationship of critic to text and who derives from failure a salutary sense of ironic distance from his own profession and its practitioners, who thus, although remaining a practicing critic and retaining his obsession with the Vereker problem, is enabled to become the author (within the fiction) of "The Figure in the Carpet" itself, whose text transmits from Vereker an art of elusive textuality, of simultaneous divulgement and withholding, but whose audience, I want to show, can only lie outside of the closed circle of the literati.

The Story of the Hero

Certainly, the commoditization of the act of critical reading, the dependence of the critic on other critics for professional advancement, and in general, the vital significance of "reputation" in determining a career are the narrator's primary concerns (and James's main targets) in the opening paragraph of the tale. It is George Corvick, we later learn, who lives by his pen (p. 248); but the narrator's first remark—his first self-estimate—is: "I had done a few things and earned a few pence." Corvick is classified in the same terms: he has "done more things" and "earned more pence" than "I"; but the narrator's judgment on him is that "there were chances for cleverness I thought he sometimes missed." The "opportunity" to review Vereker's latest book, and to review it in *The Middle* ("where my dealings were mainly with the ladies and the minor poets"—the hierarchization of the literary canon provides the measure of the critic's status), is seen as the narrator's "real start" on his "course," or career. "This was his new novel, an advance copy, and whatever much or little it should do for his reputation I was clear on the spot as to what it should do for mine." To this person, then, the literary text is very much a pretext: a pretext for cleverness, for earning "a few pence," and for advancement; and it is clear that the narrator writes less in the service of Vereker and his work than he works to position himself strategically and to build his own reputation.

His personal encounter with Vereker consequently has chastening effects. It counts as the narrator's first real engagement with the nature of text, that is, with the relationship of critic to text on which the rest—his relationship to audience and his professional status—is supposed to depend. What he discovers is that the very characteristic of text that justifies and legitimizes critical *practice* is that which simultaneously makes of the critical *profession* a hot bed of rivalry, cleverness, and "reputation." The *je ne sais quoi* of literature is the *sine qua non* of criticism: unless the text is conceived as having some undefined quality that needs defining, an inexplicit something that should be made explicit, there is no role for interpretation. This is the point that George Corvick is the first to suggest:

"But he gives me a pleasure so rare, the sense of"—he mused a little—"something or other."

I wondered again. "The sense, pray, of what?"
"My dear man, that's just what I want *you* to say!" (p. 221)

Vereker in his turn will speak of "the particular thing I've written my books most *for*" (p. 230). "The order, the form, the texture of my books will perhaps someday constitute for the initiated a complete representation of it. It strikes me . . . even as the thing for the critic to find" (p. 231). And he makes it clear that, for him also, the role of the critic is complementary to textuality conceived in this way. "I do it in my way . . . . Go *you* and do it in yours" (p. 234).

The conversation between the narrator and Vereker functions, of course, through the identification of author with text, not just as a conversation *about* literature but as an exemplification of the very critical relationship such a conception of text implies. Vereker produces discourse that both invites and refuses the effort of clarification and explicitation the narrator, in his interrogatory stance, attempts to make. He makes constant reference to a textual object, the description of which shifts—it is now his "little point" (p. 229), now a "general intention" (p. 235), now "this little trick of mine" or really "an exquisite scheme" (p. 231) that is his "secret" (p. 232)— and he defines it as the critic's task to discern and define this object to which he has at best only alluded. The discourse in which he evokes it is, moreover, blatantly figurative:

The thing's as concrete there as a bird in a cage, a bait on a hook, a piece of cheese in a mousetrap. It's stuck into every volume as your foot is stuck into your shoe. It governs every line, it chooses every word, it dots every i, it places every comma. (p. 233)

But like the references, the images are inconsistent: whereas, in the first conversation, the "thing" is contained in and separable from the text, like the items mentioned above, and the "organ of life" (p. 234) in the body or a "buried treasure" (p. 235)—all images, incidentally, of successful intercourse—it becomes in the following interview "something like a complex figure in a Persian carpet" (p. 240), "the very string . . . that my pearls are strung on" (p. 241), that is, a structural phenomenon inseparable from the text that embodies it, and hence much more elusive.

In its combination of allusiveness and elusiveness, such discourse evidently mimes the literary discourse itself of which Vereker is speaking; just as the series of communications that occur between author and critic (the first conversation by the bedroom fire, the note of retraction asking for the narrator's discretion, the final conversation in which—in spite of his "I shall never speak of that mystery again" [p. 238] —Vereker agrees, "although . . . with visible impatience" [p. 240], to answer some more questions) might be thought to mime the repetitiveness of the successive works that the secret is said to control, the "pearls" of which it is the "string." The narrator can only acquire the impression that it has constantly been a question of "something" that, however, he has not been permitted to grasp; and he chooses to express his sense of Vereker's textual "drift" first as a matter of moodiness or caprice (a standard nineteenth-century thematization of linguistic arbitrariness and the "absent" referent): ". . . I couldn't help pronouncing him a man of unstable moods. He had been free with me in a mood, he had repented in a mood, and now in a mood he had turned indifferent" (p. 240); and ultimately in the suspicion—never allayed, never confirmed—that he has been toyed with. "The buried treasure was a bad joke, the general intention a monstrous *pose*" (p. 236).

This pique is a response to the tantalizing quality of those textual characteristics on which the practice of interpretive criticism depends. Not only must there be a secret element in the text, but the secret must be formulable by the critic even though it goes unformulated in the text; and once formulated, it must be self-evidently "the" secret of the text—confirmed, that is, by its repetitiousness— so that the critic's success will be obvious to all. Consequently, the secret is both not there and very much there, said and unsaid, elusive and formulable. To the narrator's complaint: "Your description's beautiful, but it does't make what you describe very distinct," the reply is: "I promise you it would be distinct if it dawned on you at all" (p. 230); and later, when "I took refuge in repeating that his account of his silver lining was poor in something or other that a plain man knows things by," the response is similar: "That's only because you've never had a glimpse of it" (p. 232). It has been suggested, notably by W. Iser,[3] that the narrator's questions are inept: that what he is asking for—a "meaning" separable from the discourse—is the contrary of what Vereker is getting at and that consequently the conversation is the record of a communicative misunderstanding, a *dialogue de sourds*. But this is to ignore some of the inconsistencies in what Vereker himself says; and what emerges in general from exchanges such as those just quoted is rather the idea of a situational impossibility: the necessity of discovering, and saying, a "secret" that does not exist in discursive form—or that is identical with the discursive form in which it is referred to.[4] This is the theoretical necessity that grounds interpretive criticism but makes it a practical impossibility.

In two different ways, such a situation produces a struggle for power. There is a power issue in the relationship between text and critic (here dramatized in its implications by the hierarchical social relationship of established author to budding critic) and another in the relationship of critic to critic, illustrated, of course, by the story of the narrator's relationship with his friends. One might say that there is between critic and text a vertical power relationship, a question of "mastery," and between critic and critic a horizontal power relationship, expressed as "rivalry"—and it is the attainment of critical mastery in the vertical dimension that is presumed to confer an authority that dissolves rivalry on the horizontal plane by establishing the supremacy of one critic over his fellows. However, it is just this initial mastery that proves so problematical, and the difficulty, not to say impossibility, of achieving it that produces jealousy and frustration in horizontal relationships.

That Vereker's successive communications with the narrator are manifestations of *his* power and mastery of the situation, and of the narrator's relative powerlessness, is a fact that, although obvious, is not frequently discussed. He acts, in the first place, out of "compunction," that is, from the feeling that he has behaved ungraciously —"compunction for a snub unconsciously administered to a man of letters in a position inferior to his own" (p. 228). The remedy is, of course, an act of graciousness: "To make the thing right he talked to me exactly as an equal . . ."—which means that those speaking are in fact *not* equal, that Vereker is being condescending, not to say patronizing; ". . . he couldn't have done anything more intensely effective" (p. 228). It is indeed to the *effectiveness* of Vereker's social strategy, and the superiority that it implies, that the narrator succumbs.

Everything that Vereker says and does reinforces his mastery of the situation. His manner is consistently calculated to demonstrate condescension. His hand is placed protectively on the younger man's shoulder, kindly "feeling for a fracture" (p. 228), or accompanying a patent insult "to show the allusion wasn't to my personal appearance" (p. 231). Although supposedly speaking "equal to equal," he allows concern for the other to show through: a "friendly reproach" has to be defused by being "jocosely exaggerated" (p. 230), a shake of the head and a wave of the finger express anxiousness (p. 235). The narrator is aware that he is being indulged: "He indulgently shook my hand again, and I felt my questions to be crude and pitiful." "He was suitably indulgent . . . . But his amusement was over; I could see he was bored" (p. 234). "Vereker's happy accent made me appear to myself, and probably to him, a rare dunce" (p. 230). And when finally Vereker proffers his advice to abandon pursuit of the secret ("Give it up!"), the young man perceives that "this wasn't a challenge—it was fatherly advice" (p. 234). What does this make of the relationship of equals?

If the author's manner is calculated to make the young critic feel a dunce, his discursive strategies—more subtle, perhaps—are even more brilliantly successful. The narrator has, in essence, two main concerns. One is his need for clarity, for "something or other that a plain man knows things by" (p. 232). His questions are not dissimilar to the familiar disambiguation technique of everyday conversation, when someone asks "What do you mean?"[5] But Vereker's reaction is to imply that such a question is inappropriate: "I promise you it would be distinct if it should dawn on you at all" (p. 230); ". . . the critic just *isn't* a plain man" (p. 232). There is some appeal here to the young critic's "intelligence" and "subtlety"—his "cleverness"—which is flattering and stimulating; an effect that, however, is countermanded by the implication of obtuseness in impatient questions like "Have I got to *tell* you, after all these years and labours?" (p. 229) and brutal responses like "Ah, my dear fellow, it can't be described in cheap journalese!" (p. 233). The second of the narrator's concerns is technical: "Is it something in the style? or something in the thought? An element of form or an element of feeling?" or "I see—it's some idea *about* life, some sort of philosophy. Unless it be . . . something you're after in the language" (p. 234). To these questions Vereker responds with a scorn so offhand that the narrator's laborious distinctions appear hopelessly trivial and misplaced. He "indulgently" shakes the critic's hand, with a "Good-night, my dear boy—don't bother about it." Or, equally indulgently, he jokes, ". . . he only said I hadn't got the right letter. But his amusement was over: I could see he was bored" (p. 234). A certain conception of the significance of literature—which is beyond vulgar conceptions of meaning and naive formal distinctions—is being conveyed here, and it is a conception one may feel the text itself endorses; but its first effect is to make the critic feel a failure.

This is reinforced by Vereker's major discursive strategy, which consists of alternately advancing and retreating, giving the "tip" and withdrawing it. The challenge to "tell me in the morning that you've laid me bare" is shortly followed by the "fatherly advice" to "give it up" (p. 235). The (apparently) outgoing conversation by the bedroom fire is followed, soon after, by an attack of reticence: "Now that the fit's over I can't imagine how I came to be moved so much beyond my wont" (p. 238). But this is followed, in turn, by a further conversation in which more revelations are unexpectedly forthcoming: it is learned that, in Vereker's estimation, the fact that Corvick and Gwendolen are to be married "may help them"; and soon—but not before the advice to "give it up" has been repeated—two apparently key images of the secret are produced. The narrator's image—"something like a complex figure in a Persian carpet"—is highly approved" by the author, who adds in seeming confirmation his own, inconsistent, however, and rather banal one: "It's the very string . . . that my pearls are strung on!" (pp. 240-241). One recalls the reference in Vereker's note to the "game" he is playing with the narrator:

I was accidentally so much more explicit with you than it had ever entered into my game to be, that I find this game—I mean the pleasure of playing it—suffers considerably. In short, if you can understand it, I've rather spoiled my sport (p. 238)

—and this corresponds very much to the narrator's final estimation of his experience with Vereker. "He comes back to me from that last occasion . . . as a man with a safe preserve for sport" (p. 241). The game of literature, in short, is played not "as equals" but more as a cat plays with a mouse.

Recalling that this unequal relationship between Vereker and the narrator serves as a model of the literary relationship of text to critic-reader, one is led to revise somewhat one's sense of the significance of literature for the author, that is, of "the particular thing I've written my books most *for*" (p. 230). Instead of the somewhat portentous "secret," the "organ of life" pulsating in the textual body, it appears that what Vereker writes *for* is ultimately the "pleasure of playing" a game, and in particular the pleasure of playing a game in which he has, and retains, the upper hand, maintaining a "safe preserve for sport." The reader of "The Figure in the Carpet" is led, certainly, to judge the narrator for the limitations of his vision, the narrowness of his conception of literary meaning, and to wish, like Corvick, that he might have had the "gumption" to pose different, and better, questions in the face of Vereker's clearly more sophisticated understanding of text. But equally one is brought to the conclusion that Vereker's true superiority over the critic does not lie in his possession of a secret so much as it results from his successful deployment of discursive strategies for which the younger man is not a match. He is in direct line of descent from Poe's Dupin. In this light, the text-critic relationship appears as one between a rhetorically masterful text and a reader ill equipped to "lay it bare." And the narrator's eventual failure to elicit the secret from his study of Vereker's works thus comes as a confirmation of the inadequacy that can already be extrapolated from the narrative of his various encounters with the author.

But this inadequacy now becomes the motivating factor in a rivalry in which the sexual connotations of textual intercourse become explicit—I mean the rivalry that pits the narrator against his friends, or more accurately leaves him "humiliated," "out in the cold" while "Vereker's inner meaning" gives George Corvick and Gwendolen Erme "endless occasion to put and to keep their young heads together" (p. 243). "At the core of my disconcerted state . . . was the sharpness of a sense that Corvick would at last probably come out somewhere" (p. 244)—a conviction shared, incidentally, by Corvick who proudly insists on "playing fair" and on seeking no more guidance from the master himself: " 'Oh when I've run him to earth,' he also said, 'then, you know, I shall knock at his door. . . . He shall crown me victor—with the critical laurel' " (p. 246). Thus, another game begins. This time, it is a figurative chess game pitting Corvick, with the girl who hangs on his moves, against the now absent Vereker, "a ghostlier form, the faint figure of an antagonist" (p. 245), while the narrator's role is reduced to that of "a kind of coerced spectator" (p. 261). It is a "game of skill" in which "skill meant courage, and courage meant honour, and honour meant passion, meant life," and which—for that very reason —resembles rather more a game of chance such as reunites the "grim gamblers at Monte Carlo." "Gwendolen Erme, for that matter, with her white face and her fixed eyes, was of the very type of the lean ladies one had met in the temples of chance" (p. 250). But, skill or chance, the players agree on one thing: what is "life" to them is "a pastime too precious to be shared with the crowd" (p. 242). It is only among initiates that the game is worth playing: "It isn't," Corvick says, "for the vulgar" (p. 237).

The relative eclipse of Vereker from this point on is striking: the narrator does not see him again before his death, and of Corvick's eventual interview with him in Rapallo we have only the most laconic report. Foreshadowed by this eclipse, Vereker's death will signify the loss of any possible "sanction" (p. 274) for a proposed solution to the critical problem posed by his work; his withdrawal from the scene appears consequently as the natural corollary of the fact that, at this stage in the tale, the major focus is no longer on the relationship of critic to text but on that between critics, working under circumstances in which there is no absolute knowledge but only a rivalry that can never be genuinely resolved. So, Vereker's disappearance is balanced by the new prominence of Gwendolen Erme, the "author" figure who replaces him as an image of the problematics of text but who, as the object of sexual jealousy between the narrator and Corvick ("my renewed envy of Corvick's possession of a friend who had some light to mingle with his own," p. 242), and later between the narrator and Deane, figures also the text as occasion for the critics' rivalry, the text for whose mastery they vie.

Gwendolen is a worthy successor to Vereker: her two principal characteristics are her passionate self-identification with writing (she is, says Corvick, "quite incredibly literary," she "felt in italics and thought in capitals" [p. 246], and the narrator confirms that "she lived for the art of the pen" [p. 250]), and "her consummate independence" (p. 269). The measure of her status as a textual figure is, consequently, not only her three novels, the second of which is a "carpet" with a "figure" of its own (p. 267), but also the art of withholding herself she practices. The Celtic root of her name means "white, pale." Her early novel, "Deep Down," is itself a kind of void: "a desert in which she had lost herself, but in which she had dug a wonderful hole in the sand" (p. 250). From Corvick she withholds herself on what finally appears to have been the pretext (since the obstacle disappears when she becomes anxious to marry) of her mother's health. From the narrator, she withholds herself by her habitual reticence (from the start, she has "remarkably little English" for him [p. 243]), which makes it difficult for him to read her (he never gets to the bottom of her engagement to Corvick, broken off then reinstated without explanation). And, more specifically, when at last she is in possession of Vereker's secret, her refusal to communicate it exacerbates his now retrospective jealousy of Corvick, his desire to know—but also his sense of her beauty. The woman who originally was (in Corvick's unchallenged phrase) "not pretty but awfully interesting" (p. 220) grows in allure and in stature as she becomes the proud and independent possessor of the precious secret she will not impart: she is now seen as "incontestably hand-some" and "leading a life of singular dignity and beauty" (p. 264).

But for all these resemblances to the fascinating Vereker, Gwendolen is also unlike the master in that she is a woman and also in that, without being a critic ("I don't 'review' . . . I'm reviewed!" p. 268), she is like the critics of her acquaintance—the narrator, Corvick and, in due course, Deane—in being obsessed with the question of Vereker's secret. In this respect, the text draws a careful distinction between her books (the life that is constituted, for her, by "the art of the pen") and her actual life, and it is in this latter domain, not her writing, that Vereker's secret matters to her (she is also more anxious than Corvick to check with the living author rather than relying on the texts). "If her secret was, as she had told me, her life—a fact discernible in her increasing bloom . . . it had yet not a direct influence on her work" (p. 272), notes the narrator; and indeed the secret will always remain indiscernible in, and apparently unconnected with, her writing. This division of the character means that the power she wields as a figure of text is balanced, in her life, by the power to which she submits as a "critic" and as a woman. In this respect, her role is not to withhold herself but, on the contrary, to give herself to the critical "victor," to be the prize, or laurel, that rewards critical success. Her marriage to Corvick is the sign, on one hand, of her submission to the Vereker text (since she thereby tacitly admits he was right in announcing that a woman would never find the secret alone, p. 239) and, on the other, of her availability as reward for Corvick's critical coup. For her, fascination with the textual secret amounts to a certain vulnerability; in the presence of critical claims such as those of Corvick, she yields without hesitation to his presumed mastery.

What is significant is that the Vereker secret is no more laid bare in Corvick's version of it than it is in Vereker's own discourse. It is indistinguishable from the—again—succession of texts, written ones this time (cursory telegrams, reticent letters, the fragmentary article that fails to "unveil the idol" [p. 263]), that refer to it, describe it, but do not reveal it.[6] The narrator and Gwendolen have only Corvick's *word* that the secret is out—just as the narrator and Corvick had previously speculated about the value of Vereker's "word" ("nothing but the word of Mr. Snooks," p. 244) and just as, in due course, the narrator will have to make do with Gwendolen's own word ("I heard everything . . . and I mean to keep it to myself," p. 263). The power exerted by Corvick over Gwendolen is not different in kind, then, from that exerted first by Vereker, and later by Gwendolen herself, over the narrator. The only possible conclusion is that critical mastery—while it may or may not be mastery of the actual textual object—is certainly mastery over the critical audience and that such mastery is obtained by means exactly similar to those by which the literary text exerts its own mastery. The title of Gwendolen's second novel, published eighteen months after her marriage (and Corvick's death), is "Overmastered" (p. 267).

However, a critical victory such as Corvick's—vain as it may appear—is not to be undervalued. The conquest of the critical reader, like that of the literary reader, is analogous to the consummation of intimate relations. Whereas the narrator is attracted to Vereker the man ("I had taken to the man still more than I had ever taken to the books," p. 242) and then to Gwendolen the woman ("I was wondering if some day she would accept me," p. 266)—that is, in each case, to the fascinating possessor of the secret that is withheld from him—he never achieves true intimacy. It is Gwendolen's role, as a woman, to give herself sexually to Corvick, as possessor of the secret; and their marriage is metaphorically equivalent to the critical article Corvick proposed to write. In the one, he plans to "utter—oh so quietly!—the unimagined truth" (p. 260); the other takes place " 'very quietly'—as quietly, I seemed to make out, as he meant in his article to bring out his *trouvaille*" (p. 262). More accurately, since the article is never completed, although the marriage is consummated and the secret revealed, it seems that the union of Corvick and Gwendolen actually completes the critical act begun in the article, provides its missing "climax" (p. 263). Corvick's critical success, whether or not he has actually discovered the Vereker secret, amounts to a genuine union with (the figure of) text, Gwendolen, and so brings with it a true prize: the appeasement of desire. But which text does Gwendolen represent? Is she the Vereker text? Everything in the tale assimilates her to Vereker but declares her difference. Is she the text Corvick himself produces, as the coincidence of his writing and their union suggests? She stands everywhere else for the creative text, not the critical text (she does not review, she is reviewed). What she figures must be the point of union, where the critical text (Corvick) encounters the literary text proper (Vereker); but this means that she must also figure a necessary "drift" between Vereker's text and Corvick's critical account of it, a noncoincidence between the two, since it is with Gwendolen (and not with Vereker) that Corvick consummates the union.

In this light, one understands both the import of the narrator's courting of Gwendolen and the reasons for his failure. She embodies for him the secret, since possession of the secret, for Corvick, was equivalent to possession of Gwendolen. But the secret as such is not to be possessed; it is a textual phenomenon, as Corvick's actual critical performance illustrates; and its "possession" is, in fact, an act of intimacy with *text*. Gwendolen is the *reward* of an already successful critical performance, not a means of achieving such success.[7]

What the narrator encounters in Gwendolen, consequently, in pursuing the secret, is what he earlier encountered in Vereker, not the availability of the secret but the resistance of a text. Everything, in fact, now repeats itself, but raised to a higher power of frustration —that is, neurotically. Gwendolen's reserve "was something of a shock to me" (p. 264).

Certainly it added at the same time hugely to the price of Vereker's secret, precious as the mystery already appeared. I may as well confess abjectly that Mrs. Corvick's unexpected attitude was the final tap on the nail that was to fix my luckless idea, convert it into the obsession of which I'm for ever conscious.

But this only helped me the more to be artful, to be adroit, to allow time to elapse before renewing my suit. (p. 265)

The word "suit" at this stage still refers only to the narrator's request that she reveal the secret, but it anticipates quite clearly his velleitary courtship: they are, for him, one and the same action. And in giving herself finally to Drayton Deane, Gwendolen simply underscores the failure that, given the narrator's false premises, was inevitable. His jealousy of Deane then repeats his envy of Corvick, just as his desire for Gwendolen (her secret) repeats his desire for Vereker (his secret); and his exclusion from the new marriage convinces him of his "impotence," a powerlessness both sexual and critical. "His wife had told him what I wanted and he was amiably amused at my impotence" (p. 273). But what in fact the marriage *does* finally lay bare is the total insubstantiality of the "secret" as such—as object of desire and fomenter of envy—for it eventually becomes clear not only that Deane does not know the secret but that he is ignorant of its very existence. It is the narrator who will have to reveal it to him. In its consequences, then, the secret functions in exactly the same way, whether it be "real" or merely an "effect of text."

The Story of the Story

But what does it mean that finally the narrator tells Deane the story of the Vereker secret, communicating to him his own obsession and producing in him a retrospective jealousy of Gwendolen akin to his own frustrated desire? The story thus repeats itself once again, with the narrator now performing something like the initiatory function formerly accomplished by Vereker. But *this* narrative act is also, in the most specific sense, a *mise en abyme* of the act of narration that constitutes the tale of "The Figure in the Carpet."

I told him in a word just what I've written out here. He listened with deepening attention, and I became aware, to my surprise, by his ejaculations, by his questions, that he would have been after all not unworthy to be trusted by his wife. So abrupt an experience of her want of trust had now a disturbing effect on him; but I saw the immediate shock throb away little by little and then gather again into waves of wonder and curiosity—waves that promised, I could perfectly judge, to break in the end with the fury of my own highest tides. I may say that to-day as victims of unappeased desire there isn't a pin to choose between us. The poor man's state is almost my consolation; there are really moments when I feel it to be quite my revenge. (p. 277)

The story told to Deane is "just what I've written out here." Must the reader, then, react to the text in the way that Deane does to the story, becoming with respect to the secret as much the victim of "unappeased desire" as the narrator himself? The empirical reader has, of course, over the fictional narratee (Deane) the advantage of access to certain contextual information and can see, for example, the parallel between the way Vereker acted toward the narrator at Bridges and the way the narrator now acts toward Deane. Here, as there, it is a matter of repairing a social gaffe; the narrator acts out of contrition. "My compunction was real; I laid my hand on his shoulder" (p. 277). Here as there, power is exerted by the revelation that there is a secret, combined with a failure to reveal the secret—by the production of fascination.

But the differences are equally obvious. Where Vereker spoke from a position of genuine superiority, the narrator speaks only out of impotence and rage: his purpose in inoculating the other with his own "unappeased desire" is to achieve "consolation" and "revenge." "Revenge," precisely—one may assume—for the *coup de maître* of Vereker, which has forever left the narrator in a position of subservience, exclusion, and despair; "consolation" for the frustration and powerlessness in which he must consequently live. The power of "text" is here being used to put Deane in the same position of impotence as the one in which the narrator finds himself. The reader is invited by this passage to join the group of the defeated, of those whose desire has been aroused for a satisfaction that now—now that Vereker is dead ("Who alas but he had the authority?" p. 274), now that Corvick and Gwendolen are dead, now that the tale is over—has no hope of being provided. But the same reader is simultaneously warned: to respond as Drayton Deane responds to the narrator's story is to play into the narrator's hand and to offer oneself as a victim: an object of revenge and a means of consolation for a narrator who thus, strangely, comes out in the end as one still unappeased, but as a kind of victor.

In light of this ending, it is not surprising that "The Figure in the Carpet" has been the object of much critical discussion: it actually offers itself as a critical war-horse by indicating that criticism is an appropriate reader's response to the text. It *is* surprising, however, that so much of the critical response has fallen into the mold the text seems to be warning against. Drayton Deane is the model for all those critics who allow their focus to be determined by the narrator's obsession with Vereker's "secret." Given the difficulty of responding concretely to the question "What is the secret?" most discussion has, of course, centered on the narrator's suggestion that there is no secret, that "Vereker had made a fool of me" (p. 236). *Is* there a secret? Opinion has been divided among those who believe that there is no secret and for whom the tale exposes the meretriciousness of a literary world in which the pretentiousness of authors is matched only by the "evasion, deviousness and imposture" of criticism[8] and those who believe in the secret. These latter critics discuss the reasons why the narrator's manifest failure to discover the secret contrasts with the presumed success of Corvick and Gwendolen (the narrator may be guilty of a disqualifying inability to love)[9] — unless they assume, with Quentin Anderson,[10] that all the characters are victims of such failure (in which case, George, and later Gwendolen, are guilty of misrepresenting the truth).

In recent years, it is true, a structuralist and poststructuralist conception of text has begun to produce less literal views of what might be at stake in the notion of textual secrecy. Where Shlomith Rimmon has set out with exemplary clarity and exhaustiveness the conflicting evidence that makes the traditional questions (What is the secret? Is there a secret?) undecidable,[11] Tzvetan Todorov's reading of James's oeuvre as a whole in the light of the tale has proved influential in shifting the focus of critical discussion from the secret as some entity, definable per se (although undefined), to the idea of a necessary absence that founds text:

Le secret de Henry James (et, pourquoi pas, celui de Vereker) réside précisément en l'existence d'un secret, d'une cause absolue et absente, ainsi que dans l'effort pour percer ce secret à jour, pour rendre l'absence présente. Le secret de Vereker nous est donc communiqué, et ceci de la seule manière possible: s'il avait été nommé, il n'aurait plus existé, or c'est précisément son existence qui forme le secret.[12]

Such a conception, which views the secret as significant only as a necessary precondition for the existence of the narrator's tale, does not free critical perspectives from sharing the narrator's essential focus, however; on the contrary, it makes of the unavailable secret as object of the quest, the constitutive component of the text. More recently, taking a cue from Todorov (while pointing out that James's text allows not only for the cause to be absent but also for it to be nonexistent) and another from Iser's distinction between the positivist critical assumptions of the narrator and those he assigns to Corvick,[13] J. Hillis Miller has produced a brilliant deconstructionist reading of the "unreadability" of the tale, suggesting that S. Rimmon's conflicting interpretations are not so much alternative as they are intertwined, just as the word "figure" itself refers simultaneously to the secret as something hidden (for which the "figure" substitutes) and as something visible, "the overall pattern of Vereker's work." "Neither of these ideas is possible without the other."[14]

This second group of critics, although they "side" with Vereker (that is, the rhetorical sophistication of text) against the naïveté of the narrator's questions, are still persisting in defining the critical issues in terms of the narrator's quest. The present reading cannot claim to have escaped these same issues, so far; nor does it claim that they are irrelevant. It does note the irony, however, that all these descendants of Drayton Deane jostle like James's characters for Corvick's "crown" or "critical laurel." There are proponents of certainty who strive to produce a reading that will correct or displace previous readings judged inadequate or erroneous; and proponents of uncertainty, whose tactic consists of siding with the "winner" (Iser sides with Corvick against the narrator; the deconstructionists with Vereker), or else of adopting, as Rimmon does, the position of neutral adjudicator—which gives Hillis Miller the opportunity, in his polemic with her,[15] to achieve a kind of mastery on the critical plane by denouncing other critics' desire to master the text. In short, the rivalry, the struggle for power among James's characters is still pursued in the discourse of their descendants; and by a kind of transference identified by Shoshana Felman apropos of *The Turn of the Screw*,[16] the critical history of the work reproduces what, precisely, is at issue in the work.[17]

This near unanimity in adopting the concerns of the narrator is a sign of overexclusive interest in, and submission to, what Barthes would call the hermeneutic code of the text.[18] This effect results, in turn, most obviously, from the power of the characteristically Jamesian use of the "reflector," a narrative perspective strictly limited to the "consciousness" of an individual observer (in this case, the narrator). In principle, this device is mimetic and realistic in function: it is a representation of the limitations that a given individual must recognize as those of his or her own consciousness of the world. As James puts it in the Preface to *The Ambassadors*: ". . . Strether's sense of these things, and Strether's only, should avail me for showing them; I should know them but through his own groping knowledge of them, since his very gropings would figure among his most interesting motions. . . ."[19] But the device has also a more technical effect, which itself has a double aspect. It serves to produce enigma, or at least uncertainty, on the narrative plane and at the same time to focus the attention of the reader (who must espouse the narrative consciousness) onto that enigma, the unknowable object of the consciousness. In this way—which corresponds perhaps to what the Preface to *The Ambassadors* calls the "grace of intensity"[20]—the device serves less as a mimetic technique and more to produce an effect of "literariness." Since this is the secret of the textual "game" being played with the reader, it is a means of inviting participation in a fascinating game of skill—or of chance?—while ensuring that it cannot be "won." In terms of the theoretical framework of this book, the Jamesian "reflector" is a means of textual self-contextualization that, paradoxically, however, produces a crucially *limited* context; and it is in turn this limitation of context that produces the uncertainty, a degree of unreadability within a general readability, that is here the marker of the literary text.

Examples from tales related to "The Figure in the Carpet" may support this contention. They both produce a central figure whose consciousness focuses the narrative, but who is excluded, like the narrator of "The Figure in the Carpet," from carnal knowledge: "romance" or marriage. The novella *In the Cage* has as "reflector" a lady telegraphist who by virtue of her employment is partially privy to the evolution of a romantic involvement between two of her customers. The focus of consciousness is perhaps on this romantic relationship; but the text's subject is much more clearly the "gropings" of the partially informed, though crucially *un*informed, consciousness at the narrative center; and the literariness of this effect of uncertainty is underscored by the enigmatic text of the telegrams, which—like the communications of Corvick in "The Figure in the

Carpet"—function, *en abyme,* as models of textuality: "Everard, Hôtel Brighton, Paris. Only understand and believe. 22d to 26th, and certainly 8th and 9th. Perhaps others. Come. Mary." or: "Miss Dolman, Parade Lodge, Parade Terrace, Dover. Let him instantly know right one, Hôtel de France, Ostend. Make it seven nine four nine six one. Wire me alternative Burfield's."[21]

In "The Lesson of the Master," the discourse of an established author, St. George, in his book-lined study ("the room's a fine lesson in concentration") is the model of literary discourse ("The outer world . . . was so successfully excluded, and within the rich, patronizing square . . . the dream-figures, the summoned company, could hold their particular revel"). But, in retrospect, to Paul Overt, the young and aspiring author who is at once its recipient and the narrative "reflector," it is uncomfortably ambiguous. Was the advice that turned Overt away from Miss Fancourt in order to be a better writer genuine in its intention, or "Was it a plan—was it a plan?"—a plan destined to enable St. George to marry her himself? There can be no answer within the context provided by Paul Overt's limited knowledge of the context, although quite obviously the question is not in and of itself unanswerable (since St. George must know the answer).[22] There is an obvious analogy with "The Figure in the Carpet," although we cannot be *sure* that Hugh Vereker knows any more than he actually says about his supposed secret (nor indeed that he could ever *say* whatever it is he actually knows). But the sense of frustration, of an unnecessary and arbitrary limit, that the reader is expected to feel from awareness of the constraints (intellectual, psychological, social) that limit the narrator's scope and prevent him from asking those questions that might—just possibly— prove truly disambiguating, *is* inscribed in the text: the impatience of Corvick, mentioning "half-a-dozen questions he wished to goodness I had had the gumption to put" (pp. 237-238), is our own.

Textual uncertainty, then, is a function of textual limitation of context (itself a product of strict narrative perspectivism). And curiously, a device that is in principle mimetic serves to mark off the text as "literary," by contrast, precisely, with those everyday or "practical" situations in which it is possible to disambiguate the uncertain, or at least to launch a process tending toward disambiguation, through a strategy of extension of context. One cannot ask the Jamesian text any questions beyond those to which the reflecting narrative consciousness, itself striving to understand, has already provided an answer. In this sense, the text is as freestanding, as divorced from the network of infinite relationships constitutive of the canvas of "life" as the presumed monadic consciousness of an "individual" personality is divorced from all others. This is how James solves the problem defined in the Preface to *Roderick Hudson*: "Really, universally, relations stop nowhere, and the exquisite problem of the artist is eternally but to draw, by a geometry of his own, the circle within which they shall happily *appear* to do so."[23] But, as Fredric Jameson has pointed out,[24] this solution implies textual self-contextualization in terms of a bourgeois ideology of the individual, on the one hand, and, on the other, in terms of a reified conception of "literature"—as a specialized function autonomous from "life"—that is characteristic of the culture of capitalism.

Although it is true, however, that the text of "The Figure in the Carpet" offers the reader no access to a consciousness other than that of the narrator, it is not true that the state of mind in which the narrator communicates, out of a need for consolation and revenge, his own obsession to Drayton Deane is necessarily the same state of mind that presides over the narration of the tale itself. In subtle but telling ways, the narrative text distances itself from the mood—of obsession and frustration—and the situation—of involvement and unselfconsciousness—in which the tale is told to Deane. That telling is itself the object of a narration and has its place in a series of events from which the narration stands at a remove. The distance is firmly established in the opening lines of the tale, in the tense system that sets apart the moment of actual narration (the narrator has already gone some way along "the little measure of [his] course") from the earlier period ("I had done a few things and earned a few pence") when, thanks to Corvick, he got his "real start." The essential difference between the time of narration and that of the events themselves is more specifically formulated, however, some way further into the text:

Pen in hand, this way, I live the time over, and it brings back the oddest sense of my having been, both for months and in spite of myself, a kind of coerced spectator. All my life had taken refuge in my eyes, which the procession of events appeared to have committed itself to keep astare. (p. 261)

A time, then, for seeing (the eyes "astare") versus a time for writing ("pen in hand"); however, this distinction is not quite reducible to Genette's famous discrimination within narrative "point of view" between "who sees" and "who speaks/writes."[25] More relevant is Mieke Bal's concept of embedded "focalizations,"[26] for, as I will try to show, the narrator-writer, "pen in hand," is also one who sees, as spectator of a comic show, whereas in his earlier role as "hero" of the adventure, his experience consisted in *becoming*—through his enforced role as voyeur—one who sees, that is, the narrator as writer. In short, this narrative, like so many others, concerns the coming into being of the conditions of its own existence, the gradual *mise en place* of the situation of its telling.

A clear sign of this evolution is the way, as the text develops, the self-irony that the narrator-writer directs against his own past self, the narrator-hero as young man, gradually fades, and the distance between the two decreases. The young author of what Vereker calls "the usual twaddle" is seen by the narrative as self-important (aware, for example, of his own "obvious fitness for the task" of reviewing Vereker, [p. 219]), insecure (cf. his rearrangement of Lady Jane's display of periodicals so as to correct the "careless inconspicuity" of *The Middle* [p. 223]), inexperienced and jejune (capable, for instance, of thinking of a famous author's presence in his bedroom as "the brilliancy of his being there" [p. 228])—and, seen through Vereker's eyes, he is clearly a comic figure ("I hadn't lost my power to minister to his mirth," p. 239), unaware of what makes him ridiculous. He will remain obsessed and self-centered to the end (cf. his vexation at having to see to his brother's health in Germany just when Corvick is due back in England and, of course, his fixation on the innocent Drayton Deane). But, toward the end of the tale, he himself is already able to refer offhandedly and Vereker-like to "the usual ineptitudes" (p. 268) that greet the author's last novel: he has grown, learned something, and matured in some sense, as a result of the Vereker experience, which was, as the narrator-writer says, "to turn me out for more profundity" (p. 223).

And this is due not to critical success but to the salutary impact of a failure, his inability to discover the Vereker secret, his "impotence." Even while continuing to be plagued by curiosity and to envy Corvick and Gwendolen Erme their success, he derives from his "disconcerted state" (p. 244), his "bewildered hours" (p. 265) in the role of "coerced spectator," a benefit not available to those more skillful (or luckier?) members of the critical profession; and that is the gift of irony, for *they* are so caught up in their pursuit of the critical prize that they lack all sense of distance and proportion. Gwendolen "had indeed no sense of humour" and is "one of those persons whom you want, as the phrase is, to shake" (p. 242); Corvick, in his turn, is manic, "like nothing, I told him, but the maniacs who embrace some bedlamitic theory of the cryptic character of Shakespeare" (p. 244). The narrator sees him as "a chess-player bent with a silent scowl, all the lamplit winter, over his board and his moves" (p. 245). These "grim gamblers" (p. 250), totally involved as they are in those "circles" in which "we were all constructed to evolve" (p. 272), are living what the narrator-hero already sees, even as he is participating in it, as a *melodrama*.[27] Gwendolen has just received the crucial telegram from Rapallo: "At sight of me she flourished a paper with a movement that brought me straight down, the movement with which, in melodramas, handkerchieves and reprieves are flourished at the foot of the scaffold" (p. 255). And it is, of course, to this melodramatic universe of involvement that the narrator introduces Deane at the end, having for a long time eyed him ("It was therefore from her husband I could not remove my eyes," p. 273) under the mistaken impression that he was already involved in it, knew the secret, but "never told the only truth that seemed to me in these (*sic*) days to signify" (p. 272). The narrator's telling of his tale to Drayton Deane has as its function to convert a personage who is outside of the melodrama ("He wasn't acting . . ." p. 275) to one who, at first "astonished," "disconcerted" (p. 276), is by the end of the tale completely involved in it. This is what constitutes the narrator's revenge.

But it signals also, for the narrator, not just the achievement—or more accurately the near achievement—of consolation and revenge (which imply his own continued involvement in the melodrama) but also a further stage in the process of his liberation from it, an act *almost* of exorcism and release. In passing on his obsession to Deane, he does not divest himself of it ("to-day as victims of unappeased desire there isn't a pin to choose between us," p. 272), but he does manifest the aptitude to stand back and judge that has been implied all along by his role as spectator in the melodrama: "I *saw* the immediate shock throb away . . . ," "waves that promised, I could perfectly *judge*, to break . . . ." This is the judgment that marks the future narrator-writer, whose distance from the events is reflected in remarks such as "the only truth that *seemed to me in these days* to signify,"[28] a judgment that he will bring to bear in his narration, not only upon others—Corvick, Gwendolen, Deane—but also upon himself.

A melodrama contemplated with a sense of distance ceases to be a melodrama and becomes comic. Thus, it comes about that the generic intertext of "The Figure in the Carpet"—Genette's arche-text[29]—is a double one. If it is involvement that produces the melo-dramatic, it is the narrator's achieved distance that gives his text the comic flavor criticism often remarks. If he was once a "coerced spectator," he is now a more wryly amused one. Thus, the rapid series of deaths—old Mrs. Erme, Corvick, Vereker, Vereker's wife, Gwendolen—that marks the end of the tale, a "procession of events" indeed calculated to keep the narrator's (and the reader's) eyes astare (with disbelief?), has something of the melodramatic—and something of the comic. The social satire in the text (Lady Jane is its main butt) not only acts as a *pendant* to the satire of the literary crowd, with their "intellectual pride" (p. 242), their self-importance and self-involvement, but also signals a narrative distance easily transferable from one group to the other. What is most significant, however, for my present argument about the comic quality of the text is that, emanating as it does from the vision of the mature narrator, the narrator as writer, "pen in hand," it presupposes also an audience similarly mature and as much divorced from the world of professional critics as he has come to be himself. (That a professional critic may equally be divorced from the world of criticism is what the narrator's example makes clear: he remains a practicing critic even while narrating the text of his tale.) Those who are as humorless as Gwendolen and as manic as Corvick will not perceive, or at least not appreciate, the comedy. This projected audience, situated outside the narrow "circle" of literature, of course, gives the text, as communicational act, a very different function. Much less concerned with the problematics of Vereker's secret, such an audience will see rather the depiction of a specific social group—a profession not unlike Molière's doctors—an analysis of the conditions under which that profession functions, and a judgment of its stature in human terms. It will also read a story of the "getting of wisdom" —of that form of wisdom that is the indispensable precondition of the comic vision. Literature, here, therefore, is not confined to the literati: on the contrary, it is addressed to a readership that embraces the nonliterati, a readership whose interests are those of "life."

Telling and Writing

The empirical reader of "The Figure in the Carpet" who, allowing the focus of his or her reading to be controlled by the circumscribed consciousness of the narrator-hero, slips into the role of Drayton Deane, has consequently an important further evolution to accomplish. A victim, like the narrator, of "unappeased desire," this reader's "consternation" should, in turn, produce a distancing effect that will make the reader a more suitable audience for the narrator-writer, with his comic vision of the melodrama of critical involvement. The reader's evolution, in short, mimes that of the narrator, who thus stands, in this sense also, as the figure of his own text. This definition of the reader's role as a getting of wisdom is perhaps disappointing and banal: it certainly defines "The Figure in the Carpet" as a "readerly" and mimetic text, a comic-realist survey of a segment of the social world involving literary presuppositions that are a far cry from the heady and problematic atmosphere of the conversation by the fireside. But to be content with such a formulation is to ignore what is at once most significant about the narrative situation of "The Figure in the Carpet" and most original in terms of the traditional narrative of *Bildung,* that is, the third intertextual genre to which, by virtue of the narrator's conversion from critic to autobiographer, the tale comes to adhere. Here, the getting of wisdom—on the narrator's part and, by extension, on the reader's part—leads to no abatement of obsession: melodrama and comedy, spectatorhood and involvement, coexist, the ironic autobiographer remains the involved critic.

In the episode in which the narrator tells his tale to Drayton Deane, the key sentence reads: "I told him in a word *just what I've written out here*" (my emphasis). Can it be that this equivalence between the tale Deane hears and the tale the reader reads extends not only—as has so far been assumed—to the content but also to the manner of the narration (the irony, the sense of comedy)? It is easy to read the sentence as implying a more complete identity between the two acts of storytelling. "In a word" does not mean "succinctly" here but has the force of "to be brief," "to summarize"; so it does not imply a difference in length (and hence in tone) between them. To say "what I've written *out* here" (as opposed to just "written") seems to suggest a certain derivation of the written text from the spoken original; and "*just* what I've written out" further strengthens the idea of the two narratives' identity.[30] Only the difference between telling and writing out is specifically reported as significant. If indeed the two narratives are identical in tone, it means that the obsessed narrator, bent on consolation and revenge at Deane's expense, is also already the ironist who is responsible for the narration of "The Figure in the Carpet." But this in its turn must mean that the ironic narrator of "The Figure in the Carpet" is not necessarily free of obsession, involvement, unappeased desire, and the need for revenge and consolation. And the text indeed acknowledges that this is the case: "*to-day* as victims of unappeased desire there isn't a pin to choose between us" (p. 277) and earlier: "I may as well confess abjectly that Mrs. Corvick's unexpected attitude was the final tap on the nail that was to fix fast my luckless idea, convert it into the obsession *of which I'm for ever conscious*" (p. 265) (my emphases).

It seems, then, that the text of "The Figure in the Carpet" functions at one and the same time as a self-involved act of revenge and as ironically distanced comedy. Indeed, is not its very irony interpretable as a manifestation of revenge and a means of consolation? Irony is perhaps the form of satisfaction most readily available to the impotent, the type of superiority that, like the narrator's *knowing* involvement of Deane in obsession, his judicious watching of the latter's nascent curiosity and desire, fulfills the need for power of those who are otherwise powerless. To ironize is not to have escaped the reach of coerced spectatorhood but rather to have realized the full implications of such a role, for it is a way of marking one's distance while remaining involved—and the reader who follows the narrator's evolution from involvement to distance is not thereby guaranteed any escape from the text's obsession either but remains within the range of its fascination and narrative power, a "coerced spectator" in turn.

What perhaps confirms this analysis is the relative paucity of information concerning the situation of the narrator-writer, "pen in hand," as opposed to the narrator-hero whose circumscribed consciousness controls the narrative perspective and who tells the tale to Deane at the end. Apart from what can be extrapolated from his generic allegiances, we have no answers to questions such as: What exactly is the point of his narration? What use is the reader to make of the text? The narrator-writer is a shadowy and wholly undetermined figure, his separate existence defined only by that contradictory gap between "the obsession of which I'm for ever conscious" and "the only truth that seemed to me in these days to signify." By contrast with texts in which the general narrative contract is more clearly and more specifically distinguished from that of the internal narratives (for example, "Sylvie" or "Sarrasine"), the possibility of confusion between the narrator-writer and the narrator-hero is consequently very great. Except for that "pen in hand," they are indeed, to all intents and purposes, identical.

But the exception is significant: it means that in becoming a writer, the narrator is making for his text the claims of literature. What distinguishes his telling of the tale to Deane and his present writing is a difference in situation that is very specifically registered by the text. "I told him"—this is a precise and closed narrative situation, defined by the identities of narrator and narratee, respectively, the obsessed but ironic teller and the at first ignorant, then disconcerted, and finally equally obsessed listener. But "what I've written out here" refers to a much more open communicational situation, in which audience is unspecified, and the shifter "here" leaves equally open the specification of what, in fact, has been written, since the content of this self-reference (such is the nature of shifters) can only be a function of the communicational situation itself. This is true also, finally, of "I," whose existence as the otherwise asemantic subject of the writing depends similarly on the undetermined relationship of reader to text.

Therefore, there is here a communicational situation of great indeterminacy, an openness that contrasts strikingly with the focused perspective and circumscribed context that the consciousness of the narrator-hero forces upon the addressee. And where the latter produces interpretational uncertainty, this new situational openness pluralizes the text by positing the relevance of the broadest possible range of interpretive situations. Such indeterminacy is clearly no less significant as a marker of "literature" than the uncertainty of closed narrative perspective, and it produces a communicational situation no less unusual in terms of "ordinary" experience. But whereas perspectivism produces text as a closed and reified experience, it is here opened up, through the transparency of its narrative stance, onto the infinite possible situations of "life" itself. What we have been calling the narrator of "The Figure in the Carpet" is perhaps ultimately only a switching device, the embodiment of writing as the means whereby the closed perspective of textual "individuality" becomes available to the unlimited world of readers.

It is insufficient, then, to say that "The Figure in the Carpet" is both melodrama (an obsessive and fascinated tale transmitting its obsession and fascination to the hearer) and comedy (an ironically distanced vehicle for satiric observation), although it *is*, inextricably, both of these. It defines itself as a "telling" incorporated within a "writing"—a telling that is both ironic and involved, a writing that, equally, is obsessed but distanced. A telling, however, whose finality is to be *telling*, that is, to have a specific impact comparable to that of the narrator's tale on Drayton Deane, and a writing whose function is to be a writing *out*, in other words, to be addressed outward, out of the closed situation of individual communication toward an undefined world of possibility, to which it transmits, or redirects, the "telling" text. This is its function as autobiography, in which the circumscribed world controlled by the "auto-" (individual consciousness) and the open situation of writing (the "-graphy") coincide, brought together by an element of life (the "-bio-") that is, here, that almost imperceptible fissure in the narrator's identity by which he is both teller and writer. The concept of literary communication to which the text subscribes is consequently one that assumes the essential problematics of the "readerly" text, one whereby a circumscribed relationship involving a carefully programmed individual reader in the grip of a monadic, "telling" text doubles simultaneously with a text that remains open and looks beyond the individual reader to an undefined world in which "writing" is available for a whole history of interpretation.

The duality of telling and writing in "The Figure in the Carpet" is not without analogy to the doubleness of "Un cœur simple." Mimetic duplicity has the compelling force of "telling," while textual simplicity, like "writing," presupposes a more simple and open text-reader relationship. But where Flaubert equates involvement and frustration with the social world and loving simplicity with aesthetic relationships, it is, to the contrary, the little self-enclosed world of letters that James sees as obsessed, neurotic, and sexual and the wider, unforeseeable world of society and history that offers a salving distance, and a broader context. The result is that, whereas the Flaubert text defines its situation as an invitation to love, the James story is not far from situating its reader as a "coerced spectator" — one who, like the narrator in both the "telling" and the "writing," is at once involved and distanced, obsessed and ironic. "You fire me," the narrator had said to Vereker in the fireside interview (p. 232), "as I've never been fired" — this state of arousal in him (while Corvick and Gwendolen achieve consummation, and death) is never satisfied and never subsides. It defines his life, and it is the same state he communicates (through telling) to Deane and (through writing) to the reader. The function of his text is to produce, through a combination of involving and distancing techniques (whose ultimate model is, of course, the rhetorical tactics of Vereker) an "unappeased desire" that makes the reader a voyeur of the text, "out in the cold" yet intrigued by a sense of "inner meaning." This is not quite seduction, nor is it a "simple" invitation to love; it is a holding off combined with an intense deployment of techniques of involvement. We are already quite close to the situational themes of "The Dead," in which the "writerly" text fuels desire through refusal, exclusion, and exile.

NOTES

1. Page references are to *The Novels and Tales of Henry James* (New York Edition), 15 (New York: Augustus M. Kelley, 1970 [originally, Scribner's, 1909]), 217-277.

2. See H. James, *The Art of the Novel: Critical Prefaces* (New York: Scribner's, 1938), p. 228; also New York Edition, 15, p. xv.

3. See *The Act of Reading: A Theory of Aesthetic Response* (Baltimore: Johns Hopkins University Press, 1978), 3-10 ("Henry James, *The Figure in the Carpet:* In Place of an Introduction").

4. On the paradox that there is no secret except in the divulgence, see my "Le secret est un œuf: Lecture d'une fable de La Fontaine," *Versants*, 2 (1982), 75-85.

5. A technique whose relevance the text implies by its mimesis of it in the final conversation between Vereker and the narrator: " 'I have told somebody,' I panted, 'and I'm sure that person will by this time have told somebody else! It's a woman into the bargain.' — 'The person you've told?' — 'No, the other person' " (p. 239).

6. Compare particularly the discussion between the narrator and Gwendolen as to whether the "immense" secret can be "got into a letter" (where "letter" is readable as a figure of textuality) (p. 252) and the metaphor finally produced by Gwendolen that makes the unfinished critical article, in intention, a work of art: "that great study which was to have been a supreme literary portrait, a kind of critical Vandyke or Velasquez" (p. 266).

7. It is worth noting, in confirmation of this, that, whereas the narrator courts Gwendolen with a view to being able, as a result, to produce a critical text, both Corvick (pp. 221, 250) and Deane (p. 267) (i.e., the two successful suitors) use critical texts (relating to Gwendolen's work) as a means of courting her.

8. See G. A. Finch, "A Retreading of James's Carpet," *Twentieth Century Literature*, 14 (1968), 98-101 (quotation, p. 100); and already, much earlier, Perry D. Westbrook, "The Supersubtle Fry," *Nineteenth Century Fiction*, 8 (1953), 134-140.

9. See Seymour Lainoff, "Henry James's 'The Figure in the Carpet': What Is Critical Responsiveness?" *Boston University Studies in English*, 5 (1961), 122-128 (in which Deane is linked with the narrator); and Leo B. Levy, "A Reading of 'The Figure in the Carpet,' " *American Literature*, 33 (1962), 457-465 (in which Deane is grouped with the successful critics).

10. This was the seminal reading, in *The American Henry James* (New Brunswick, N.J.: Rutgers University Press, 1957), 148-149: "The critics in *The Figure in the Carpet* . . . have before them an authentically great novelist, whose intention they cannot discover because they have no power to love."

11. *The Concept of Ambiguity: The Example of James* (Chicago: University of Chicago Press, 1977).

12. *Poétique de la prose* (Paris: Éd. du Seuil, 1971), 151-185 ("Le secret du récit"), quotation, p. 183.

13. *The Act of Reading*, 3-10.

14. "The Figure in the Carpet," *Poetics Today*, 1, 3 (spring 1980), 107-118, quotation, p. 114. See also Suzanne Kappeler's argument that, in James, "with respect to the literary text, we have to assume a total relativism, a scepticism towards any reconstruction of the plane of reference . . ." in *Writing and Reading in Henry James* (New York: Columbia University Press, 1980), p. 55.

15. See S. Rimmon-Kenan, "Deconstructive Reflections on Deconstruction: In Reply to Hillis Miller," *Poetics Today*, 2, 1b (winter 1980-1981), 185-188; and J. Hillis Miller, "A

Guest in the House: A Reply to Shlomith Rimmon-Kenan's Reply," *Poetics Today*, 2, 1b (winter 1980-1981), 189-191.

16. "Turning the Screw of Interpretation," *Yale French Studies*, 55/56 (1977), 94-207. See also Norman J. Holland, "Re-covering 'The Purloined Letter': Reading as a Personal Transaction," in S. Suleiman and I. Crosman, eds., *The Reader in the Text: Essays on Audience and Interpretation* (Princeton, N.J.: Princeton University Press, 1980), 350-370.

17. Less mimetic criticism from which I have benefited includes: H. Cixous, "Henry James: L'Écriture comme placement ou de l'ambiguïté de l'intérêt," *Poétique*, 1 (1970), 35-50; Jean Perrot, "L'Anamorphose dans les romans d'Henry James," *Critique*, 383 (avril 1979), 334-354, and "Énigme et fiction métalinguistique chez James," *Poétique*, 45 (février 1981), 53-66; J.-B. Pontalis, *Après Freud* (Paris: Gallimard, 1971), 336-355 ("Le lecteur et son auteur: À propos de deux récits de Henry James"). Of these, only the last includes a detailed study of "The Figure in the Carpet."

18. *S/Z* (Paris: Éd. du Seuil, 1970).

19. *The Art of the Novel*, pp. 317-318.

20. *The Art of the Novel*, p. 318.

21. New York Edition, 11. Quotations on pp. 376, 425.

22. New York Edition, 15. Quotations on pp. 63, 64, 88.

23. *The Art of the Novel*, p. 5.

24. *The Political Unconscious* (Ithaca, N.Y.: Cornell University Press, 1981), 220-221.

25. See *Figures*, III (Paris: Éd. du Seuil, 1972).

26. See *Narratologie* (Paris: Klincksieck, 1977) and "Notes on Narrative Embedding," *Poetics Today*, 2, 2 (winter 1981), 41-59.

27. On the "melodrama of the interpretive consciousness" in James, see P. Brooks, *The Melodramatic Imagination* (New Haven, Conn.: Yale University Press, 1976), chapter 6, and especially the pages (from 173) concerning the "abyss" – "all the evacuated centers of meaning in the fiction that nonetheless animate lives, determine quests for meaning, and which confer on life, particularly on consciousness, the urgency and dramatics of melodrama" (pp. 173-174).

28. One would expect "those." "These," while marking distance by deixis (a distance reinforced by the past-tense verb), also expresses a sense of closeness that is consonant with the narrator's continuing involvement.

29. See *Introduction à l'architexte* (Paris: Éd. du Seuil, 1979).

30. Note, however, that, whereas the text cites the story told to Deane as its model, the only model it gives for this story is "just what I've written out here," that is, the text itself. Moreover, logically speaking, the last four sentences of the text (concerning Deane's reception of the tale) cannot form part of the tale Deane hears. In these two ways, the hierarchical priority of the text over the tale told to Deane is assured.

Chapter Eight
Gabriel Conroy Sings for His Supper,
or Love Refused ("The Dead")

> Little Tom Tucker sang for his supper.
> What shall we give him? White bread and butter.
> How shall he cut it without a knife?
> How shall he marry without a wife?

Parasites

Gabriel and Michael are the messenger angels, charged the one with the Annunciation, the other with heralding the Day of Judgment.[1] In "The Dead," Gabriel Conroy and Michael Furey figure in a story about messages, set at Epiphany time,[2] and inviting consideration of its own status as message, that is, its relationship to noise.

It is a commonplace of communication theory that there is no message without "noise": since there must always be a channel of communication, there is also a degree of interference between the message's transmission and its reception. But, putting it another way, this means that noise is a *condition* of communication and less an accidental condition of disorder, perhaps, opposing the message's order, than the fundamental and primary ongoing circumstance of chaos against which the message labors to constitute itself. If so, to be in touch with "noise" is to be in touch, not with some accidental happenstance, but with something fundamental, and indeed a message in its own right.

We know that in certain circumstances, say, the ringing of the telephone that interrupts the guests' conversation at the dinner table, noise *can* be a message in its own right. And my telephone conversation, when I answer the phone, becomes a message (or exchange of messages) against which the table talk now functions as "noise," just as the phone conversation is "noise" to the talk around the table. One message, therefore, can be noise to another, and that is why there may be rivalry between messages and a need to distinguish between them in terms, for example, of their quality, urgency, significance, or value. This is the issue raised in "The Dead" by the Misses Morkan's Twelfth Night party, with its music, speeches, dancing, laughter, and applause, for this social intercourse figures as noise against the background of which are received intimations of another sort, or epiphanies—manifestations that function in turn as cosmic noise interfering with the cozy world of the party.[3]

In an extraordinary book by Michel Serres, from which I have borrowed the example of the dinner conversation and the phone message,[4] a case is made for relating communicational "noise," as the *parasite* in the channel (the French word *parasite* translates "interference" or "static"), to parasitism in its biological and social senses: the organism that lodges in the host's body and derives life from it (and whose presence may sometimes be vital to the health and well-being of the host) and the guest who eats at the host's table without reciprocating in kind (but without whose presence, perhaps, the party would not "go"). "Sans lui," says Serres of the latter, "le festin n'est qu'un repas froid."[5]

Le parasite est invité à table d'hôte. Il doit, en retour, égayer les convives de ses histoires et de ses ris. En toute exactitude, il échange de bons morceaux contre de bons mots, il paie son repas, il l'achète en monnaie de langue. C'est le plus vieux métier du monde.[6]

Here is a description of a parasite that reads like a comment on the character of Gabriel Conroy, the person who, however uncomfortable and out of place he feels in the company of his two old aunts—"ignorant old women," as he thinks them[7]—their niece and their guests, is regarded by them as indispensable to the success of their gathering and who willingly carves the goose, supplies an after-dinner speech carefully calculated to please, and in an awkward moment provides relief in the form of an anecdote. In the English idiom, he sings for his supper, exchanging words for hospitality: and since he has artistic pretensions, as a school teacher with an awareness of the languages and culture of the Continent and as a book reviewer for *The Daily Express* (two other forms of parasitism), he can be seen as a figure of the artist as parasite. I mean the artist who is nourished materially, but also culturally and spiritually, by a society to which, in return, he gives words that please and entertain, words without which the party would not "go" and "le festin serait un repas froid"—the artist, then ("c'est le plus vieux métier du monde"), who prostitutes himself. But singing for one's supper is also a byword for exclusion, and the admonition to "sing for your supper" rings sometimes like the Ant's rejection of the Cicada, in La Fontaine:

Vous chantiez? j'en suis fort aise:
Et bien! dansez maintenant

—just so, the problem in "The Dead" will arise from the fact that parasitism as social inclusion is incompatible with another form of "parasitism" (as affinity with cosmic "noise") and, as such, amounts to an exclusion from love. As in the nursery rhyme, singing for one's supper poses Gabriel the problem of being married "without a wife."

Noise Within and Without

"It was always a great affair, the Misses Morkan's annual dance. . . . For years and years it had gone off in splendid style as long as anyone could remember . . ." (p. 175); that this should again be the case is the aunts' great concern, and the secret of their reliance on Gabriel. However, their soirée is readable, and in the context of *Dubliners* inescapably so, as a figure of Irish society or, more accurately, of Dublin life. Gabriel, in his speech, insists on the Irishness of the occasion and on the exemplary quality of the three ladies' hospitality:

Of one thing, at least, I am sure. As long as this one roof shelters the good ladies aforesaid . . . the tradition of genuine warm-hearted courteous Irish hospitality, which our forefathers have handed down to us and which we in turn must hand down to our descendants, is still alive among us.

A hearty murmur of assent ran around the table. (p. 203)

But there are, of course, many ironies here, and the culture being so warmly praised by the speech maker speedily reveals significant deficiencies when one takes the party as a genuine reflection of it. The absence of Miss Ivors, the militant nationalist ("It shot through Gabriel's mind that Miss Ivors was not there and that she had gone away discourteously") strikes a dissenting note amid the congeniality. And the living tradition of hospitality, as many readers have remarked, succeeds only partially in masking a pervasive sense of death, or at least of that moral "paralysis," the cultural "hemiplegia"[8] —half-life or half-death—that is a central concern of *Dubliners*.

For "tradition" it is easy to read "repetition," and to recall—thinking of Johnny the horse—that the Misses Morkan have been giving the same annual party, with the same guests, the same menu, the same entertainment, the same jokes and anecdotes and speeches, for "a good thirty years." "Never once had it fallen flat" (p. 175).

But the *danger* of its falling flat is always close to the consciousness of reader and characters alike, and the Misses Morkan and their guests (Gabriel foremost among them) work hard to ensure that everything goes off, as it should, "in splendid style" (p. 175). An awareness of the imminent death of the more aged participants (Aunt Julia and Mrs Malins) is complemented by more subtle hints of the "last end" (p. 201) toward which all are proceeding, and if Gretta is thought on her arrival to be "perished" with cold, it is Gabriel's turn, at the end, to dwell on thoughts of mortality ("Soon, perhaps, he would be sitting in that same drawing-room, dressed in black . . . . Yes, yes: that would happen soon" (p. 222). The "funferal," as Joyceans enjoy saying, is akin to a "funeral." Meanwhile, the cultural chatter of the party reveals a society isolated in its own provincialism, and turning—again like Johnny the horse—in the circle of its own past experience, a milieu in which not only is Browning alien but the opera singers of the local past are deemed superior to those of a European present that includes Caruso. And the few dissident voices (Gabriel with his partiality to Continental "fads" like galoshes, Bartell D'Arcy with his awareness of foreign musical life, and Mary Jane, who would "give anything to hear Caruso sing") serve largely to point up the general complacency.

A gloomy feast, then, were it not for the effort being made by those present to enjoy themselves and—on the part of those who, like Gabriel, are not enjoying themselves—to make the party nevertheless "go," for the others, at the price of words and actions that are, from one angle, warm and well intentioned; from another, forced, mendacious, or hypocritical. The irony is patent in the words of the ritual song with which the guests salute their hosts:

> For they are jolly gay fellows, [etc.]
> Which nobody can deny.
>
> Unless he tells a lie,
> Unless he tells a lie.

The cohesiveness of the group ("the singers turned towards one another, as if in melodious conference . . . then, turning once more towards their hostesses . . . ," p. 205) is at its height here, but their harmony is built, precisely, on a lie: the lie of their "jollity" and "gaiety," a lie akin to that of the toastmaster who calls the Misses Morkan "the Three Graces of the Dublin musical world" and wishes three "ignorant old women" "health, wealth, long life, happiness and prosperity" (p. 205). Without such lies, the feast would indeed be a cold one.

Putting this another way, the party appears poised precariously between the order of its harmony, warmth, and good feeling and the disorder—the sense of a dying world—that constantly threatens it. In similar fashion, music competes—as an expression of the festive mood—with noise. But the music is formalized and contained within the conventions of the well-programmed soirée. Aunt Julia sings her piece in a voice of great purity: "To follow the voice, without looking at the singer's face, was to feel and share the excitement of swift and secure flight" (p. 193); but the face bears a "haggard look" (p. 222) that foretells her death, and the choice of her aria, "Arrayed for the Bridal," contrasts pathetically and ludicrously with her spinsterhood and advanced age. As for Mary Jane's party piece, "full of runs and difficult passages," it "has no melody" for the listeners, who drift away bodily, or mentally (Gabriel thinks of death, connoted by the engravings of Romeo and Juliet and the little princes in the tower, and of the resentment he feels toward his dead mother); and they return just in time to furnish the lie of their acclamation. It is something of a relief, one feels in both cases, for the listeners to be able to lapse into the noise making of applause (be it genuine, as in Aunt Julia's case, or hypocritical, as in Mary Jane's); just as it is, perhaps, in the case of the acclamation that follows the rendition of "For they are jolly gay fellows" or the burst of "applause and laughter" that greets Gabriel's sally about the Three Graces. Such noise is a response to slight embarrassment. But it still has the quality of expressing social cohesion and harmony, as does the dancing, where, however, music borders more perilously still on disorder and disharmony. It is while dancing the lancers that Miss Ivors "picks her crow" with Gabriel; and in the preparatory hush preceding Gabriel's speech, one hears the piano "playing a waltz tune and . . . the skirts sweeping against the drawing-room door" (p. 202) (for the young people have supped first). So, it is against a background of insistent disturbance that he must make himself heard throughout his address, the parasite's words of comfort being themselves accompanied by the parasitical presence of noise in the communicational situation.

The self-same sound of waltzing had greeted Gabriel on his arrival at the party: "He waited outside the drawing-room door until the waltz should finish, listening to the skirts that swept against it and the shuffling of feet" (p. 179); and it accompanies the initial conversation between Gabriel and Gretta and their hostesses, itself punctuated by laughter (Gretta "broke out into a peal of laughter . . . . The two aunts laughed heartily too," p. 180). But noise, of course, characterizes the description of the whole party. The "clapping of hands" that signals the end of the waltz also accompanies Julia's announcement: "Here's Freddy" (p. 182) (a noisy entry that will be significantly repeated at a later point). Gabriel "recognized Freddy Malins' laugh. Then he went down the stairs noisily" (p. 182). Meanwhile, laughter and the excited clapping of hands accompanies Mr Browne's pleasantries and the organization of quadrilles (p. 183), and when Gabriel reappears with Freddy, "he was laughing heartily in a high key at a story which he had been telling Gabriel on the stairs" (pp. 184-185) (another anticipation of a significant later event). Soon Freddy is again exploding, in midnarration, "in a kink of high-pitched bronchitic laughter" (p. 185)—a first instance in the narrative of storytelling traversed by noise.

If the early stages of the party are thus interspersed with laughter and clapping, supper—announced by "the clatter of plates and knives" (p. 192)—is the occasion for considerable din: "There was a great deal of confusion and laughter and noise, the noise of orders and counter-orders, of knives and forks, of corks and glass-stoppers" (p. 197); and the aunts refuse for a long time to settle, "toddling around the table, walking on each other's heels, getting in each other's way and giving each other unheeded orders" (pp. 197-198). After a new "clatter of forks and spoons" (p. 200) accompanying dessert, the anticipatory lull preceding Gabriel's toast is "broken only by the noise of the wine and the unsettlings of chairs" while a few gentlemen pat the table, both as encouragement for the speaker and as "a signal for silence" (p. 201); the speech itself being given, as has been noted, against the background of waltzing in the next room.

At departure time, laughter again breaks out (Mary Jane's, Aunt Kate's, Mr Browne's [p. 206]); and general merriment accompanies Gabriel's anecdote of Johnny the horse (p. 208), the conclusion of which is greeted by renewed "peals of laughter" that are interrupted in turn by Freddy's "resounding knock at the hall door" (p. 208). As the guests enter their cab, there is "a great deal of confused talk." "Aunt Julia and Mary Jane helped the discussion from the doorstep with cross-directions and contradictions and abundance of laughter"

(p. 209). Finally, the cab "rattle[s] off" "amid a chorus of laughter and adieus" (p. 209). The relative silence of the walk, and drive, to the hotel and of Gabriel's and Gretta's *coucher* forms a perceptible contrast with all this festive noise.

And festive it is, warm and expressive of social cohesion, whatever communication disorder it may introduce into the situation. But it is associated also with a long series of small incidents—ineptnesses, gaffes, maladroit behavior, all the "noise" of social intercourse—that are themselves suggestive of an underlying cultural disarray. I am not thinking so much of the major divisions and dissensions that center mainly on Gabriel and D'Arcy, the two artist figures: the contrast between Continental culture and Dublin parochialism, that between the anglicized East and the deeper, rural roots of West Ireland, whence Gretta comes, and which Miss Ivors reproaches Gabriel for betraying (to these we will return). It is more a matter of a series of uncomfortable moments. The aunts are at first worried because Gabriel is late (p. 176); Freddy Malins, on the other hand, "always came late," but they are "dreadfully afraid that [he] may turn up screwed" (p. 176)—which proves to be the case (although this time he is only slightly tipsy). Gabriel's conversational failure with Lily, which draws a bitter retort, and his failure to make amends by a Christmas tip "discompose" him (p. 179) and crystallize his feelings of disquiet about the speech he has prepared: "Their grade of culture differed from his. He would only make himself ridiculous by quoting poetry to them which they could not understand . . . . His whole speech was a mistake from first to last" (p. 179)—this while he listens to the rustling and clacking and shuffling of the dancing within. The strained conversation about galoshes ("—O, on the Continent, murmured Aunt Julia, nodding her head slowly. Gabriel knitted his brows . . . ," p. 181) comes as a confirmation of this intuition.

But soon it is Mr Browne's turn to make three young ladies uncomfortable, by an innuendo in "a very low Dublin accent" (p. 183), and Mary Jane's to be embarrassed, "blushing and rolling up her music nervously" at the applause for her miscalculated show-piece (a lesson for Gabriel, this) (p. 187). Miss Ivors is a major source of social discomfort: not only does her accusation of "West Briton" grate on Gabriel so that he retorts "suddenly": "—O, to tell you the truth, I'm sick of my own country, sick of it!" (p. 189), but she goads him into public conflict with his wife over the proposed vacation in Galway (p. 191). Finally, she departs abruptly from the party before supper and on a most unconvincing excuse, leaving

Mary Jane "puzzled" (p. 196) and Gabriel reflecting that "she had gone away discourteously" (p. 203). Another center of disruption is Mr D'Arcy, who at first refuses to sing, provoking Gretta's opinion that he is "full of conceit" (p. 191), then sings (apparently for his own pleasure or at least on his own whim) just as the guests are departing (p. 210), and who, when reproached for having told a "great fib" in alleging a cold, responds "roughly" to poor Aunt Kate, leaving everyone "taken aback by his rude speech" and making it necessary for all to make embarrassed amends, the ones by displaying excessive solicitude for the slighted cold, the other by relating its history in circumstantial detail. (It is Mr D'Arcy, too, who, not realizing there is to be a toast, at first refuses wine.) But the gracious hostesses themselves are not exempt from social errors: Mary Jane's and Aunt Julia's musical performances are both, in different ways, poorly judged for the occasion; Aunt Kate gives "scandal" to Mr Browne, "who is of the other persuasion," by speaking ill of the Pope and working herself into an indecorous state of passion over her sister's eviction from the choir in favor of boy singers (p. 194). It is Kate, too, who incautiously expresses irritation with Mr Browne ("He has been laid on here like the gas all during the Christmas") before adding sheepishly, "I hope to goodness he didn't hear me" (p. 206).

It is against noise, then, both in the literal sense and as a metaphor of social ineptitude, that Gabriel works to maintain order. In spite of his own social lapses and mental discomfort, his behavior stands out on at least two occasions for its smoothness and felicity. The after-dinner speech is, of course, one of them, and the other is his telling of the story of the "old gentleman" and his horse Johnny. At departure time, there is an awkward pause in the hall while Gretta is still upstairs (her slowness, one remembers, is the reason for the couple's symmetrically late arrival). Gabriel smoothes over the moment of waiting with an amusing anecdote concerning a treadmill horse that, when taken out for a ride, ends up obstinately circling the statue of King Billy (that is, William of Orange, the victor of the Boyne and hence a major oppressor of Ireland). Critics, who seem to have read the account of "noise" at the party as simple, realistic detail (for they do not discuss it), have also universally interpreted this story in terms of its content, as a comment on the containment and mechanical repetition that characterize Dublin's moral paralysis, that is, as a *mise en abyme de l'énoncé* (both with respect to "The Dead" and with respect to *Dubliners* as a whole). But the circumstances of the telling (the story as *mise en abyme de l'énonciation*) are also interesting and can begin to suggest to us something of the status of "The Dead" itself as a message.

In this respect, two factors are especially relevant. First, like the speech, the story is told in order to please: it is an example of Gabriel's parasitism at its most successful. His manner is droll, he is willing even to clown for the amusement of his hearers ("Everyone laughed, even Mrs Malins . . . Gabriel paced in a circle round the hall in his goloshes amid the laughter of the others," p. 208)—an action that incidentally identifies him with the treadmill society the story is perceived to be about. This is Gabriel smoothing tension and producing group cohesion, as is his wont. But second, the story is told against a background of noise—a noise that manifests itself here in a way familiar to us, but also in a new way, for the sound that accompanies the initial awkward pause and the storytelling proper is slightly eerie: it is associated in the conversation with the cold, with a journey homeward, and by suggestion, with death.

> —Someone is strumming at the piano, anyhow, said Gabriel.
>
> Mary Jane glanced at Gabriel and Mr Browne and said with a shiver:
>
> —It makes me feel cold to look at you two gentlemen muffled up like that. I wouldn't like to face your journey home at this hour. (p. 207)

The strumming is in preparation for D'Arcy's song, which means that the story will be accompanied by a sound of "distant music"—a noise that, associated as it is with the cold and a "homeward" journey, will come, as we will see, to constitute for Gabriel a message of deep significance, although it is here disregarded by the revelers in favor of the amusing anecdote.

A more familiar noise, which interrupts the concluding jollity, is associated with Freddy Malins, who manifests himself, not as facing a journey in the cold, but as coming back into the warmth of the house, out of the cold. There is a "resounding knock" that suggests some dramatic intervention from without, but it proves to be only the familiar drunkard, returning with a cab. Freddy, like Bartell D'Arcy, although in a different way, is something of an alter ego of Gabriel's: at the start, the two come upstairs together, as Freddy tells a story, and now, as Gabriel tells *his* story, their departures coincide. And it is not coincidental that Gabriel, with his concern for the smooth order of the party, would be told by the aunts to watch over Freddy throughout the evening, for the chronic drunkard with his high-pitched laugh stands as a major figure of festive disorder and misrule, everything, that is, that the aunts most fear and that Gabriel, in his parasitic way, does his best to counteract. Freddy personifies noise: his voice, like that of his mother (who also stutters), has a "catch" in it that interferes with communication: "Freddy Malins bade the Misses Morkan good-evening in what seemed an off-hand fashion by reason of the habitual catch in his voice . . ." (p. 185). It seems, then, that the two types of noise that accompany Gabriel's storytelling are polarized, as between the noise of festive warmth (Freddy) and something more uncanny, cold, and distant (D'Arcy); but Gabriel himself, whose message (the story of the horse) it is that defines both D'Arcy's hoarse ballad and Freddy's noisy knock at the door as interference, suggests in this refusal of both that they may well have something in common.

And indeed, Freddy's "catch" relates him to the scratch in the voice of the singer, who by reason of his cold is "as hoarse as a crow." The crow, in turn, is not only (as a vulgar version of the raven) a harbinger of death; it relates to yet another aspect of social dissension, the "crow" Miss Ivors wished to pluck with Gabriel—and hence, by contrast, to the goose, to the carving of which Gabriel was so relieved to turn on the departure of that intense lady.[9] Gabriel in his role as entertainer and resident "goose" thus is seen to be quite deliberately masking the insistent presence of noise at the party, a noise that distributes itself along a kind of continuum that goes from the unruly disturbance of Freddy's disruptive presence to the distant sound of D'Arcy's singing, via the abruptness of Miss Ivors's intervention. And if D'Arcy's song relates to the cold outside and if Freddy is one who comes in to the party warmth, there is another sense again in which Miss Ivors—this time by her upsetting midparty departure—provides a mediating link between "inner" and "outer" noise.

It is important to see that the speech, too, functioning as it does to counter the "noise" of social ineptitude and discord so as to produce a mood of happy harmony, does so to the accompaniment of a form of party ("inner") noise that, in the reader's mind, comes gradually to be associated less with the merrymaking than with intimations from without, the cold external world where the snow is "general over Ireland." I am thinking of the rustling of skirts and shuffling of dancing feet, which relate in due course to the soft fall of snow (while the waltz tune in the other room provides its own "distant music"). Thus, running nervously over the heads of his speech as he stands outside the drawing-room door and waits to make his entrance, Gabriel is already aware of the music within and listens to "the skirts that swept against it and the shuffling of feet" (p. 179)—and this is the moment when he makes his decision to eliminate "noise" from the speech by omitting the Browning quotation as an impediment to communication. The speech proper is delivered to the same background of music and dancing: "The piano was playing a waltz tune and he could hear the skirts sweeping against the drawing-room door" (p. 202)—but here the repressed Browning snippet makes its inevitable return in the form of an allusion to the words ("thought-tormented music") that Gabriel had used to describe the poet's art: "But we are living in a sceptical, and, if I may use the phrase, a thought-tormented age . . ." (p. 203). The little phrase not only tells us much about the form of art that Gabriel considers alien to this milieu, and about its affinity with noise; but his apology for it also conveys his sense that the phrase itself is out of place—functions as noise—in the cliché-ridden speech.

But throughout the evening, whenever Gabriel has begun to envision his speech, his mind has not only noted the noise from the other room, it has also swung to the world without, with its snowy but seductive alternative to the oppressive warmth of the party and its speechifying obligations:

Gabriel's warm trembling fingers tapped the cold pane of the window. How cool it must be outside! How pleasant . . . ! The snow would be lying on the branches of the trees and forming a bright cap on the top of the Wellington Monument. How much more pleasant it would be there than at the supper-table!

He ran over the headings of his speech . . . . (p. 192)

and:

The patting at once grew louder in encouragement and then ceased altogether. Gabriel leaned his ten trembling fingers on the tablecloth . . . . The piano was playing a waltz-tune and he could hear the skirts . . . . People, perhaps, were standing in the snow on the quay outside, gazing up at the lighted windows and listening to the waltz music. The air was pure there. In the distance lay the park where the trees were weighted with snow. The Wellington Monument wore a gleaming cap of snow that flashed westward over the white field of Fifteen Acres.

He began:
— Ladies and Gentlemen. (pp. 201-202)

Tappings and pattings of fingers, swishings of skirts and shufflings of feet, remote and thought-tormented music, leading to . . . the snow. This is not the place to rehearse the many complex and subtle readings that the "symbol" of the snow has given rise to in "The Dead." The association with death (and the West) is inescapable;[10] but my purpose is to suggest that the association with noise is both germane and firmly written into the text and that, in contra-distinction to the form of social disorder that Gabriel combats in making his speech, the snow figures a form of noise that encompasses social noise but transcends it and forms an insistent alternative to his speech, that is, another message. In this respect, snow relates, of course, to the figure of Michael Furey, Gabriel's West of Ireland alter ego out of the past, here evoked in an anticipatory way both by the motif of "gazing up" (as we will learn that Michael once gazed up, from the garden below, at Gretta's window) and by the association with the West. But later the reader will realize also that it is the lost sound of Michael Furey's "gravel thrown up against the window" that now lives on eerily—not only in the pattings and tappings of the party, not only in Freddy's rat-a-tat-tat at the door as he returns with the cab, but also (as Gabriel's final perceptions make clear) in the flutter of snow against the windowpane.

A few light taps upon the pane made him turn to the window. It had begun to snow again. He watched sleepily the flakes, silver and dark, falling against the lamplight. The time had come for him to set out on his journey westward. . . . His soul swooned slowly as he *heard* the snow falling faintly through the universe and faintly falling, like the descent of their last end, upon all the living and the dead. (p. 223) (my emphasis)

Here, then, the association with the dead Michael has become some-thing more general, an association with the universal "last end," while the snow appears as noise made visible and "falling faintly through the universe"—a background of cosmic disorder, then, that has all the evening through accompanied the party, with its own internal component of social disorder.[11] And although the party excludes this disorder as best it can, it has been ever present at the windows, so that Gabriel's tapping on the pane from the inside with his own nervous fingers seems in retrospect to have been the sign of some response within him to this message from without.[12]

Gabriel's parasitic words are proof against social disorder, as we have seen. But against the noise, the rival message—cosmic in its reach—of death? Against grief (the noise-traversed narrative of Aunt Kate, "crying and blowing her nose and telling him how Julia had died" [p. 222]), Gabriel knows that his comfortable clichés are impotent. "He would cast about in his mind for some words that might console her, and would find only lame and useless ones. Yes, that would happen soon." We must now investigate more closely Gabriel's relationship to the message of cosmic disorder.

Distant Music

Gabriel's storytelling and speech making spring from a deep and good-hearted instinct: the desire to maintain social harmony in a situation in which it is patently threatened by disorder. But a strain of negative judgment on social parasitism runs through the story, from Lily's memorable definition of men as sexual parasites (that is, seducers), "The men that is now is only all palaver and what they can get out of you" (p. 178), to Gabriel's own bitter self-evaluation at the end:

A shameful consciousness of his own person assailed him. He saw himself as a ludicrous figure, acting as a pennyboy for his aunts, a nervous well-meaning sentimentalist, orating to vulgarians and idealising his own clownish lusts, the pitiable fatuous fellow he had caught a glimpse of in the mirror. (pp. 219-220)

That one feels the latter judgment to be excessive is evidence of the sympathy the story generates for what is warm and human in Gabriel; but what forces general agreement with the thrust of his self-estimate is, of course, the reader's understanding of the experience that provokes it in Gabriel, the "epiphany" of which he is distantly cognizant but that finally excludes him, as Gretta excludes him from love. There is a form of "parasitism" that is not directed *against* disorder but expresses an alliance with the *source* of noise; and the story makes it clear, on the one hand, that this is much the more significant form of artistic parasitism and, on the other, that, sensitive as the socially seductive Gabriel is to *its* seductions, he is inadequately equipped—emotionally and aesthetically—to respond to them.

For what was noise to Gabriel's storytelling proves soon to be a genuine act of communication, taking place between Bartell D'Arcy, the singer identified with the world of European art, and Gretta, with her origins in the West of Ireland (that is, the two characters who, apart from Gabriel himself, are least identified with Dublin); and of this act Gabriel can only be an intrigued spectator. D'Arcy, it will be recalled, is the man who *refused* to "sing for his supper," a social gaffe he now compounds by choosing to sing, without audience and as it were for his own pleasure, just as the guests are leaving, adding final insult to injury by being ungracious when reproached with this:

—I have been at him all the evening, said Miss O'Callaghan, and Mrs Conroy too and he told us he had a dreadful cold and couldn't sing.

—O, Mr D'Arcy, said Aunt Kate, now that was a great fib to tell.

—Can't you see that I'm as hoarse as a crow? said Mr D'Arcy roughly.

He went into the pantry hastily and put on his overcoat. (p. 211)

His affinity with cosmic noise expresses itself first of all as social ineptitude, in direct contrast with Gabriel's smoothness.

But D'Arcy's cold is not just an excuse, it is quite real and it is associated, at least in Mary Jane's mind, with the snow, being the occasion of her key pronouncement: "I read this morning in the newspapers that it is general all over Ireland" (p. 211). And, partly as a result of his cold (which gives him something in common with Gretta, who is also so afflicted), his singing has qualities that distinguish him from the other characters. If his hoarseness recalls the "catch" in Freddy Malins's voice, D'Arcy is a singer whereas Freddy only produces laughter; and although his voice, conversely, is like Aunt Julia's in being a trained and "lovely" one, which "all Dublin is raving about" (p. 184), it differs precisely from hers (which is "strong and clear in tone," p. 193) in that it is "made plaintive by distance and the singer's hoarseness," the performer seeming "uncertain both of his words and of his voice" (p. 216). Moreover, although D'Arcy shares Gabriel's taste for things Continental, he differs from the latter in his affection for Irish folk culture: the song "seemed to be in the old Irish tonality" (p. 210) and is identified in due course as a folk song from the West, "The Lass of Aughrim." Finally, the singer's art, combining noise and loveliness, the Continental and the deeply Irish, is an expression of grief: in this it contrasts by its genuineness both with Aunt Julia's inopportune "Arrayed for the Bridal" and with the lying chorus of "For They Are Jolly Gay Fellows." It contrasts, too, with the laughter-traversed storytelling, not only of Freddy but also of Gabriel. In short, dissonant as it is with the whole mood of the Dublin party, D'Arcy's singing is a manifestation of all that the party excludes. It is in this that it so clearly figures an artistic alternative to lenitive speechifying and jolly storytelling.

It comes, this music, from such a distance—social, cultural, and metaphysical—and the communication of its message is so tenuous that the listener has to strain to hear it. If the preparatory piano strumming is background noise to Gabriel's anecdote of the "old gentleman" and Johnny, the noise of joyous leave-taking interferes much more drastically with Gabriel's reception of the song:

. . . He could hear little save the noise of laughter and dispute on the front steps, a few chords sung on the piano and a few notes of a man's voice singing.

He stood still in the gloom of the hall, trying to catch the air that the voice was singing . . . . (p. 209)

And a moment later:

The hall-door was closed; and Aunt Kate, Aunt Julia and Mary Jane came down the hall, still laughing. . . .

Gabriel said nothing but pointed up the stairs towards where his wife was standing. Now that the hall-door was closed the voice and the piano could be heard more clearly. (p. 210)

Gabriel, then, grasps the music and its message only imperfectly. The person who truly *hears* it, thanks to her position closer to the source—although she, too, must concentrate with full attention—is his wife, the "country cute" Gretta from Galway, less well educated than he but more attuned to genuine Irish culture. *She* is illumined by it: "There was grace and mystery in her attitude as if she were a symbol of something" (p. 210).

Gabriel watched his wife who did not join in the conversation. She was standing right under the dusty fanlight and the flame of the gas lit up the rich bronze of her hair which he had seen her drying at the fire a few days before. She was in the same attitude and seemed unaware of the talk about her. At last she turned towards them and Gabriel saw that there was colour in her cheeks and that her eyes were shining. (pp. 211-212)

But *he,* who does not receive the direct impact of the message, can only wonder at its significance and imagine how, as an artist, he might render it.

He asked himself what is a woman standing on the stairs in the shadow, listening to distant music, a symbol of. If he were a painter he would paint her, in that attitude. Her blue felt hat would show off the bronze of her hair against the darkness and the dark panels of her skirt would show off the light ones. *Distant Music* he would call the picture if he were a painter. (p. 210)

There is, then, a distance between him and the prime recipient of the already distant message, which not only increases the message's faintness but also alters the whole problematics of the situation: Gabriel is here less concerned with capturing and transmitting the message of D'Arcy's singing than with communicating, through the conventional techniques of art (symbolism and composition—the showing off of part against part), a sense of its impact on another.

His concept of art has little to do with the noise-traversed music of the distant singer.

Yet it is this distance—not between him and D'Arcy but between him and Gretta—that the rest of the narrative, as the story of his aroused desire and its disappointment, now shows him attempting to traverse. Gabriel does not know it, but his relationship to Gretta and hers to the distant song map directly onto the love triangle, soon to come to light in the final embedded act of storytelling, involving Gabriel, Gretta, and the long-dead Michael Furey, who "had a very good voice" as she says (p. 221) and sang "The Lass of Aughrim" before dying for her. And his desire for Gretta's body, "musical and strange and perfumed" (p. 215), is a desire for conjunction with that place that is itself in direct communication with the music that comes from so far away. The distance to be traversed is in part a distance in time—the time separating the estranged present from the honeymoon period of his and Gretta's shared "secret life": her first letter to him in the heliotrope envelope; the ticket he slipped into her warm glove; the strange episode of the glassmaker, when they were together looking *in* from the cold, toward the warmth and noise of the furnace. And the arrival at the hotel does give Gabriel a sense of having revived that period, of escaping from "their lives and duties" and running away "together with wild and radiant hearts to a new adventure" (p. 215).

But—of this Gabriel is less consciously aware—the distance to be traversed involves also a journey into death. Only the reader, perhaps, catches the connotations in the crossing of O'Connell Bridge, with its eerie encounter confirming the significance of the snow ("—I see a white man this time, said Gabriel," p. 214) and the grimly ironic equivalence between the funereal, and noisy, cab ("The horse galloped along wearily under the murky, morning sky, dragging his old rattling box after his heels") and Gabriel's honeymoon memories ("galloping to catch the boat, galloping to their honeymoon," p. 214). So, too, in the dark and silent hotel, where the "soft thuds" of their feet, the sound of falling candle wax and the thumping of Gabriel's heart (p. 215) correspond to the faint sounds of the falling snow, recorded elsewhere, and where the porter with his light figures the psychopomp conducting the couple to their resting chamber (Gabriel here feels his soul stirring with life), the reader perceives something like an entry into the land of the dead. A "ghostly light" illumines the bedroom, and Gretta, turning from her mirrored reflection and walking "along the shaft of light towards him," is herself like a shade, coming to greet Gabriel and to accept him into that world.

From the past, Gabriel has retained the sense both of the power of words and of their inadequacy:

In one letter that he had written to her then he had said: *Why is it that words like these seem to me so dull and cold? Is it because there is no word tender enough to be your name?*

Like distant music these words that he had written years before were borne towards him from the past. He longed to be alone with her. When the other had gone away, when he and she were alone in their room in the hotel, then they would be alone together. He would call her softly:

— Gretta!

Perhaps she would not hear at once: she would be undressing. Then something in his voice would strike her. She would turn and look at him . . . . (p. 214)

There is a word "tender enough," there is "something in the voice" that Gabriel is aware of "like distant music" and that would have the power of making accessible the object of his desire. Can he produce this word? As Gretta turns from the mirror, it is indeed in response to her husband's naming of her: "—Gretta!" (p. 216). But, for Gabriel, it is a moment of failure. "Her face looked so serious and weary that the words would not pass Gabriel's lips. No, it was not the moment yet" (p. 216). Gabriel's failure of nerve, in this whole eipsode with Gretta, is the sign of an artistic and indeed metaphysical inadequacy, a fatal lack of initiative, an impotency. There follows the "false" little conversation about the loan repaid by Freddy Malins, Gretta's kiss, and finally—"in an outburst of tears"—her confession: "O, I am thinking about that song, *The Lass of Aughrim*" (p. 218). Words are not the means of their coming together, of the satisfaction of Gabriel's desire: *his* words do not break down the distance between him and the recipient of the distant singing, so *her* words—noise-tormented like D'Arcy's song and like the tearful narrative of Aunt Kate, whom Gabriel will imagine "telling him how Julia died"—will be the measure of their separation.

When Gretta tells the tale of Michael Furey, she speaks in a voice "veiled and sad," a voice threatened each moment by tears ("She paused for a moment to get her voice under control," p. 221), a voice of grief. This, now, is the distant song communicating itself to Gabriel. But the words convey a message of exclusion, since the tale of Furey's selfless passion and simple devotion, the picture of him in the streaming rain outside the window, Gretta's confession: "I think he died for me" (p. 220) contrast so painfully with Gabriel's own emotional timidity and passionlessness, and with the self-image he now has as "pennyboy for his aunts." "Shy of intruding on her grief" (all of Gabriel's failure is in this phrase), he abandons all thought of possessing her and walks—once more—"to the window" (p. 221). Storytelling, we know, is frequently an act of seduction; but the point of Gretta's story has been, on the contrary, to mark an exclusion and ratify a distance: the communication it establishes concerns the impossibility of a communion.

As such, it confirms the situation already produced by D'Arcy's singing—a situation of exclusion that, one can now see, echoes redundantly throughout the text of "The Dead." "The Lass of Aughrim" is *mise en abyme de l'énoncé*: it is the story of a sexual rejection, and the words quoted in the text (p. 210) are those spoken by the lass as she stands, seduced and abandoned, in the rain—like Michael in Gretta's grandmother's garden—outside the Lord's tower. And Gabriel's exclusion from intercourse with Gretta, like his exclusion from the rapt communication between D'Arcy and Gretta through his song, repeats his sense of exclusion from the cold, snowy world that is the ultimate object of his desire—an exclusion that, by virtue of his own self-willed inclusion in the warm world of the Misses Morkan's party, he has brought on himself but that, so many times in the course of the evening, has brought him, in thought or deed, "to the window." If the "noise" that so insistently traverses the jolliness and warmth of the party is itself a message, and a message of great attractiveness to both Gabriel and Gretta, then that message is nevertheless a message about the necessity, the inevitability of exile for those who heed it. Gretta is an exile—from the West, from the past, from the love of Michael, from all the "distant music"—just as Gabriel is himself an exile from her love.

It is only in sleep, with the cessation of desire, that Gabriel achieves some sensation of union, or near union, with the world of cosmic disorder that fires his longing. Turning "unresentfully" from Gretta, he contemplates the hotel room, with its disorder reflecting the "riot" of his recent emotions and recalling the evening's merry-making; and his mind then adverts to the alternative pole, to the universality of death. "One by one they were all fast becoming shades" (p. 222). Drifting into sleep, he seems to approach, although not quite to attain, the world of death. His tears of pity—for the aging Gretta, for himself—fuse now with a vision of Michael "standing under a dripping tree." "Other forms were near. His soul had approached that region where dwell the vast hosts of the dead. He was conscious of, but could not apprehend, their wayward and flickering existence" (p. 223). As his identity fades and the world dissolves, the falling of the snow, "general all over Ireland," represents the dissolving, impalpable universe, its solidity gone; and as his soul swoons, he continues to hear the soft noise of its faint descent. Gabriel has left the world of order and is now at the very threshold of an alluring new world, of disorder perhaps, but of disorder soft and inviting. "The time had come for his journey westward" — westward into death, no doubt, but also to the source of the allurement he had felt when watching the effect of D'Arcy's singing on Gretta—westward toward Michael's snow-clad burial ground, but farther westward still to where the snow falls into the "dark mutinous Shannon waves." Westward into the heart of the storm. The universe of meteorological disorder has become *the* world, for Gabriel, and it is time for his journey. But the journey has yet to be made.

"The Dead," it seems, poses a clear alternative in the choice between the artistic parasitism exemplified by Gabriel's speech making and the affinity with noise embodied in D'Arcy's song. But the narrative models it offers are, in fact, three in number; and they constitute a group of options to all of which the text can be seen, in some sense and to some degree, to conform. All are ways of relating to cosmic noise. Gabriel as speech maker and storyteller relates negatively to such noise; Gretta as storyteller, like D'Arcy the singer, mediates noise as a message; Gabriel, finally, as spectator of Gretta's rapt listening and rejected lover, mediates the sense of cosmic noise in a more remote and distanced fashion.

In light of the contrast with the epiphanic episodes, Gabriel's speechifying and storytelling cannot be seen as a positive model of the story's own narrative situation. Yet there is an uncomfortable sense in which, like the other stories in *Dubliners,* "The Dead" is parasitic on the Dublin society from which it takes nourishment (subject matter) and to which it gives, in return, words (information). The words, to be sure, are bitter, ironic, and scarifying, as opposed to Gabriel's flattery and clowning; but in "The Dead," at least, they are not without a redeeming, positive side. We know that, writing this story some time later than the others in the collection, Joyce was anxious to correct its uniformly negative tone, in particular by acknowledging the warmth of "Irish hospitality."[13] In a sense, then, Gabriel's speech does function as a direct model of the story's own narrative situation; and it is, of course, ironic that such artistic parasitism should be pointed up precisely apropos of the national gift for hospitality. It is ironic, too, and significant, that—precisely because it was written later, after the collection was completed, and from a changed angle of vision—the story functions, within the structure of *Dubliners,* as a parasitic and disordering element. Not only does it, in thematic terms, introduce an unwonted positive note, but the story interrupts also the chronological ordering, in terms of the stages of life, that controls the other stories as a group. We might do well, instead of struggling to make this story cohere with the rest, to see that its function is not to cohere but to introduce *in extremis* a new note and a new message. In this it is not unlike Mr D'Arcy's belated singing at the party, both *of* the party and *not* of it, a disturbance to its harmony.

For it is clear that the story's major commitment is to noise, to noise as social disturbance and cosmic disorder, the two functions performed by D'Arcy's singing. Noise is everywhere present in "The Dead," like the laughter that convulses Freddy in midstory or the tears that traverse Gretta's narrative; but unlike these models—unlike Aunt Kate's grief-stricken story, as imagined by Gabriel, also, and unlike D'Arcy's hoarse song—the story speaks *of* noise without itself constituting noise. It does not speak noise or speak noisily; its narrative technique is, on the contrary, entirely coherent and indeed conventional—it is the technique of Joyce the Irish Maupassant or Zola. So, we learn from it about noise without actually hearing in its own narrative "voice" the noise with which it is concerned. This is because the story is told, broadly speaking (the opening pages are focused through Lily), from Gabriel's viewpoint, and it is Gabriel's distance from the phenomenon of noise that the reader is made to share. It is not accidental that Gabriel's model for dealing aesthetically with the epiphany of D'Arcy and Gretta is painting—an art combining realistic portrayal (the woman, her clothing, her attitude) with symbolic intent (conveyed in the title), but one from which, most obviously and inevitably, the single most important missing element is D'Arcy's voice itself. His hoarse song cannot be embodied in words that conform to the aesthetic to which Joyce subscribes in his story, an aesthetic in which there is no place, except as subject matter, for communicational noise.

Does such an aesthetic exist? Is there a form of literary art that would place the reader, with respect to the song, not in Gabriel's distant position but in that of Gretta, the more direct and immediate recipient? This would be an art speaking not the conventional language of storytelling that excludes us from "noise," but a discourse of noise, conveying directly and with immediate impact the message of disorder and death, an art destructive of order yet "melodic" in its own way and in its own terms. With hindsight, and mindful of the connection between the combination of deep Irishness and European sophistication in the epiphany of Gretta and D'Arcy and the self-same combination in the character, biography, aesthetic formation, and artistic practice of James Joyce himself, it is easy to see that the art for which D'Arcy is the model, the art of verbal noise and snowy disorder, will eventually be embodied in the author's future writing, in modernist, "writerly" texts such as *Ulysses* and *Finnegans Wake*. Like Gabriel drifting into sleep, "The Dead" has brought us to a point at which "readerly" narrative is at the threshold of its crossing over into the unleashed energy, the disorder, and the soft, alluring beauty of the "writerly" snowstorm.

A bird is missing, then, from the aviary of (edible) fowl in "The Dead." If Gabriel is a "brown goose" (brown being the color, in *Dubliners,* of the city's paralysis), he is destined to "eat crow," less at the hands of Miss Ivors (whose connection with the West is nevertheless highly relevant) than at those of D'Arcy, who has the crow of death in his throat. But the model for the story is neither the goose nor the crow, but something in between, for it is a swan song. It is the swan song of *Dubliners* as D'Arcy's song is the swan song of the party, but as such it constitutes a farewell to its own aesthetic and the announcement of an aesthetic yet to be discovered. The swan, as Socrates pointed out,[14] is not mourning its own death but, knowing beforehand "the good things of the other world," acts as prophet of a better future "in the presence of the god." One may imagine its song a little like D'Arcy's, melodious and beautiful but with a hint of "crow," or like the narrative of "The Dead," couched in the aesthetic language of "this side" but traversed by many hints of the beauty and allure of the "other side." Joyce's story, strangely, speaks from out of an aesthetic space, a situation that is, as yet, absent, using discourse that belongs, by its own reckoning, to an already outmoded past.

No more fitting exemplification could be found than this of the "spectral" character of narrative situation in texts, always of the text and constructed by its discourse, but always dependent on a construing in the future, from outside of the text and independently of it. That is why the reader must be both seduced by the text, with all its alluring requirements of "understanding" or love, and yet maintained in his or her own freedom, refused by the text, as Gabriel is excluded by Gretta, the better to constitute that always future situation indispensable to its life. If, as narrative texts approach the "writerly" — "Un cœur simple," "The Figure in the Carpet," "The Dead" — the reading situation they construct tends progressively toward greater and greater openness, none of them neglects the seduction of the reader, whose involvement is ensured by mimetic duplicity, coerced spectatorhood, or here, exacerbated desire. The reader's participation in the perspective and emotions of Gabriel does not go without a certain distancing from Gabriel, whose deficiencies, inadequacies, and "unresentfulness" — human as they are — are difficult to share. As readers of "The Dead," we share the perspective of exclusion — from the love of Gretta, from the source of cosmic noise — that is his, but our desire does not abate so easily as we follow him in his slow swoon toward death; for our perspective is also that of Michael Furey, who does not take rejection by Gretta quite so tamely, and whose desire, far from abating, becomes strengthened as it merges with a desire for death. Gabriel, lying beside Gretta, can easily picture "that image of her lover's eyes when he had told her that he did not wish to live" (p. 223), and he knows that such tenacity as Michael's, as opposed to his own "shy[ness] of intruding on her grief," is the sign of genuine passion. "He had never felt like that himself towards any woman but he knew that such a feeling must be love."

The loving reader, whose desire remains alive even as Gabriel drifts into the death of sleep, is the shadowy figure — "the form of a young man standing under a dripping tree" — that the text projects, as the ghost of Michael, into its own future. "Other forms were near. . . . He was conscious of, but could not apprehend, their wayward and flickering identity." These "hosts of the dead" with whom, as his own identity "fade[s] out," Gabriel gradually merges occupy the situation from which the story asks to be read, the perspective that Gabriel's own perspective will eventually rejoin, but only when he has completed the journey on which he is as yet only setting out. Not the unloving living but the dead, the loving dead, whose messages reach the world of the living as tempest and noise, are the readership the story craves but cannot define. The dead of its title are of the future, not the past.[15]

NOTES

1. See Florence Walzl, "Gabriel and Michael: The Conclusion of 'The Dead,' " *James Joyce Quarterly*, 4, 1 (fall 1966), 17-31.

2. See Florence Walzl, "The Liturgy of the Epiphany Season and the Epiphanies of Joyce," *PMLA*, 80, 4/5 (September 1965), 436-450; and for a confirmation, Bernard Benstock, "The Dead," in Clive Hart, ed., *James Joyce's "Dubliners"* (New York: Viking, 1969), 153-169.

3. Apart from essays more explicitly referred to, I have derived valuable suggestions for my reading of "The Dead" from Warren Beck, *Joyce's "Dubliners": Substance, Vision and Art* (Durham, N.C.: Duke University Press, 1969); Samuel N. Bogorad, "Gabriel Conroy as 'Whited Sepulchre': Prefiguring Imagery in 'The Dead,' " *Ball State University Forum*, 14, 1 (1973), 52-58; John D. Boyd and Ruth A. Boyd, "The Love Triangle in Joyce's 'The Dead,' " *University of Toronto Quarterly*, 42, 3 (spring 1973), 202-217; John W. Foster, "Passage through 'The Dead,' " *Criticism*, 15, 2 (spring 1973), 91-108; Peter K. Garrett, ed., *Twentieth Century Interpretations of "Dubliners"* (Englewood Cliffs, N.J.: Prentice-Hall, 1968); Don Gifford, *Notes for Joyce: "Dubliners" and "A Portrait of the Artist as a Young Man"* (New York: Dutton, 1967); William T. Going, "Joyce's Gabriel Conroy and Robert Browning: The Cult of 'Broadcloth,' " *Papers on Language and Literature*, 13 (1977), 202-207; Epifanio San Juan, *James Joyce and the Craft of Fiction: An Interpretation of "Dubliners"* (Cranbury: Associated University Presses, 1972), 209-233.

4. *Le Parasite* (Paris: Grasset, 1980), p. 93.

5. Ibid., p. 255.

6. Ibid., p. 49.

7. James Joyce, *Dubliners*, ed. R. Scholes (London: Penguin Books, 1976), p. 192. All page references in parentheses are to this edition.

8. Cf. Joyce's letter to Constantine Curran (early July 1904) and Grant Richards (5 May 1906), in Richard Ellmann, ed., *Selected Letters of James Joyce* (New York: Viking, 1975), pp. 22 and 81-84.

9. On the crow, see John P. McKenna, "Joyce's 'The Dead,' " *Explicator*, 30, 1 (1971), 1-2, and more appositely Dorothy Logan, "Joyce's "The Dead,' " *Explicator*, 32, 2 (1973), 16; on the goose, see Eleanor M. Robinson, "Gabriel Conroy's Cooked Goose," *Ball State University Forum*, 11, 2 (spring 1970), 25.

10. See especially Brewster Ghiselin, "The Unity of *Dubliners*," in Morris Beja, ed., *James Joyce: "Dubliners" and "A Portrait of the Artist as a Young Man." A Casebook* (London: Macmillan, 1973), 100-116 (also in Garrett, *Twentieth Century Interpretations of "Dubliners"*); and Jack Barry Ludwig, "The Snow," in James R. Baker and Thomas F. Staley, eds., *James Joyce's "Dubliners": A Critical Handbook* (Balmont, Calif.: Wadsworth, 1969), 159-162.

11. Ludwig, "The Snow," has seen the connection between snow and disorder, but he relates it solely to social disorder. On the significance of storms and meteorological disorder generally, see, of course, M. Serres, *Hermès IV: La distribution* (Paris: Éd. de Minuit, 1977). In "The Dead," the snowstorm over Ireland relates to the pouring rain of Galway in Gretta's past involvement with Michael Furey and in the present to her "outburst of tears" (p. 218).

12. The message does occasionally penetrate, however (and always in the form of noise), as characters come in from outside. Thus, Gabriel, on his arrival, scrapes his feet vigorously and "as the buttons of his overcoat slipped with a squeaking noise through the snow-

stiffened frieze, a cold fragrant air from out-of-doors escaped from crevices and folds" (p. 177); and at the end, after his dramatic knock at the door, Freddy stands "puffing and steaming."

13. Letter to Grant Richards (25 September 1906), in Ellmann, *Selected Letters.*

14. Plato, *Phaedo,* 84e.

15. On the reader as ghost in the text, see also my essay "La lecture comme hantise: *Spirite* et *Le Horla,*" *Revue des Sciences Humaines,* 177 (1980-1981), 105-117.

Chapter Nine
Authority and Seduction:
The Power of Fiction

A Theory of Theory

Jonathan Culler would probably include this book among those works of theory that fall into the "temptations of interpretation."[1] Such works are misguided, in his view, because, theory being a conceptualization, or explicitation, of the norms and conventions by which the literary community (authors in their writing, readers in their reading) produce the phenomenon of literature, a theory that attempts to "prove" itself by demonstrating that it can generate "new" interpretations of literary works, is self-contradictory. One should rather expect of a theory that it give an account of the interpretations we already possess.

But it is surely imposing unnecessary limits on theory to require of it that it be content to formalize what is, in a sense, already known. May it not be that there are features of literary communication that ordinary interpretive practice, as we know it, ignores or underestimates or marginalizes? If attention to such features would enhance the power of texts to produce meanings, theory would be wrong not to attempt to bring them into sharper focus, so that reading could become to that extent a more comprehensive practice. Such, at least, has been a primary aim of mine, to draw attention to a specific component of the narrative text, its situational self-reflexivity, that not only has been neglected by theoreticians but to which it would be rewarding for readers to become more attentive. It happens that the very self-situating devices by which texts achieve interpretability (or "point") are themselves open to interpretation (that, as I tried to explain in chapter 2, is how the phenomenon of "readability" arises), and my essays can stand as demonstrations of that fact.

A more pointed critique of the book, however, might concern its relatively narrow range. When it has been demonstrated that a handful of nineteenth-century "art stories" are situationally self-referential, what then? Early readers of my draft consistently asked: What of the novel? If what you say is true of the "short story" (or of some "short stories"), is it also true of much longer, and perhaps less tightly organized, narrative texts? I might have included a section on the novel in this volume, at the price of considerably increasing its length; but if, finally, I have decided to devote only a few pages of this concluding chapter to the question of longer narratives, it is because in the last analysis an extension of the textual corpus in the direction of the novel would do relatively little to broaden the theoretical focus; indeed, it might begin, rather repetitively, to produce interpretations for interpretation's sake. In fact, the very *obviousness* of the question concerning the novel, the automatic movement of the mind whereby a study of short literary narratives should next take account of long literary narratives, could be regarded almost as danger signals. They point to a certain specialization of perspective to which literary theory is subject. They assume without question the ideology that has made literature itself a specialized or autonomous practice, valuable in and for itself, and so constitute yet another example of the phenomenon of alienation, or reification, characteristic of the capitalist era.

My point is that, following a study of the "art story," the question "What of the novel?" ought perhaps to be no more automatic than the question "What of non-art storytelling?" It might, in other words, be a more productive perspective to take seriously the view of theory of literature that sees it as part of a more general theory of discourse and of communication and to try to situate the specific phenomena of literary communication within the total range of modes of verbal communication available to social beings. The practice of Barbara Herrnstein Smith is exemplary from this point of view.[2] Literary theorists are, or at least could be, people to whom the specific phenomena we call literary provide models in light of which other, nonliterary, modes of communication can be examined, both as to similarities and differences. Indeed, given the constitutive feature of literary communication, which in our culture I take to be its deferral, we are in a position to bring a worthwhile corrective to some of the commonsense views still prevalent among certain semioticians and "ordinary language" philosophers—those who tend to rely on an unproblematic view of the nature of the communicational subject and of the addressee, as well as of the relationship that prevails between them. To those who assume an equally unproblematic distinction between discourse and its context, the evidence in this book concerning the self-contextualizing power of literary discourse must also constitute some kind of challenge, for, as was pointed out in chapter 2, it renders dubious the formal separability of context from the discourse that assumes it (and, in so doing, produces it).

The question I should like to open here, however, is a more straightforward one. It arises less from the situational character of meaning and the self-situating referentiality of the texts that have been studied than it does from what the foregoing series of interpretations has identified: their common analysis of the situation pertinent to narrative acts. What was defined in chapter 3 as "narrational" authority, as opposed to "narrative" authority (the type of authority that derives from the production of *art* as opposed to the communication of *information*), has displayed a strikingly consistent reliance, in the six texts under analysis, on techniques of seduction, ranging from the denial of seduction (in "Sarrasine") to the refusal of love (in "The Dead"). Supposing this consistency to be not accidental, but the sign of some broader consensus among literary texts, one might ask what can be learned from their analysis concerning storytelling in the broader sense, stories (written or oral) that are "narrative" rather than "narratorial," and stories ("narratorial" or "narrative" as to their source of authority) that are oral rather than written. Consequently, the brief discussion of novels that follows has a double purpose: (1) to suggest that an affirmative answer is possible to the question whether, like some "art tales," some novels also self-contextualize situationally and in so doing confirm the frequency of the situational analysis of narrative in terms of authority and seduction; but also (2) to lead into some comments about storytelling itself in a situational perspective. The novels I wish to discuss consequently have been chosen for their relevance to these purposes, and specifically the latter one, rather than, in purely literary-historical or even literary-theoretical terms, for their homogeneity (with respect to historical period or to culture of provenance) with my corpus of nineteenth-century "art tales."

Seduction in Opposition

However, the art stories studied in this book were not themselves initially selected for the homogeneity they proved to have as interpreters of narrative situation. I wanted rather to choose texts with which it could be assumed that, through their canonical prominence or critical notoriety, a good number of readers would be familiar; and the consistency of their situational analysis came as a surprise to me as, text by text, my work proceeded. Similarly, it happens that the only two novels I was teaching in the period when I was pondering these concluding pages were neither of them of the nineteenth century, and both were by French-speaking authors from outside France. Yet, Cheikh Hamidou Kane's *L'Aventure ambiguë*[3] and Hubert Aquin's *Prochain épisode*[4] are nevertheless both spectacularly self-contextualizing novels in situational terms; and the narrative situation they produce raises the questions, now familiar to us, of authority and seduction. (The same, incidentally, is true of the one novel briefly mentioned in chapter 1, Manuel Puig's *El beso de la mujer araña,* with its relationship between Valentin and Molina; and it is true also of the two short stories briefly analyzed in chapter 2, with the "self-possession" of Vera in "The Open Window" and the use of love as a metaphor for reading in "Les Sans-Gueule.")

L'Aventure ambiguë concerns the cultural pain of a West African society (the Diallobé) forced, as it believes, to choose between its traditional Islamic past and the knowledge, or know-how, of the West, embodied here in the educational institutions of the colonial power, France. The pain is lived in intensified form by the protagonist, Samba Diallo, who—having first imbibed a passionate Islamic mysticism in Coran school—finds himself transferred to the French school where he learns (in the post-Cartesian sense of the term, one virtually unknown, it seems, in Islamic tradition) to "philosophize." After an abortive stay in France, he returns to his native land, "le pays des Diallobé," in a self-contradictory and finally destructive attempt to reunite, as an "atheist," with the theocentric cultural tradition of his ancestors. But Samba is an oddly passive hero, and the question the novel seems to be asking—and to be asking by the very fact of its existence as a novel—is whether such pain must inevitably lead to defeat and destruction or whether it cannot be overcome. In the opening scene, set in the Coran school, we see the young Samba Diallo learning to overcome physical pain in order to recite to perfection the perfect Word of God, as God *shaped* it ("telle qu'il lui avait plu de la façonner," pp. 14-15). For each faltering of the voice, for each mispronunciation of the alien Arabic, he is cruelly punished by the Master, until he achieves perfect delivery of the verse—for it is not just a matter of getting the words right, it is a matter of overcoming the agony.

L'enfant réussit à maîtriser la souffrance. Il répéta la phrase sans broncher, calmement, posément, comme si la douleur ne l'eût pas lanciné.

Le maître lâcha l'oreille sanglante. Pas une larme n'avait coulé sur le fin visage de l'enfant. Sa voix était calme et son débit mesuré. La Parole de Dieu coulait, pure et limpide, de ses lèvres ardentes. . . . Cette parole qu'il enfantait dans la douleur, elle était l'architecture du monde, elle était le monde même. (p. 15)

But such words—"voix calme," "débit mesuré," "l'architecture du monde"—apply so compellingly to the narrative voice of the text itself, and describe so well its own narrative project, that it is difficult not to see in the child's suffering here a model, less of the future hero's "ambiguous adventure" than of the place out of which emerges, calm and measured, with its classical French phrasing giving the lie, as it were, to the aggressively Islamic stamp of the author's name on the cover, the text's own discourse. This is the discourse of one who has learned, in pain, to master the alien language of the master, in its most sacred and perfect form—that of its "classical" texts—and who is using it now to set out the true architecture of the world (that is, of the painful world in which the Diallobé flounder and Samba Diallo is destroyed). The narrative voice thus achieves for itself, through language, a mastery that gives it equality with the colonial masters themselves (there is some suggestion of awareness, in the novel, that Islam itself was once, similarly, a colonizing force in West Africa). But through this mastery of the rhythms and phraseology to which French readers most deeply and intuitively respond, the text is claiming also not just equality in mastery but even a certain unobtrusive power over its hearers, the insidious power of involving them willy-nilly, through language, in the sufferings that are its subject matter and for which the French must take responsibility. In this way, *L'Aventure ambiguë* turns a position of weakness into eloquence and strength, not by confrontational means, but by tactics more indirectly, more discreetly, but also more deeply persuasive. And the narrative voice, while it identifies the reader very strongly with the situation of its defeated hero, speaks itself from a place of strength and control.

Questions of power and weakness are even more explicitly to the fore in the narrative situation with which the Québec novel, *Prochain épisode*, is obsessively concerned. Arrested by the Mounties for suspect activities in the cause of Québec independence, the narrator languishes in a psychiatric clinic, a prey to the characteristic prisoner's agonies: a sense of self-doubt and impotence, both in terms of personal identity and of political action, together with sexual frustration, the three (identity weakness, political failure, and amorous deprivation) combining, then, in a generalized sense of powerlessness. In this situation, there is nothing to do but write, as a compensatory and time-filling activity, but also, although less obviously, as some kind of last-resort *response* to situational weakness. The narrator launches into an enterprise that, at least on the plane of identity, is to be a justification of self: he plans to "faire original" in the genre (conventional par excellence) of the spy story. But, as the proposed story develops, episode by episode, in fits and starts, it evolves less as a tale of heroism and mastery than as one of ineffectualness, error, doublecrossing, and defeat. In short, as the narrator also adumbrated from the start ("mes mémoires"), it is the story of failure that brought him to his present fix. Not coincidentally, he realizes at the same time the folly of his ambition to "faire original" in a world where the precise place of his writing has already been foreseen in the Dewey decimal system. The narrative that leads out of prison leads back into prison, and no more economical way could be imagined of embodying in story form the thesis of this book concerning the identity (or at least inseparability) of story and situation.

The narrative of *Prochain épisode* presents itself, then, as an attempt to gain authority, the authority of authorship, as compensation for the loss of power. But, on the other hand, it appears also as a seductive enterprise: it describes itself as a long love letter, addressed to a Eurydice-like figure, K, with whom the narrator recalls having shared idyllic scenes and passionate nights in the past and who stands symbolically for his Québec patriotism, and indeed for a free Québec itself. The illocutionary success of this love letter, then, would not only confirm the acquisition of authority/authorship but would also signify the attainment of liberty—the narrator's freedom, the political and national emancipation of Québec. "Nous n'avons jamais cessé de préparer la guerre de notre libération, mêlant notre intimité délivrée au secret terrible de la nation qui éclate, la violence armée à celle des heures que nous avons passées à nous aimer" (p. 143). What the novel records, however, is the failure of these two conjoined enterprises: authorship, as we have seen, is a vicious circle and leads back into prison; and it is perhaps K herself who has betrayed the narrator to the double agent H. de Heutz, and hence to the imprisoning authorities.

But, as in the example of *L'Aventure ambiguë*, there is a case for distinguishing between the defeat of which the novel talks and its own situational success. Indeed, *Prochain épisode*, in two embedded episodes, makes its own strong claim for the power of fiction. Caught by H. de Heutz and held at gunpoint, the narrator disguises his identity by telling a cock-and-bull story: he is a Belgian businessman who has run away from his wife, children, and debts; all he wants to do is to commit suicide (the narrative as a whole presents itself as a metaphoric suicide). This story—whose stress on failure and escapism parallels that of the novel itself—works well enough for the narrator to achieve freedom, by surprising and overpowering H. de Heutz— who soon, however, manages to turn the tables, now that it is the narrator who has the upper hand, by telling the *same* cock-and-bull story ("la même salade") and by taking advantage of the narrator's dismay at this effrontery in order to escape in his turn. Even as the narrator's sense of identity collapses in this confrontation with the counterspy who functions as a strange alter ego, the power of narrative to convert defeat into victory—and to do it through barefaced fictionality (something like Vera's "self-possession"?)—is twice affirmed. And what is true of these episodes is also true, *mutatis mutandis*, of the narrative as a whole, which talks of defeat but in fact exerts a compelling fascination, even on novice readers, who are so caught up in the twists and turns of its arrant fictionality—like the zigzags of the Alpine highways on which much of the action occurs—that they join the narrator in his own "suicide," the sinking mood that is also a "descente au fond des choses" and a rehearsal of the "mots-clés qui ne me libéreront pas" (p. 7). This union in death and defeat, although it cannot produce the desired freedom, is evidence, certainly, that the narrative does have powers greater than those claimed for it by the narrator and that these are powers of seduction.

In the opening pages of this book, the first power of fiction, it was claimed, was the power to theorize itself, and the second (which amounts perhaps to the same thing), the power to control its own impact through situational self-definition. The third power is the one claimed by the stories studied at some length in the previous chapters and the novels more briefly evoked here: it specifies fictional "impact" in terms of the power of seduction. But whereas the power of text to theorize itself and the power of self-definition are analytic powers, the claim to seductive power is a claim of perlocutionary force, another *kind* of power. It is not self-directed but other-directed; and it is definable as the power to achieve authority and to produce involvement (the authority of the storyteller, the involvement of the narratee) within a situation from which power is itself absent. If such power can be called the power of seduction, it is because seduction is, by definition, a phenomenon of persuasion: it cannot rely on force or institutional authority ("power"), for it is, precisely, a means of achieving mastery in the absence of such means of control. It is the instrument available to the situationally weak against the situationally strong. Pierre Bourdieu, it is true, believes, to the contrary, that authority is in itself seductive: "Tout incline à penser que . . . l'autorité de quelque ordre que ce soit enferme un *pouvoir de séduction* qu'il serait naïf de réduire à un effet de servilité intéressée."[5] But the production of authority is *itself* a phenomenon that needs accounting for, and without wishing to deny the strength and value of Bourdieu's insight, I will be suggesting rather that narrative authority is the outcome of seduction even while it exerts a seduction of its own and that the two finally fold into each other in a mutually reinforcing way, so that in the end it becomes difficult to say which is the primary phenomenon.

In any case, the historical situation in which novels like *El beso de la mujer araña*, *L'Aventure ambiguë*, and *Prochain épisode* were written (all of them, in different ways, products of an experience of political oppression) perhaps helps them to give some sharpness of definition to a claim that is made more diffusely and more implicitly in the nineteenth-century texts, which themselves emanate, however, from a situation of historical weakness, that of the marginalized artist (as a "dominated" subgroup) in an age of bourgeois dominance. I suggested at the outset that narrative seduction is a consequence of the alienation undergone by literary discourse in the text, and a condition of its interpretability. But the further claim is now made that such seduction, producing authority where there is no power, is a means of converting (historical) weakness into (discursive) strength.[6] As such, it appears as a major weapon against alienation, an instrument of self-assertion, and an "oppositional practice"[7] of considerable significance. This is the proposition I plan to explore further, and whose limits I wish to test, in another volume.

But the question that remains and that must be asked straightaway, concerns, of course, the extent to which such an analysis can be generalized. Is the evidence of "narrational" (artistic) texts valid for "narrative" (informational) situations? Can an analysis deriving from texts so deeply rooted in situations of historical alienation and/or oppression be legitimately extended and, in what sense, to all narrative acts? Are the circumstances of written narrative comparable to those of oral narrative? And conversely, is there a specificity of literary narrative? What, more particularly, of the tension that must arise between the seductive thrust of storytelling and the power of literary narrative to analyze itself and reveal its mechanisms, that is, between an agency favoring blindness, on the one hand, and lucidity, on the other? These—and others like them—are not questions to which one would wish to give short, definitive, or even simple answers. What follows is only an attempt to suggest some lines of thought and to conclude this very limited investigation in a way that does not close it off from some more general significance.

Authority and Seduction

It does seem that there is something defensive in even the most accomplished storyteller, and that it is a situational defensiveness. "Pointless stories," as Labov remarks, "are met in English with the withering rejoinder: 'So what?' Every good narrator is continually warding off this question . . . ."[8] There are situations of great confidence in which the "point" of a story is a matter that can very largely be assumed to be tacitly agreed between two, say, long-standing life partners and situations of stress for the storyteller in which the "point" must continually be established and reestablished, but the right to tell stories always depends on there being a point recognizable to, and accepted by, the hearer. In this sense, "point" and the establishment of "authority"—the authority to narrate—are, if not exactly synonymous, two ways of describing the same situational circumstances. Some kinds of authority—professional authority, for example, that of judges, doctors, or professors—derive support from institutional structures and power; but the authority of the storyteller is essentially without external support and derives almost totally from the "interest" of the tale. Those who are recognized in their community as accomplished storytellers perhaps benefit from the authority of reputation, but even this can be quickly lost as a result of a few flops in performance. As was pointed out in chapter 3, the storyteller's authority must be first obtained, then maintained, until the end of the tale by means that are essentially discursive.

Such authority, then, is highly vulnerable. It rests on an act of authorization on the part of the addressee(s), and one that (taking the form of a suspension of conversational turn taking) can very easily be withdrawn (either by a return to turn taking or by leaving the storytelling situation altogether). A miscalculation of effect, a failure of *tactics,* and the hearers have lost interest, the narrator has lost control. As Michel de Certeau has pointed out, the storyteller in his or her exposed position is forced to be a tactician. If "strategy" is the practice of those who are masters of the terrain and "tactics" that of those who are not, at the outset, in control of the situation, the narrator, who is situationally condemned to operate without preexistent authority and to earn the authority to narrate in the very act of storytelling, must be a master of certain "tactical" devices that ensure his or her *survival* as storyteller. Such a person must display "a capacity to inhabit the space of the other without possessing it" and exercise an art that is "the art of 'scoring' . . . . Here too, discourse is characterized more by the way it makes its moves, than by what it tries to show."[9] Narrative moves, then, produce "authority," and "authority" is an acknowledgment that the story has "point." But another name for narrative "moves," addressed as they are to another whose adherence to the story must be gained, is seduction, as a way of "inhabiting the space of the other without possessing it."

For a storyteller who seeks authority, two obvious tactics are available at the outset. One is Dupin's method (and Vera's): the tranquil assumption of a mastery that is, literally, *taken for granted.* The possession of a superior insight or of information urgently required can be implied by a refusal to divulge (Dupin's approach to the chief of police), followed perhaps (Dupin's approach to his friend and admirer) by a "divulgation" so calculated that it acts more as a smoke screen, behind which the essential fact—which itself, perhaps, is a void—may remain undivulged. In this connection, secrecy—the claim to be in possession of a secret, together with an implied willingness to divulge it—forms the paradigm of all such tactics of narrative authority, as doubtless Balzac's narrator in "Sarrasine" is fully aware, and as Hugh Vereker, in "The Figure in the Carpet," also demonstrates to perfection. With what willing attention the narrator interrogates him and listens to his responses, then interrogates Vereker's writing: with what attention the reader in his or her turn scrutinizes James's text for some glimmer of insight into the nature and meaning of the alleged secret. It matters little, in light of this willing granting of attention, that the secrets in question are dubious (the narrator in "Sarrasine" may be inventing his story; both Dupin and Vereker may well be bluffing); what matters is the authority they confer. Vera's "self-possession" is matched by Nuttal's willingness to give credence to the family "secret" she imparts. Indeed, so strong is the presumption, in a reader or listener, that a narrator who embarks self-assuredly on a tale has something of significance to impart that the truly skillful storyteller is perhaps the one who, far from making portentous claims (like those just mentioned) or emphatic expostulations (like Labov's storytellers), simply launches calmly into a quiet narrative— as does the narrator of "Un cœur simple"—secure in the knowledge that the more confidence he or she displays, the more the narratee will trust the narrator to *deliver*, that is, will attend to the narrative discourse with a view to discovering the point it is assumed to have. In short, such confidence (Bourdieu's idea) is itself seductive.

A more defensive procedure, however, is to lay claim to a *derived* authority, intertextual reference being the clearest mode by which literary narratives exploit such secondary authority. In the discourse of everyday life, the gambit takes such forms as: "Guess what X told me . . ." or "I have it on good authority that . . . ." In literary narrative, one might think, for example, of Balzac's narrator suggesting to Mme de Rochefide that the story he is about to tell her has the appeal of those passionate romances between Northerners and Southern women of which she is so fond; but the hint in Balzac's own text that his story has Hoffmann-like significance functions in exactly the same way. So, too, in "Sylvie," the precedent of Rousseau (as romancer and as philosopher) is constantly put forward to bolster the interest of the narrator's own adventure. This ploy is more obviously seductive in that the message it delivers boils down to saying "What you have enjoyed before, in Hoffmann or Rousseau, you will enjoy again in my own narrative." In more subtle form, it may well rely on the intertext as an antimodel: "where X was only partially successful, I will do better," or "where X was wrong, I will be right." But, in this light, the function of the intertext appears to not simply provide the narratee with interpretive guidance; it also makes a powerful claim to authority and is a device of seduction in its own right.

Once established, however (whether by a show of self-assurance or an appeal to precedent), such authority must be maintained, and it is here that seductive devices "proper" come into their own. Seduction as a narrative tactic takes the form of recruiting the desires of the other in the interests of maintaining narrative authority, so it is a duplicitous act to the extent that it introduces into the concept of "point" a *cleavage*, a conflict of motives, since the story that conforms to the hearer's desires has also the function of satisfying other desires (e.g., the desire to tell the story) in the storyteller. It is the failures of seduction that reveal this duplicity most clearly: Balzac's narrator miscalculates the effect of his narrative on Mme de Rochefide and pays the price (loss of authority); in "Sylvie," the young hero, in his storytelling ventures, constantly confuses his own desires with those of his hearers, so that the former stand condemned as "illusions." But the narrator of "Sylvie" has learned from this lesson, and we saw his "fixer sans beaucoup d'ordre" as a *switching device* enabling him to combine *distanced* narration and reader *involvement* in such a way as to produce "understanding." A similar point of cleavage is the "fissure" we perceived in "The Figure in the Carpet" between telling and writing. That storytelling as seduction—the art of "inhabiting the space of the other," the art of "moves"—is very frequently successful is a fact sufficiently demonstrated by these and the other stories whose performance has been analyzed in this book. So, the problem is not so much, perhaps, to recognize the seductive power of narrative as it is to understand it; for here is without doubt a case where the *practice* of narrative, the *savoir-faire* of the texts, far outstrips our ability to theorize and to analyze it. Despite the contributions of rhetoric (from the rhetoric of persuasion in antiquity to more modern versions, such as Michel Charles's rhetoric of desire[10]), we urgently need a detailed theory of narration as seduction.

What the texts studied here could most cogently contribute to such a theory is their demonstration of the seductive power inherent in the device of denying seduction. Taking them together, one might easily derive from them a conception of nineteenth-century aesthetic ideology as vigorously antiseductive in its thrust. If there is a rather thin line, in texts like "The Purloined Letter" and "The Figure in the Carpet," between the *exposure* of seductive discursive techniques (in protagonists like Dupin and Vereker) and textual *exploitation*, through the dominance of these characters, of the same techniques, other narratives draw very careful distinctions between narrative seduction and their own program. In "Sylvie" and "Sarrasine," the values of "understanding" are thus opposed to seductive attitudes (sexual in one case, *romanesque* in the other), and these "readerly" texts undertake an education of the reader designed to make him or her receptive to their "philosophical" project. Texts that, although still firmly "readerly," are beginning to approach more "writerly" conceptions of art also distance themselves from seduction: in "Un cœur simple," seductive discourse figures as mimetic duplicity and is opposed to textual simplicity; while "The Dead" exposes Gabriel Conroy as a pennyboy, a seductive parasite ("only all palaver and what they can get out of you") by contrast with artistic values that are, through their affinity with cosmic "noise," socially dissonant. In such texts, as in "The Figure in the Carpet," the reader is maintained at a greater distance, so that it seems that "writerly" values presuppose a less thoroughly programmed reader, one capable of bringing to the text his or her own *disponibilité* in a situation of less involvement, and greater openness.

Yet all these texts, as I have suggested, have seductive programs of their own. Denial or renunciation of one form of narrative seduction may merely mask another form of reader recruitment, a seduction of a different kind, as is the case in "Sarrasine" or "Sylvie." These texts are *actively* seductive in their mechanisms for ensuring the appropriate form of reader involvement in the mode of understanding they assume to be crucial. But "Un cœur simple" can also be readily seen as combining the seductive—in this case, control of the reader through mimetic duplicity—with the more open stance of textual simplicity; here there is a less active mode of seduction and, correspondingly, a greater reliance on the reader's willingness to love, while the reader is nevertheless recruited and indeed controlled by the realist text, guided, that is, into responding to the textual "invitation." Similarly, the reader of "The Figure in the Carpet" is both distanced by the text as "writing out" and involved in the text as "telling," and "The Dead" contrives to make the reader experience the text, Gabriel-like, as a refusal of love while ensuring that, Michael-like, his or her desire remains unabated; for there is a form of seduction that consists of holding the "seducee" at arm's length. Narrative seduction, then, seems as complex and varied in its tactics as are the erotic seductions of everyday life; and its range, from active enterprise, through the "simple" invitation, to a carefully calculated "refusal," is not dissimilar to what can be observed wherever people relate sexually to one another. What is constant is the basic duplicity whereby a seductive program is condemned so that a seductive program can be pursued.

Duplicity is a word that has occurred many times in this book, and in a number of different senses. The "duplicitous" narrative, itself opposed to self-designating narrative (chapter 2), splits, as we have seen (chapters 3 and 6), into mimetic duplicity and the doubleness (or "duplicity" in quotation marks) that arises from textual, and therefore situational, simplicity. Self-designating narratives, on the other hand, although they are open as to their status as narrative, tend to be situationally duplicitous, their openness as narrative coinciding with seductive programs (chapters 4 and 5). But the conclusion to which our current analysis tends is that all narratives are necessarily seductive, seduction being the means whereby they maintain their authority to narrate; and if that is so, then the duplicity of seduction, whereby narrative conforms to the (projected) desires of the other in order to bring about its own desire to narrate, is *constitutive of the narrative situation* as such. If "authority" and "seduction" are in a sense interchangeable, so too are "seduction" and "duplicity"; but the latter term introduces firmly into the analysis of narrative "point" the *double* perspective, the cleavage that arises from a *dual* input into the narrative situation, that of the narrator and that of the narratee. Duplicity—and this is true, in the final analysis, of all the senses in which I have employed the word— is a manifestation of the "gap" between discourse and its presumed recipient, of the assumed *otherness* of the instance that has the power of determining the success or failure of the communicational act. It is, in short, a product—whether in literary discourse or in life—of alienated relationships.[11] In this light, the duplicity involved in the seductive tactic of denying seduction appears as a particular case of a more general rule. Denial of seductive intent signals respect of the reader's desires: but this is, in fact, a *recruitment* of the reader's desire (the desire not to be seduced) and the trust thus gained can then be channeled in the direction of the narrative's own program ("understanding," "textual simplicity," the aesthetic of "noise," or whatever).

The Power of Fiction

The question is, however, whether there can be a narrative that is not, in some sense and to some degree, duplicitous because seductive. Can there be, in Othello's words, a "round, unvarnish'd tale," *simple* (or unalienated) storytelling? Everything in the foregoing analysis suggests the contrary: because there can be no narrative without the authority to narrate, and no authority without the authorization of another, whose desire must consequently be inscribed, however spectrally, in the narrative discourse itself, it is difficult to see the possibility of a narrative act—at least in the present state of Western culture—that is not at the same time, in small or large measure, an act of seduction. And it is this characteristic of narrative acts that, I believe, throws light on the *power of fiction*.

There is, of course, for practical purposes, a convention that distinguishes between those stories that we choose to regard as informative (and give "narrative" authority to), and those we regard as fictional (and look to for "narratorial" interest): fiction, in this sense (which is the sense that has been assumed in the greater part of this book) is the fiction we recognize as fiction. But such distinctions (like other similar ones: "literature" versus "nonliterature," for example) are at best distinctions of degree, not of kind; and we seem, in fact, to be dealing with a polarized continuum. It is, after all, a matter of everyday experience that one person's "fact" is another's "fiction"; that what is "information," "history," "knowledge," et cetera for one period or culture is read, in another, as "fiction," "literature," "imagination," et cetera. The dividing line between fiction and nonfiction, the "narrative" and the "narratorial," being conventional, is one that constantly shifts; and, since Nietzsche, the pervading fictional quality of *all* discourse has been, for many, axiomatic.

I should like, then, from the perspective of this book, to suggest that "fiction" might be most fruitfully (if radically) defined as the name we give to the narrative moves that, in a given narrative situation, produce authority through seduction. It is, in short, that "mighty magic" that Othello denies using but that Shakespeare shows his tale putting into effect (in repetition of the seductive effect of his storytelling on Desdemona). The Duke and the Senators of Venice, as the Duke acknowledges with his comment, "I think this tale would win my daughter too," are subject to the action of a narrative "charm." (So, this—incidentally—is yet another seduction that operates, in Othello's claim to plain speaking, through the denial of seduction.) Such a definition of fictionality is not intended to deny the possibility of there being, in a given communicational circumstance, a greater or lesser presence of what might be called "fiction effect"; but it does suggest that, because narrative is one of the principal ways by which human beings *relate,* it is necessarily characterized, as a discursive phenomenon, by the duplicity that has been analyzed here as resulting from the duality of the storytelling situation itself. "Fiction," in this analysis, is simply the way narrative interacts with narrative situation; or, put in another way, it is what arises, in language, out of this interaction. There is something emblematic from this point of view in the ambivalence of the narrator of "Sarrasine," whose desire to seduce Mme de Rochefide produces a narrative I felt justified in calling "fiction," although it is presented as truth, and without it being possible to be *certain* that the narrator is deliberately "inventing." It is, of course, an implication of this definition that the production of fiction is always, in the first place, *involuntary* (because situational), although it *may* become intentional as a second-order phenomenon.

However, the interaction between narrative and narrative situation does itself function differently in different communicational situations, and this remark will bring us back to the specificity of the literary. The tactics of the *oral* storyteller, whose audience is *in presentia*, are determined by the phenomenon of *feedback*: thus, the "same" story may be long or short, elaborate and digressive, or brief and to the point, ornamented or plain, according to the narrator's sense of audience reaction. In this sense, the story is truly the product of a collaboration, or at least of a negotiation, and the good storyteller is one who has the flexibility to make necessary adjustments in different circumstances, for different audiences, and—for the same audience—as the narrative proceeds.[12] "Upon this hint I spake"—so Shakespeare records a successful feedback operation; whereas, in "Sarrasine," it is the narrator's inflexibility, his maladroitness in the feedback situation represented by Mme de Rochefide's reactions, that Balzac illustrates. Feedback is, of course, not absent from situations of written communication, where it plays a smaller or greater role according to the degree to which audience reaction can by hypothesized or anticipated; thus, in a letter to a friend, I can adjust my narrative as a function of the probable impact it will have, that is, of the feedback I have received in the past. But as the deferral of communication becomes more clearly constitutive of the situation, which is the case in the literary text, and as the audience becomes a more crucially hypothetical construct, then for the flexibility, the sensitivity to feedback characteristic of the oral narrator is substituted a greater degree of insistence, that is, a form of textual *redundancy.* This compensates for the deficiency in feedback by establishing, in a way calculated to survive the unpredictable variety of historical reading situations, that communicational situation in which the narrative (in its own self-understanding) "makes sense," or "has point." Some of these techniques of redundancy, whereby the audience *in absentia* becomes spectrally "present" in the discourse of literary narrative, have been the object of study and interpretation in the essays that compose the body of this book.

However, such a need for situational redundancy in the literary text produces, in turn, a phenomenon that is certainly not absent from narrative acts in general (it is Labov's "evaluation" discourse, for example) but that seems particularly characteristic of literary texts, exemplifying as they do the deferral that may be taken to exist to some degree in all communicational situations. I mean, of course, their self-reflexivity. In order to exert their power, as fiction, these texts are obliged to include in their discursive texture elements that, in their turn, not only permit but require the analysis of the communicational situation on which their fictional power depends. Alongside their seductive power, they have necessarily an analytic power that dismantles the elements of their "charms," their "magic." It is not possible to reflect for long on the storytelling episodes included in the texts studied here without concluding that they have a double function: *without* them the story could not "work," but *with* them it cannot work since they reveal the conditions under which it works and thus defuse its action. *Nec tecum nec sine te —* such is, with respect to situational self-reflexivity, the paradoxical law of narrative power in these texts: it is a power dependent for its force on the power to undo itself.

In a moral perspective, one could say that this is the essential honesty of literature. In a certain literary-philosophical mode, one recognizes something like the deconstructive model of the Yale critics. I see it, rather, less as a universal quality of texts than as a situational necessity, tied to the current position of literature in our culture, with respect to the overall phenomenon of narrative it exemplifies. So long as concepts like readability, implying the ongoing production of meaning combined with a certain channeling of textual productivity, continue to dominate our understanding of literature, situational self-reflexivity of this kind is likely to be a prominent feature of texts. It is, in short, a product of the alienated status literature has among us, as the very type not just of deferred communication, but of deferred communication that is self-aware.

* * *

Imagine a husband whose wife had committed suicide a few hours before by throwing herself out of a window and whose dead body is lying on the table. His mind is in a state of confusion, and he has not as yet had time to collect his thoughts. He keeps pacing the room, trying to find some reason for what has happened, "to gather his thoughts to a point."

That, says Dostoevsky, is the point of his story "A Gentle Creature." "So there he is, talking to himself, telling the whole story, trying to *explain* it to himself."[13] The intuition is very clear here that *narrative* "point" is indistinguishable from the "point" of human *relationships*—one might as well say (for humans as communicating creatures) the point of existence. My own conclusion must necessarily be along the same lines. It is a disappointing conclusion in a sense, for it collapses what was apparently a manageable subject (concerning narrative) into an issue so large as to be, for purposes of practical study, completely elusive. But it is an exciting one also, because it suggests yet another way in which the study of literature escapes the specialization and the technical definitions we impose on it and shades into a study of human beings' understanding of human beings. At a recent University of Chicago conference on narrative, Ursula Le Guin, unconsciously echoing Dostoevsky, expressed at one and the same time her discontent with the merely technical study of literary narrative and her concern for the more philosophical question of point, her sense that the whys and wherefores of storytelling are bound up, in a fundamental way, with the whys and wherefores, if such there be, of our existence together, as social beings. Her little ditty provides me with the best possible ending, not because it asks an unanswerable question, but because the unanswerable question it asks is the one that all studies of narrative should ideally lead up to and leave in their reader's mind:

> The *histoire* is the what
> and the *discours* is the how
> but what I want to know, Brigham,
> is *le pourquoi*
> *Why* are we sitting here around the campfire?[14]

NOTES

1. See *The Pursuit of Signs: Semiotics, Literature, Deconstruction* (Ithaca, N.Y.: Cornell University Press, 1981), especially pp. 3-17 ("Beyond Interpretation") and pp. 80-99 ("Riffaterre and the Semiotics of Poetry"). Quotation on p. 98.

2. See in particular *On the Margins of Discourse* (Chicago: University of Chicago Press, 1978).

3. (Paris: Julliard, 1961). My references are to the 10/18 edition (Paris: Union Générale d'Éditions, 1972).

4. (Montréal: Tisseyre, 1965).

5. *La distinction* (Paris: Éd. de Minuit, 1979), p. 229.

6. In *De la séduction* (Paris: Éd. Galilée, 1979), Jean Baudrillard argues similarly that "la séduction représente la maîtrise de l'univers symbolique, alors que le pouvoir ne représente que la maîtrise de l'univers réel" (p. 19). I would reformulate as "la maîtrise *dans* l'univers symbolique" and remove the restrictive "ne . . . que" from the description of power. And I do not subscribe to Baudrillard's extension of his argument in the direction of the supposed nature of femininity.

7. Cf. Michel de Certeau, "On the Oppositional Practices of Everyday Life," *Social Text*, 3 (fall 1980), 3-43.

8. *Language in the Inner City: Studies in the Black English Vernacular* (Philadelphia: University of Pennsylvania Press, 1972), p. 366.

9. "On the Oppositional Practices of Everyday Life," pp. 41 and 35.

10. See *Rhétorique de la lecture* (Paris: Éd. du Seuil, 1977).

11. I have pursued this analysis of narrative duplicity in two articles: "Narrative as Oppositional Practice: Nerval's *Aurélia*" (to appear in *Stanford French Review*) and especially "Récits d'aliénés, récits aliénés: Nerval et John Perceval," *Poétique*, 53 (février 1983), 72-90.

12. Walter J. Ong, S.J., has made this point in a number of places, most recently (to my knowledge) in *Interfaces of the Word* (Ithaca, N.Y.: Cornell University Press, 1977), passim.

13. *The Best Short Stories of Dostoevsky* (New York: Modern Library, n.d.), p. 241 ("Short Preface by the Author"). I am grateful to Tobin Siebers for drawing my attention to this text.

14. "It Was a Dark and Stormy Night: Or Why Are We Huddling around the Campfire," *Critical Inquiry*, 7, 1 (autumn 1980), 191-199. Quotation on p. 192.

Appendixes

Appendix A
Saki, "The Open Window"

"MY AUNT WILL BE DOWN presently, Mr. Nuttel," said a very self-possessed young lady of fifteen; "in the meantime you must try and put up with me."

Framton Nuttel endeavored to say the correct something which should duly flatter the niece of the moment without unduly discounting the aunt that was to come. Privately he doubted more than ever whether these formal visits on a succession of total strangers would do much toward helping the nerve cure which he was supposed to be undergoing.

"I know how it will be," his sister had said when he was preparing to migrate to this rural retreat; "you will bury yourself down there and not speak to a living soul, and your nerves will be worse than ever from moping. I shall just give you letters of introduction to all the people I know there. Some of them, as far as I can remember, were quite nice."

Framton wondered whether Mrs. Sappleton, the lady to whom he was presenting one of the letters of introduction, came into the nice division.

"Do you know many of the people round here?" asked the niece, when she judged that they had had sufficient silent communion.

"Hardly a soul," said Framton. "My sister was staying here, at the rectory, you know, some four years ago and she gave me letters of introduction to some of the people here."

He made the last statement in a tone of distinct regret.

"Then you know practically nothing about my aunt?" pursued the self-possessed young lady.

"Only her name and address," admitted the caller. He was wondering whether Mrs. Sappleton was in the married or widowed state. An undefinable something about the room seemed to suggest masculine habitation.

"Her great tragedy happened just three years ago," said the child; "that would be since your sister's time."

"Her tragedy?" asked Framton; somehow in this restful country spot tragedies seemed out of place.

"You may wonder why we keep that window wide open on an October afternoon," said the niece, indicating a large French window that opened onto a lawn.

"It is quite warm for the time of year," said Framton; "but has that window got anything to do with the tragedy?"

"Out through that window, three years ago to a day, her husband and her two young brothers went off for their day's shooting. They never came back. In crossing the moor to their favorite snipe-shooting ground they were all three engulfed in a treacherous piece of bog. It had been that dreadful wet summer, you know, and places that were safe in other years gave way suddenly without warning. Their bodies were never recovered. That was the dreadful part of it." Here the child's voice lost its self-possessed note and became falteringly human. "Poor aunt always thinks that they will come back some day, they and the little brown spaniel that was lost with them, and walk in at that window just as they used to do. That is why the window is kept open every evening till it is quite dusk. Poor dear aunt, she has often told me how they went out, her husband with his white waterproof coat over his arm, and Ronnie, her youngest brother, singing, 'Bertie, why do you bound?' as he always did to tease her, because she said it got on her nerves. Do you know, sometimes on still, quiet evenings like this, I almost get a creepy feeling that they will all walk in through that window—"

She broke off with a little shudder. It was a relief to Framton when the aunt bustled into the room with a whirl of apologies for being late in making her appearance.

"I hope Vera has been amusing you?" she said.

"She has been very interesting," said Framton.

"I hope you don't mind the open window," said Mrs. Sappleton briskly; "my husband and brothers will be home directly from shooting, and they always come in this way. They've been out for snipe in the marshes today, so they'll make a fine mess over my poor carpets. So like you men-folk, isn't it?"

She rattled on cheerfully about the shooting and the scarcity of birds, and the prospects for duck in the winter. To Framton it was all purely horrible. He made a desperate but only partially successful effort to turn the talk on to a less ghastly topic; he was conscious that his hostess was giving him only a fragment of her attention, and her eyes were constantly straying past him to the open window and the lawn beyond. It was certainly an unfortunate coincidence that he should have paid his visit on this tragic anniversary.

"The doctors agree in ordering me complete rest, an absence of mental excitement, and avoidance of anything in the nature of violent physical exercise," announced Framton, who labored under the tolerably widespread delusion that total strangers and chance acquaintances are hungry for the least detail of one's ailments and infirmities, their cause and cure. "On the matter of diet they are not so much in agreement," he continued.

"No?" said Mrs. Sappleton, in a voice which only replaced a yawn at the last moment. Then she suddenly brightened into alert attention — but not to what Framton was saying.

"Here they are at last!" she cried. "Just in time for tea, and don't they look as if they were muddy up to the eyes!"

Framton shivered slightly and turned toward the niece with a look intended to convey sympathetic comprehension. The child was staring out through the open window with dazed horror in her eyes. In a chill shock of nameless fear Framton swung round in his seat and looked in the same direction.

In the deepening twilight three figures were walking across the lawn toward the window; they all carried guns under their arms, and one of them was additionally burdened with a white coat hung over his shoulders. A tired brown spaniel kept close at their heels. Noiselessly they neared the house, and then a hoarse young voice chanted out of the dusk: "I said, Bertie, why do you bound?"

Framton grabbed wildly at his stick and hat; the halldoor, the gravel-drive, and the front gate were dimly noted stages in his headlong retreat. A cyclist coming along the road had to run into the hedge to avoid imminent collision.

"Here we are, my dear," said the bearer of the white mackintosh, coming in through the window; "fairly muddy, but most of it's dry. Who was that who bolted out as we came up?"

"A most extraordinary man, a Mr. Nuttel," said Mrs. Sappleton; "could only talk about his illness, and dashed off without a word of good by or apology when you arrived. One would think he had seen a ghost."

"I expect it was the spaniel," said the niece calmly; "he told me he had a horror of dogs. He was once hunted into a cemetery somewhere on the banks of the Ganges by a pack of pariah dogs, and had to spend the night in a newly dug grave with the creatures snarling and grinning and foaming just above him. Enough to make anyone lose their nerve."

Romance at short notice was her specialty.

Appendix B
Marcel Schwob, "Les Sans-Gueule"

On les ramassa tous deux, l'un à côté de l'autre, sur l'herbe brûlée. Leurs vêtements avaient volé en lambeaux. La conflagration de la poudre avait éteint la couleur des numéros; les plaques de maillechort etaient émiettées. On aurait dit de deux morceaux de pâte humaine. Car le même fragment tranchant de tôle d'acier, sifflant en oblique, leur avait emporté la figure, en sorte qu'ils gisaient sur les touffes de gazon, comme un double tronçon à tête rouge. L'aide-major qui les empila dans la voiture les prit par curiosité surtout: le coup, en effet, etait singulier. Il ne leur restait ni nez, ni pommettes, ni lèvres; les yeux avaient jailli hors des orbites fracassées, la bouche s'ouvrait en entonnoir, trou sanglant avec la langue coupée qui vibrait en frissonnant. On ne pouvait s'imaginer une vie si étrange: deux êtres de même taille, et *sans figure*. Les crânes, couverts de cheveux ras, portaient deux plaques rouges, simultanément et semblablement taillées, avec des creux aux orbites et trois trous pour la bouche et le nez.

Ils reçurent à l'ambulance les noms de Sans-Gueule n° 1 et Sans-Gueule n° 2. Un chirurgien anglais, qui faisait le service de bonne volonté, fut surpris du cas, et y prit intérêt. Il oignit les plaies et les pansa, fit des points de suture, opéra l'extraction des esquilles, pétrit cette bouillie de viande, et construisit ainsi deux calottes de chair, concaves et rouges, identiquement perforées au fond, comme les fourneaux de pipes exotiques. Placés dans deux lits côte à côte,

231

les deux Sans-Gueule tachaient les draps d'une double cicatrice arrondie, gigantesque et sans signification. L'éternelle immobilité de cette plaie avait une douleur muette: les muscles tranchés ne réagissaient même pas sur les coutures; le choc terrible avait anéanti le sens de l'ouïe, si bien que la vie ne se manifestait en eux que par les mouvements de leurs membres, et par un double cri rauque qui giclait par intervalles entre leurs palais béants et leurs tremblants moignons de langue.

Cependant il guérirent tous deux. Lentement, sûrement, ils apprirent à conduire leurs gestes, à développer les bras, à replier les jambes pour s'asseoir, à mouvoir les gencives durcies qui revêtissaient encore leurs mâchoires cimentées; ils eurent un plaisir, qu'on reconnut à des sons aigus et modulés, mais sans puissance syllabique: ce fut de fumer des pipes dont les tuyaux étaient tamponnés de pièces de caoutchouc ovales, pour rejoindre les bords de la plaie de leur bouche. Accroupis dans les couvertures, ils respiraient le tabac; et des jets de fumée fusaient par les orifices de leur tête: par le double trou du nez, par les puits jumeaux de leurs orbites, par les commissures des mâchoires, entre les squelettes de leurs dents. Et chaque échappement du brouillard gris qui jaillissait entre les craquelures de ces masses rouges était salué d'un rire extra-humain, gloussement de la luette qui tressaillait, tandis que leur reste de langue clapotait faiblement.

Il y eut une émotion dans l'hôpital, quand une petite femme en cheveux fut amenée par l'interne de service au chevet des Sans-Gueule, et les considéra l'un après l'autre d'une mine terrifiée, puis fondit en larmes. Dans le cabinet du médecin en chef elle expliqua, entre des sanglots, qu'un de ces deux-là devait être son mari. On l'avait noté parmi les disparus; mais ces deux blessés, n'ayant aucune marque d'identité, étaient dans une catégorie particulière. Et la taille ainsi que la largeur d'épaules et la forme des mains lui rappelaient invinciblement l'homme perdu. Mais elle était dans une affreuse perplexité: des deux Sans-Gueule, quel était son mari?

Cette petite femme était vraiment gentille: son peignoir bon marché lui moulait le sein; elle avait, à cause de ses cheveux relevés à la chinoise, une douce figure d'enfant. La douleur naïve et l'incertitude presque risible se mélangeaient dans son expression et contractaient ses traits comme ceux d'une petite fille qui vient de casser un joujou. De sorte que le médecin en chef ne se tint pas de sourire; et, comme il parlait gras, il dit à la petite femme qui le regardait en dessous: "Eh ben!—quoi!—emporte-les, tes Sans-Gueule, tu les reconnaîtras à l'essai!"

Elle fut d'abord scandalisée, et détourna la tête, avec une rougeur d'enfant honteuse; puis elle baissa les yeux, et regarda de l'un à l'autre lit. Les deux coupes rouges couturées reposaient toujours sur les oreillers, avec cette même absence de signification qui en faisait une double énigme. Elle se pencha vers eux; elle parla à l'oreille de l'un, puis de l'autre. Les têtes n'eurent aucune réaction,—mais les quatre mains éprouvèrent une sorte de vibration,—sans doute parce que ces deux pauvres corps sans âme sentaient vaguement qu'il y avait près d'eux une petite femme très gentille, avec une odeur très douce et d'absurdes manières exquises de bébé.

Elle hésita encore pendant quelque temps, et finit par demander qu'on voulût bien lui confier les deux Sans-Gueule pendant un mois. On les porta dans une grande voiture rembourrée, toujours l'un à côté de l'autre; la petite femme, assise en face, pleurait sans cesse à chaudes larmes.

Et quand ils arrivèrent dans la maison, une vie étrange commença pour eux trois. Elle allait éternellement de l'un à l'autre, épiant une indication, attendant un signe. Elle guettait ces surfaces rouges qui ne bougeraient jamais plus. Elle regardait avec anxiété ces énormes cicatrices dont elle distinguait graduellement les coutures comme on connaît les traits des visages aimés. Elle les examinait tour à tour, ainsi que l'on considère les épreuves d'une photographie, sans se décider à choisir.

Et peu à peu la forte peine qui lui serrait le cœur, au commencement, quand elle pensait à son mari perdu, finit par se fondre dans un calme irrésolu. Elle vécut à la façon d'une personne qui a renoncé à tout, mais qui vit par habitude. Les deux moitiés brisées qui représentaient l'être chéri, ne se réunirent jamais dans son affection; mais ses pensées allaient régulièrement de l'un à l'autre, comme si son âme eût oscillé en manière de balancier. Elle les regardait tous deux comme ses "mannequins rouges", et ce furent les poupées falotes qui peuplèrent son existence. Fumant leur pipe, assis sur leur lit, dans la même attitude, exhalant les mêmes tourbillons de vapeur, et poussant simultanément les mêmes cris inarticulés, ils ressemblaient plutôt à des pantins gigantesques apportés d'Orient, à des masques sanglants venus d'Outre-mer, qu'à des êtres animés d'une vie consciente et qui avaient été des hommes.

Ils étaient "ses deux singes", ses bonshommes rouges, ses deux petits marins, ses hommes brûlés, ses corps sans âme, ses polichinelles de viande, ses têtes trouées, ses caboches sans cervelle, ses figures de sang; elle les bichonnait à tour de rôle, faisait leur couverture, bordait leurs draps, mêlait leur vin, cassait leur pain; elle les menait marcher par le milieu de la chambre, un à chaque côté, et les faisait sauter sur le parquet; elle jouait avec eux, et, s'ils se fâchaient, les renvoyait du plat de la main. D'une caresse ils étaient auprès d'elle, comme deux chiens folâtres; d'un geste dur, ils demeuraient pliés en deux, semblables à des animaux repentants. Ils se frôlaient contre elle et quêtaient les friandises; tous deux possesseurs d'écuelles en bois où ils plongeaient périodiquement, avec des hurlements joyeux, leurs masques rouges.

Ces deux têtes n'irritaient plus la petite femme comme autrefois, ne l'intriguaient plus à la façon de deux loups vermeils posés sur des figures connues. Elle les aimait également, avec des moues enfantines. Elle disait d'eux: "Mes pantins sont couchés; mes hommes se promènent." Elle ne comprit pas qu'on vînt de l'hôpital demander lequel elle gardait. Ce lui fut une question absurde: c'était comme si on avait exigé qu'elle coupât son mari en deux. Elle les punissait souvent à la manière des enfants avec leurs poupées méchantes. Elle disait à l'un: "Tu vois, mon petit loup—ton frère est vilain—il est mauvais comme un singe—je lui ai tourné sa figure contre le mur; je ne le retournerai que s'il me demande pardon." Après, avec un petit rire, elle retournait le pauvre corps, doucement soumis à la pénitence, et lui embrassait les mains. Elle leur baisait aussi parfois leurs affreuses coutures, et s'essuyait la bouche tout de suite après, en fronçant les lèvres, en cachette. Et elle riait aussitôt, à perte de vue.

Mais insensiblement elle s'accoutuma plus à l'un d'eux, parce qu'il était plus doux. Ce fut inconscient, certes, car elle avait perdu tout espoir de reconnaissance. Elle le préféra comme une bête favorite, qu'on a plus de plaisir à caresser. Elle le dorlota davantage et le baisa plus tendrement. Et l'autre Sans-Gueule devint triste, aussi, par degrés, sentant autour de lui moins de présence féminine. Il resta plié sur lui-même, souvent accroupi sur son lit, la tête nichée dans le bras, pareil à un oiseau malade. Il refusa de fumer; tandis que l'autre, ignorant de sa douleur, respirait toujours du brouillard gris qu'il exhalait avec des cris aigus par toutes les fentes de son masque pourpre.

Alors la petite femme soigna son mari triste, mais sans trop comprendre. Il hochait la tête dans son sein en sanglotant de poitrine; une sorte de grognement rauque lui parcourait le torse. Ce fut une lutte de jalousie dans un cœur obscurci d'ombre; une jalousie animale, née de sensations avec des souvenirs confus peut-être d'une vie d'autrefois. Elle lui chanta des berceuses comme à un enfant, et le calma de ses mains fraîches posées sur sa tête brûlante. Quand elle le vit très malade, de grosses larmes tombèrent de ses yeux rieurs sur le pauvre visage muet.

Mais bientôt elle fut dans une angoisse poignante; car elle eut la sensation vague de gestes déjà vus dans une ancienne maladie. Elle crut reconnaître des mouvements autrefois familiers; et les positions des mains émaciées lui rappelaient confusément des mains semblables, autrefois chéries, et qui avaient frôlé ses draps avant le grand abîme creusé dans sa vie.

Et les plaintes du pauvre abandonné lui lancinèrent le cœur; alors, dans une incertitude haletante, elle dévisagea de nouveau ces deux têtes sans visages. Ce ne furent plus deux poupées pourpres—mais l'un fut étranger—l'autre peut-être la moitié d'elle-même. Lorsque le malade fut mort, toute sa peine se réveilla. Elle crut véritablement qu'elle avait perdu son mari; elle courut, haineuse, vers l'autre Sans-Gueule, et s'arrêta, prise de sa pitié enfantine, devant le misérable mannequin rouge qui fumait joyeusement, en modulant ses cris.

Bibliography

Bibliography

Altieri, C. "Presence and Reference in a Literary Text: The Example of Williams' 'This Is Just to Say,' " *Critical Inquiry*, 5, 3 (spring 1979), 489-510.

Altieri, C. *Act and Quality: A Theory of Literary Meaning and Humanistic Understanding* (Amherst: University of Massachusetts Press, 1981).

Anderson, Q. *The American Henry James* (New Brunswick, N.J.: Rutgers University Press, 1957).

Austin, J. L. *How to Do Things with Words* (New York: Oxford University Press, 1965).

Baker, J. R., and Staley, T. F., eds. *James Joyce's "Dubliners": A Critical Handbook* (Belmont, Calif.: Wadsworth, 1969).

Bal, M. *Narratologie* (Paris: Klincksieck, 1977).

Bal, M. "Notes on Narrative Embedding," *Poetics Today*, 2, 2 (winter 1981), 41-59.

Barbéris, P. "À propos du *S/Z* de Roland Barthes," *L'Année Balzacienne* (1971), 11-123.

Barthes, R. "L'analyse structurale des récits," *Communications*, 8 (1966), 1-83.

Barthes, R. *Critique et vérité* (Paris: Éd. du Seuil, 1966).

Barthes, R. *S/Z* (Paris: Éd. du Seuil, 1970). (Translated as *S/Z* [New York: Hill and Wang, 1974].)

Bateson, G. *Mind and Nature* (New York: Dutton, 1979).

Baudrillard, M. *De la séduction* (Paris: Éd. Galilée, 1979).

Beaujour, M. "Exemplary Pornography: Barrès, Loyola and the Novel," in S. Suleiman and I. Crosman, eds., *The Reader in the Text: Essays on Audience and Interpretation* (Princeton, N.J.: Princeton University Press, 1980), 325-349.

Beck, W. *Joyce's "Dubliners": Substance, Vision and Art* (Durham, N.C.: Duke University Press, 1969).

Beja, M., ed. *James Joyce: "Dubliners" and "A Portrait of the Artist as a Young Man." A Casebook* (London: Macmillan, 1973).

Benjamin, W. *Illuminations*, ed. H. Arendt (New York: Schocken Books, 1969).

Benveniste, E. *Problèmes de linguistique générale*, I and II (Paris: Gallimard, 1966 and 1974).

Benstock, B. "The Dead," in Clive Hart, ed., *James Joyce's "Dubliners"* (New York: Viking, 1969), 153-169.

Bertrand, M. "Parole et silence dans les *Trois contes* de Flaubert," *Stanford French Review*, 1, 2 (fall 1977), 191-203.

Blackmur, R. P. "In the Country of the Blue," in F. W. Dupee, ed., *The Question of Henry James: A Collection of Critical Essays* (New York: Holt, 1945), 191-211.

Bogorad, S. N. "Gabriel Conroy as 'Whited Sepulchre': Prefiguring Imagery in 'The Dead,' " *Ball State University Forum*, 14, 1 (1973), 52-58.

Bonnet, H. *"Sylvie" de Nerval* (Paris: Hachette, 1975).

Bonnet, H. "Nerval et la fête continue," *Cahiers de l'Herne*, 37 (1980), 139-155.

Booth, W. C. *The Rhetoric of Fiction* (Chicago: University of Chicago Press, 1961).

Booth, W. C. *A Rhetoric of Irony* (Chicago: University of Chicago Press, 1974).

Borowitz, H. O. "Balzac's *Sarrasine*: The Sculptor as Narcissus," *Nineteenth Century French Studies*, 5 (1976-1977), 171-185.

Bourdieu, P. *La distinction* (Paris: Éd. de Minuit, 1979).

Boyd, J. D., and Boyd, R. A. "The Love Triangle in Joyce's 'The Dead,' " *University of Toronto Quarterly*, 42, 3 (spring 1973), 202-217.

Bremond, Cl. *Logique du récit* (Paris: Éd. du Seuil, 1973).

Brombert, V. *The Novels of Flaubert* (Princeton, N.J.: Princeton University Press, 1966).

Brombert, V. *Flaubert par lui-même* (Paris: Éd. du Seuil, 1971).

Brooks, P. *The Melodramatic Imagination* (New Haven, Conn.: Yale University Press, 1976).

Brooks, P. "Godlike Science/Unhallowed Arts: Language and Monstrosity in *Frankenstein*," *New Literary History*, 10, 3 (1978), 592-605.

Brooks, P. "Un rapport illisible: *Cœur des Ténèbres*," *Poétique*, 44 (1980), 472-489.

Brooks, P. "The Novel and the Guillotine; or Fathers and Sons in *Le rouge et le noir*," *PMLA*, 97, 3 (May 1982), 348-362.

Brooks, P. "Incredulous Narration: *Absalom, Absalom!*" *Comparative Literature*, 34, 3 (summer 1982), 247-268.

Budniakewitz, T. "A Conceptual Survey of Narrative Semiotics," *Dispositio*, 3, 7/8 (1978), 189-217.

Cellier, L. *De "Sylvie" à "Aurélia"* (Paris: Minard, 1971).

Certeau, M. de. "On the Oppositional Practices of Everyday Life," *Social Text*, 3 (fall 1980), 3-43.

Chambers, R. *Gérard de Nerval et la poétique du voyage* (Paris: Corti, 1969).

Chambers, R. *L'Ange et l'automate: Variations sur le mythe de l'actrice, de Nerval à Proust* (Paris: Minard, 1971).

Chambers, R. "Gautier et le complexe de Pygmalion," *Revue d'Histoire Littéraire de la France*, 72, 4 (1972), 641-658.

Chambers, R. "Le poète fumeur," *Australian Journal of French Studies*, 16, 1/2 (1979), 138-150.

Chambers, R. "Pour une poétique du vêtement," *Michigan Romance Studies*, 1 (1980), 18-46.

Chambers, R. "La lecture comme hantise: *Spirite* et *Le Horla*," *Revue des Sciences Humaines*, 177 (1980-1981), 105-117.

Chambers, R. "Le secret est un œuf: Lecture d'une fable de La Fontaine," *Versants*, 2 (1982), 75-85.

Charles, M. *Rhétorique de la lecture* (Paris: Éd. du Seuil, 1977).

Charles, M. "Digression, régression (Arabesques)," *Poétique*, 40 (1979), 395-407.

Chatman, S. *Story and Discourse: Narrative Structure in Fiction and Film* (Ithaca, N.Y.: Cornell University Press, 1978).

Citron, P. "Interprétation de *Sarrasine*," *L'Année Balzacienne* (1972), 81-95.

Cixous, H. "Henry James: L'Écriture comme placement, ou de l'ambiguïté de l'intérêt," *Poétique,* 1 (1970), 35-50.

Culler, J. *Flaubert: The Uses of Uncertainty* (London: Paul Elek, 1974).

Culler, J. *The Pursuit of Signs: Semiotics, Literature, Deconstruction* (Ithaca, N.Y.: Cornell University Press, 1981).

Dällenbach, L. *Le récit spéculaire* (Paris: Éd. du Seuil, 1977).

Dällenbach, L. "Du fragment au cosmos (*La comédie humaine* et l'opération de lecture, I)," *Poétique,* 40 (novembre 1979), 420-430.

Dällenbach, L. "Le tout en morceaux (*La comédie humaine* et l'opération de lecture, II)," *Poétique,* 42 (avril 1980), 156-169.

Dällenbach, L. "Réflexivité et lecture," *Revue des Sciences Humaines,* 177 (1980-1981), 23-37.

Daniel, R. "Poe's Detective God," in W. L. Howarth, ed., *Twentieth Century Interpretations of Poe's Tales* (Englewood Cliffs, N.J.: Prentice-Hall, 1971).

Debray-Genette, R. "Les figures du récit dans *Un cœur simple,*" *Poétique,* 3 (1970), 348-364.

Debray-Genette, R. "Du mode narratif dans les *Trois contes,*" *Littérature,* 2 (1971), 39-62.

Debray-Genette, R. "La technique romanesque de Flaubert dans 'Un cœur simple': Étude de genèse," in M. Issacharoff, ed., *Langages de Flaubert: Actes du Colloque de London* (Paris: Minard, 1976), 95-114.

Denommé, R. "Félicité's View of Reality and the Nature of Flaubert's Irony in 'Un cœur simple,' " *Studies in Short Fiction,* 7 (197), 573-581.

Derrida, J. "Le facteur de la vérité," *Critique,* 21 (1975), 96-147.

Donato, E. "The Museum's Furnace: Notes toward a Contextual Study of *Bouvard et Pécuchet,*" in J. Harrari, ed., *Textual Strategies* (Ithaca, N.Y.: Cornell University Press, 1979), 213-238.

Ducrot, O. *Dire et ne pas dire* (Paris: Herman, 1972).

Ducrot, O., et al. *Les mots du discours* (Paris: Éd. de Minuit, 1980).

Eisenzweig, U. *L'Espace imaginaire d'un récit: "Sylvie" de Gérard de Nerval* (Neuchâtel: La Baconnière, 1976).

Ellis, J. M. *The Theory of Literary Criticism* (Berkeley: University of California Press, 1974).

Fairlie, A. "An Approach to Nerval," in *Studies in Modern French Literature Presented to P. Mansell Jones* (Manchester: Manchester University Press, 1961), 87-103.

Fairlie, A. "La contradiction créatrice: Quelques remarques sur la genèse d'*Un cœur simple,*" in C. Carlut, éd., *Essais sur Flaubert en l'honneur de Don Demorest* (Paris: Nizet, 1979), 203-231. (Reprinted in *Imagination and Language* [Cambridge: Cambridge University Press, 1981], 337-380.)

Felman, S. "Turning the Screw of Interpretation," *Yale French Studies,* 55/56 (1977), 94-207.

Felman, S. *La folie et la chose littéraire* (Paris: Éd. du Seuil, 1979).

Felman, S. "Psychoanalysis and Education: Teaching Terminable and Interminable," *Yale French Studies,* 63 (1982), 21-44.

Finch, G. A. "A Retreading of James's Carpet," *Twentieth Century Literature,* 14 (1968), 98-101.

Fish, S. *Is There a Text in This Class?* (Cambridge, Mass.: Harvard University Press, 1980).

Flahault, F. "Sur *S/Z* et l'analyse des récits," *Poétique,* 47 (septembre 1981), 303-314.

Foster, J. W. "Passage through 'The Dead,' " *Criticism,* 15, 2 (spring 1973), 91-108.

Frappier-Mazur, L. "Le régime de l'aveu dans *Le lys dans la vallée:* Formes et fonctions de l'aveu écrit," *Revue des Sciences Humaines,* 47, 175 (1979), 7-16.

Gaillard, F. "L'en-signement du réel, ou la nécessaire écriture de la répétition," in Cl.

Gothot-Meersch, éd., *La production du sens chez Flaubert: Colloque de Cerisy* (Paris: U.G.E. [10/18], 1975), 197-226.

Garrett, P. K., ed. *Twentieth Century Interpretations of "Dubliners"* (Englewood Cliffs, N.J.: Prentice-Hall, 1968).

Geertz, C. *The Interpretation of Cultures* (New York: Basic Books, 1973).

Genette, G. *Figures, III* (Paris: Éd. du Seuil, 1972). (Translated as *Narrative Discourse* [Ithaca, N.Y.: Cornell University Press, 1980].)

Genette, G. *Introduction à l'architexte* (Paris: Éd. du Seuil, 1979).

Geninasca, J. "De la fête à l'anti-fête: Reconnaissance et construction de l'équivalence sémantique des chapitres IV et VII de *Sylvie* de Gérard de Nerval," *Versants*, 1 (1981), 93-108.

Ghiselin, B. "The Unity of *Dubliners*," in M. Beja, ed., *James Joyce's "Dubliners" and "A Portrait of the Artist as a Young Man." A Casebook* (London: Macmillan, 1973), 100-116.

Gifford, D. *Notes for Joyce: "Dubliners" and "A Portrait of the Artist as a Young Man"* (New York: Dutton, 1967).

Girard, R. *Mensonge romantique et vérité romanesque* (Paris: Grasset, 1961). (Translated as *Deceit, Desire and the Novel* [Baltimore: Johns Hopkins University Press, 1966].)

Girard, R. *La violence et le sacré* (Paris: Grasset, 1972). (Translated as *Violence and the Sacred* [Baltimore: Johns Hopkins University Press, 1974].)

Going, W. T. "Joyce's Gabriel Conroy and Robert Browning: The Cult of 'Broadcloth,' " *Papers on Language and Literature*, 13 (1977), 202-207.

Gordon, R. B. "Dentelle: Métaphore du texte dans *Sylvie*," *Romanic Review*, 73, 1 (January 1982), 45-66.

Greimas, A.-J. *Sémantique structurale* (Paris: Larousse, 1966).

Greimas, A.-J. *Du Sens* (Paris: Éd. du Seuil, 1970).

Grice, H. P. "Logic and Conversation," in P. Cole and J. L. Morgan, eds., *Speech Acts* (New York: Academic Press, 1975), 41-58.

Hart, C., ed. *James Joyce's "Dubliners"* (New York: Viking, 1969).

Hernadi, P., ed. *What Is Literature?* (Bloomington: Indiana University Press, 1978).

Holland, N. R. "Re-covering 'The Purloined Letter': Reading as a Personal Transaction," in S. Suleiman and I. Crosman, eds., *The Reader in the Text: Essays on Audience and Interpretation* (Princeton, N.J.: Princeton University Press, 1980), 350-370.

Iqbal, F. M. *Hubert Aquin romancier* (Québec: Presses de l'Université Laval, 1978).

Iser, W. *The Implied Reader* (Baltimore: Johns Hopkins University Press, 1974).

Iser, W. *The Act of Reading: A Theory of Aesthetic Response* (Baltimore: Johns Hopkins University Press, 1978).

Issacharoff, M. *L'Espace et la nouvelle* (Paris: Corti, 1976).

Issacharoff, M., ed. *Langages de Flaubert: Actes du Colloque de London* (Paris: Minard, 1976).

James, H. *The Art of the Novel: Critical Prefaces* (New York: Scribner's, 1938).

Jameson, F. *The Political Unconscious: Narrative as a Socially Symbolic Act* (Ithaca, N.Y.: Cornell University Press, 1981).

Jauss, H. R. *Pour une esthétique de la réception* (Paris: Gallimard, 1978).

Jauss, H. R. *Toward an Aesthetic of Reception* (Minneapolis: University of Minnesota Press, 1982).

Jean, R. *Nerval par lui-même* (Paris: Éd. du Seuil, 1964).

Jeanneret, M. *La lettre perdue: Écriture et folie dans l'œuvre de Nerval* (Paris: Flammarion, 1978).

Jenny, L. "Sémiotique de collage intertextuel," *Revue d'Esthétique*, 3/4 (1978), 165-182.

Johnson, B. *The Critical Difference: Essays in the Contemporary Rhetoric of Reading* (Baltimore: Johns Hopkins University Press, 1980).

Kappeler, S. *Writing and Reading in Henry James* (New York: Columbia University Press, 1980).

Kaufmann, V. "De l'interlocuteur à l'adresse," *Poétique*, 46 (avril 1981), 171-182.

Kofman, S. *Nerval: Le charme de la répétition* (Lausanne: l'Âge d'Homme, 1979).

Kristéva, J. *Séméiotiké: Recherches pour une sémanalyse* (Paris: Éd. du Seuil, 1969).

Labov, W. *Language in the Inner City: Studies in the Black English Vernacular* (Philadelphia: University of Pennsylvania Press, 1972).

Lacan, J. "Le séminaire sur *La lettre volée*," in *Écrits*, I (Paris: Éd. du Seuil Coll. "Points," 1970), 19-75.

La Fontaine, G. E. de. *Hubert Aquin et le Québec* (Montréal: Parti Pris, 1978).

Lainoff, S. "Henry James's 'The Figure in the Carpet': What Is Critical Responsiveness?" *Boston University Studies in English*, 5 (1961), 122-128.

Lanser, S. S. *The Narrative Act: Point of View in Prose Fiction* (Princeton, N.J.: Princeton University Press, 1981).

Le Guin, U. "It Was a Dark and Stormy Night: Or Why Are We Huddling around the Campfire?" *Critical Inquiry*, 7, 1 (autumn 1980), 191-199.

Lejeune, P. *Le pacte autobiographique* (Paris: Éd. du Seuil, 1975).

Levy, L. B. "A Reading of 'The Figure in the Carpet,'" *American Literature*, 33 (1962), 457-462.

Logan, D. "Joyce's 'The Dead,'" *Explicator*, 32, 2 (1973), 16.

Lubbock, P. *The Craft of Fiction* (London: Jonathan Cape, 1957).

Ludwig, J. B. "The Snow," in J. R. Baker and T. F. Staley, eds., *James Joyce's "Dubliners": A Critical Handbook* (Belmont, Calif.: Wadsworth, 1969), 159-162.

Lukács, G. *History and Class Consciousness* (Cambridge, Mass.: MIT Press, 1971).

Mabbott, T. O., ed. *Collected Works of Edgar Allan Poe*, vol. III (Cambridge, Mass.: Belknap Press, Harvard University Press, 1978).

McKenna, J. P. "Joyce's 'The Dead,'" *Explicator*, 30, 1 (1971), 1-2.

Marin, L. *Le récit est un piège* (Paris: Éd. de Minuit, 1978).

Miller, J. H. "'The Figure in the Carpet,'" *Poetics Today*, 1, 3 (spring 1980), 107-118.

Miller, J. H. "A Guest in the House: A Reply to Shlomith Rimmon-Kenan's Reply," *Poetics Today*, 2, 1b (winter 1980-1981), 189-191.

O'Connor, J. R. "Flaubert: *Trois contes* and the Figure of the Double Cone," *PMLA*, 95, 5 October 1980), 812-826.

Ong, W. J., S.J. *Interfaces of the Word* (Ithaca, N.Y.: Cornell University Press, 1977).

Perrot, J. "L'Anamorphose dans les romans d'Henry James," *Critique*, 383 (avril 1979), 334-354.

Perrot, J. "Énigme et fiction métalinguistique chez James," *Poétique*, 45 (février 1981), 53-66.

Perruchot, Cl. "Le style indirect libre et la question du sujet dans *Madame Bovary*," in Cl. Gothot Meersch, éd., *La production du sens chez Flaubert: Colloque de Cerisy* (Paris: U.G.E., 1975), 253-285.

Peytard, J. *Voix et traces narratives chez Stendhal: Analyse sémiotique de "Vanina Vanini"* (Paris: Éditeurs Français Réunis, 1980).

Piwowarczyk, M. A. "The Narratee and the Situation of Enunciation," *Genre*, 9, 2 (1976), 161-177.

Polanyi, L. *The American Story: Social and Cultural Constraints on the Meaning and Structure of Stories in Conversation* (doctoral dissertation, University of Michigan, 1978).

Polanyi, L. "So What's the Point?" *Semiotica*, 25, 3/4 (1979), 207-241.

Polanyi, L. "What Stories Can Tell Us about Their Teller's World," *Poetics Today*, 2, 2 (winter 1981), 97-112.

Pontalis, J.-B. *Après Freud* (Paris: Gallimard, 1971).

Poulet, G. "*Sylvie* ou la pensée de Nerval," in *Trois essais de mythologie romantique* (Paris: Corti, 1966), 13-81.

Powers, L. H. "A Reperusal of James's 'The Figure in the Carpet,'" *American Literature*, 33 (1961), 224-228.

Pratt, M. L. *Towards a Speech-Act Theory of Literary Discourse* (Bloomington: Indiana University Press, 1977).

Prince, G. *A Grammar of Stories* (The Hague: Mouton, 1973).

Prince, G. "Introduction à l'étude du narrataire," *Poétique*, 14 (1973), 178-196.

Prince, G. "Aspects of a Grammar of Narrative," *Poetics Today*, 1, 3 (spring 1980), 49-63.

Prince, G. "Notes on the Text as Reader," in S. Suleiman and I. Crosman, eds., *The Reader in the Text: Essays on Audience and Interpretation* (Princeton, N.J.: Princeton University Press, 1980), 225-240.

Propp, V. *The Morphology of the Folktale* (2nd ed.) (Austin: University of Texas Press, 1968).

Rabinowitz, P. J. "'What's Hecuba to Us?' The Audience's Experience of Literary Borrowing," in S. Suleiman and I. Crosman, eds., *The Reader in the Text: Essays on Audience and Interpretation* (Princeton, N.J.: Princeton University Press, 1980), 241-263.

Ricardou, J. *Problèmes du nouveau roman* (Paris: Éd. du Seuil, 1967).

Riffaterre, M. *Semiotics of Poetry* (Bloomington: Indiana University Press, 1978).

Riffaterre, M. *La production du texte* (Paris: Éd. du Seuil, 1979).

Rimmon, S. *The Concept of Ambiguity: The Example of James* (Chicago: University of Chicago Press, 1977).

Rimmon-Kenan, S. "Deconstructive Reflections on Deconstruction: In Reply to Hillis Miller," *Poetics Today*, 2, 1b (winter 1980-1981), 185-188.

Robinson, E. M. "Gabriel Conroy's Cooked Goose," *Ball State University Forum*, 11, 2 (spring 1970), 25.

Rougemont, D. de. *L'Amour et l'Occident* (Paris: Plon, 1939). (Translated as *Love in the Western World* [New York: Harcourt Brace, 1940].)

Rousset, J. *Forme et signification* (Paris: Corti, 1964).

Rutten, F. "Sur les notions de texte et de lecture dans une théorie de la réception," *Revue des Sciences Humaines*, 177 (1980-1981), 67-83.

San Juan, E. *James Joyce and the Craft of Fiction: An Interpretation of "Dubliners"* (Cranbury: Associated University Presses, 1972).

Schaeffer, G. *Une double lecture de Nerval: "Les Illuminés" et "Les Filles du Feu"* (Neuchâtel: La Baconnière, 1977).

Schmidt, S. J. "Empirical Studies in Literature: Introductory Remarks," *Poetics*, 10, 4/5 (1981), 317-336.

Scholes, R. "Language, Narrative and Anti-Narrative," *Critical Inquiry*, 7, 1 (autumn 1980), 204-212.

Schor, N. "Fiction as Interpretation/Interpretation as Fiction," in S. Suleiman and I. Crosman, eds., *The Reader in the Text: Essays in Audience and Interpretation* (Princeton, N.J.: Princeton University Press, 1980), 165-182.

Segal, O. *The Lucid Reflector: A Study of the Role of the Observer in Henry James's Fiction* (New Haven, Conn.: Yale University Press, 1969).

Serres, M. *Feux et signaux de brume* (Paris: Grasset, 1975).

Serres, M. *Hermès, IV: La distribution* (Paris: Éd. de Minuit, 1977).

Serres, M. *Le parasite* (Paris: Grasset, 1980).

Sherrington, R. J. *Three Novels by Flaubert* (Oxford: Clarendon Press, 1970).

Smart, P. *Hubert Aquin, agent double* (Montréal: Presses de l'Université de Montréal, 1973).

Smith, B. H. *On the Margins of Discourse* (Chicago: University of Chicago Press, 1978).

Smith, B. H. "Narrative Versions, Narrative Theories," *Critical Inquiry*, 7, 1 (autumn 1980), 213-236.

Stolzfus, B. "Point of view in *Un cœur simple*," *French Review*, 35, 1 (October 1961), 19-25.

Suleiman, S. "Redundancy and the 'Readable' Text," *Poetics Today*, 1, 3 (spring 1980), 119-142.

Suleiman, S., and Crosman, I., eds. *The Reader in the Text: Essays on Audience and Interpretation* (Princeton, N.J.: Princeton University Press, 1980).

Tanner, T. *Adultery in the Novel* (Baltimore: Johns Hopkins University Press, 1979).

Thompson, G. R. *Poe's Fiction* (Madison: University of Wisconsin Press, 1973).

Todorov, T. *Grammaire du Décaméron* (La Haye: Mouton, 1969).

Todorov, T. *Poétique de la prose* (Paris: Éd. du Seuil, 1971).

Tranouez, P. "L'Efficacité narrative: Étude du *Rideau cramoisi*," *Poétique*, 41 (février 1980), 51-59.

Turner, V. "Social Dramas and Stories about Them," *Critical Inquiry*, 7, 1 (autumn 1980), 141-168.

Uitti, K. "Figures and Fiction: Linguistic Deformation and the Novel," *Kentucky Romance Quarterly*, 17, 2 (1970), 149-169.

Vitoux, P. "Le jeu de focalisation," *Poétique*, 51 (septembre 1982), 359-368.

Wagner, B. *Innenbereich und Äusserung: Flaubertsche Formen indirekter Darstellung und Grundtypen der erlebten Rede* (München: Fink, 1972).

Walzl, F. "The Liturgy of the Epiphany Season and the Epiphanies of Joyce," *PMLA*, 80, 4/5 (September 1965), 436-450.

Walzl, F. "Gabriel and Michael: The Conclusion of 'The Dead,' " *James Joyce Quarterly*, 4, 1 (fall 1966), 17-31.

Wanuffel, L. "Présence d'Hoffmann dans les œuvres de Balzac (1829-1835)," *L'Année Balzacienne* (1970), 45-56.

Weinberg, H. "A Note on Irony and *style indirect libre* in *Madame Bovary*," *Travaux du cercle méthodologique* (Toronto: Department of French, University of Toronto), 7 (1979).

Wellek, R. "What Is Literature?" in P. Hernadi, ed., *What Is Literature?* (Bloomington: Indiana University Press, 1978), 16-23.

Westbrook, P. D. "The Supersubtle Fry," *Nineteenth Century Fiction*, 8 (1953), 134-140.

White, H. *Metahistory* (Baltimore: Johns Hopkins University Press, 1973).

White, H. *Tropics of Discourse* (Baltimore: Johns Hopkins University Press, 1978).

Wilson, W. D. "Readers in Texts," *PMLA*, 96, 5 (October 1981), 848-863.

Wyers (Weber), F. "Manuel Puig at the Movies," *Hispanic Review*, 49, 2 (spring 1981), 163-181.

Index

Index

N. B. Texts that are the subject of chapter- or section-length discussion are indexed only when mentioned elsewhere. Within such chapters and sections, only items relevant to the general concerns of the book are indexed.

Ross Chambers, born in Australia, was educated at the University of Sydney and the University of Grenoble, where he earned his *doctorat d'université* in 1967. He served as McCaughey Professor and head of the French department at the University of Sydney from 1971 till 1975, and is now professor of French at the University of Michigan. Chambers is the author of *Gérard de Nerval et la poétique du voyage, La comédie au château, L'Ange et l'Automate: Variations sur le mythe de l'actrice, de Nerval à Proust,* and a collection of essays, *Meaning and Meaningfulness: Studies in the Analysis and Interpretation of Texts.*